Designing for Biodiversity

A TECHNICAL GUIDE FOR NEW AND EXISTING BUILDINGS

Second Edition

Kelly Gunnell,
Brian Murphy
and Carol Williams

RIBA Publishing

© Kelly Gunnell and Dr Carol Williams, 2013

First edition published in 2010 as *Biodiversity for Low and Zero Carbon Buildings: A Technical Guide for New Build*

Published by RIBA Publishing,
15 Bonhill Street, London EC2P 2EA

ISBN 978 1 85946 491 5

Stock code 79859

The rights of Kelly Gunnell, Dr Carol Williams and Brian Murphy to be identified as the Authors of this Work has been asserted in accordance with the Copyright, Design and Patents Act 1988, sections 77 and 88.

British Library Cataloguing in Publications Data
A catalogue record for this book is available from the British Library.

Sketch line drawings provided by: Brian Murphy
SketchUp drawings provided by: Dan Ward
Designed and typeset by: Alex Lazarou
Printed and bound by: W.G. Baird, Antrim

While every effort has been made to check the accuracy and quality of the information given in this publication, neither the Author nor the Publisher accept any responsibility for the subsequent use of this information, for any errors or omissions that it may contain, or for any misunderstandings arising from it.

RIBA Publishing is part of RIBA Enterprises Ltd.
www.ribaenterprises.com

CONTENTS

ACKNOWLEDGEMENTS

A book of this scope, even a second edition, cannot be completed without the input of a great many people and organisations. In particular, I would like to thank the RSPB, who generously provided funding for the updated drawings from which this book greatly benefits.

Special thanks to Daniel Ward (Archisan) for his incredible effort and skill in producing the 2D and 3D technical drawings.

The following people contributed to specialist sections: John Day (RSPB), Steven Falk (Buglife), Gary Grant and Dr Liat Wicks (BCT). For review and input I am thankful for the assistance of Edward Mayer (Swift Conservation), Dick Newell (Action for Swifts), John Day (RSPB), Stephen Fitt (RSPB), Matthew Twiggs and David Marsden (Barn Owl Trust), Heather McFarlane (BCT) and Phil Briggs (BCT).

Many people heeded our call for case studies and I thank you all for your time. Unfortunately, due to space limitations not all the case studies could be included in the book.

I would like to express my gratitude to Lucy Harbor and Sharon Hodgson at RIBA Publishing for their continued enthusiasm for this topic and dedication to producing a great book.

Brian Murphy (GreenSpec) has been a wealth of information for all things technical and building related. His passion and hard work have made him a fantastic co-author.

Special thanks to Dr Carol Williams for letting us build on all her great work in the first edition and for her thoughtful advice and insight on this new edition.

This book would not have been possible without the support of the Bat Conservation Trust, who have given me space and time to work on it.

KELLY GUNNELL
Built Environment Specialist
Bat Conservation Trust

Action for Swifts

GreenSpec

FOREWORD

There has been a tendency in the environmental movement to focus on one issue at a time, when what are really required are integrated solutions that address multiple challenges simultaneously. The shift towards low carbon buildings has been successful in many respects, but one unintended consequence of creating highly insulated and sealed buildings has been a negative impact on biodiversity. While old draughty buildings, often with open roof voids and generous overhangs, were terrible in terms of heat conservation, they provided numerous niches for a wide range of birds, bats, insects and plants to become established. This book shows how it is possible to do both: to design buildings that are low carbon and accommodate biodiversity.

Some sceptics might ask why it is necessary to go to such lengths to preserve biodiversity. There are obviously moral arguments about whether it is acceptable to allow as many as half of all species to drift towards extinction by the end of the century. More persuasive for sceptics is an anthropocentric argument, that much of our quality of life is dependent on the health and diversity of the natural world. The variety of our food, the sources of existing and future medical treatments, the wilderness areas we go to for recreation and the whole subject of ecosystem services (the services nature provides without ever submitting an invoice, such as pollination, water filtration, coastal protection, etc.) – all are dependent on biodiversity. The 1997 Millennium Ecosystem Assessment – a UN-funded study – calculated the value of ecosystem services and concluded that they were worth $33 trillion per year.

Biophilia is a term popularised by the biologist E.O. Wilson. It refers to a hypothesis that there is an instinctive bond between human beings and other living organisms. There is considerable experimental evidence demonstrating that humans are healthier and more productive when they are in regular contact with nature. It could be argued that sustainability ultimately is about enabling all the world's inhabitants to live happy, healthy lives within their fair share of the earth's resources. If one accepts this definition then it is clear that designing for biodiversity is an essential part of achieving this ideal.

Architects, compared with most other construction professionals, are almost uniquely powerful to influence the subject of biodiversity in the built environment – this book is an essential manual for those committed to making a difference.

MICHAEL PAWLYN
Director of Exploration Architecture
and Founding Partner of the Sahara Forest Project

PREFACE

The first edition of this book came about to fill a gap in the information available on how to make provision for building-reliant species when designing new low or zero carbon buildings. This second edition remains true to that need for practical information. It shows how to comply with the requirement to reduce the carbon footprint while at the same time achieving a biodiversity gain, thereby creating truly sustainable buildings. The focus of the book is unchanged: the provision of enhancement for biodiversity. It is not about mitigation measures for existing roosts and nesting places. Nor is it intended to take the place of an experienced ecologist, whose input will be needed to guide decisions about which measures are most appropriate and where they should be applied.

While the aims remain unchanged, this second edition includes updates to legislation, policy and regulations and presents new bespoke products and techniques. From listening to the feedback on the first edition, we are delighted that ongoing collaborations have resulted in this edition. We include new sections on enhancing for biodiversity at the wider development level, plus a chapter on enhancement for biodiversity when considering the refurbishment of our existing housing stock. While this is by no means exhaustive, we hope you find the second edition comprehensive, practical and relevant at all scales of sustainable building and design.

Kelly Gunnell

Carol Williams

Brian Murphy

INTRODUCTION

When sustainable building is being considered, there has been a tendency to focus on carbon- and material-related issues, while biodiversity has been given limited consideration. However, buildings can only be truly sustainable if they enhance and sustain life. The Strategy for Sustainable Construction published in 2008 by the Department for Business, Enterprise and Regulatory Reform (now the Department for Business, Innovation and Skills) lists the need to preserve and enhance biodiversity alongside energy and waste considerations. In addition, the recent National Planning Policy Framework (NPPF) published by the Department for Communities and Local Government identifies sustainable development as the purpose of the planning system and conserving and enhancing the natural environment as a 'Core Planning Principle'. The NPPF states that 'the planning system should contribute to and enhance the natural and local environment by … minimising impacts on biodiversity and providing net gains in biodiversity where possible, contributing to the Government's commitment to halt the overall decline in biodiversity, including by establishing coherent ecological networks that are more resilient to current and future pressures'.

This is all for a very good reason. Biodiversity is not an additional option in an ideal world, but a fundamental need – not only in the context of truly sustainable building, but also for our quality of life and the long-term sustainability of our planet. The loss of biodiversity is one of the biggest threats facing our planet.

But what do we mean when we say that biodiversity is a fundamental need? Biological diversity (biodiversity) of wildlife, plants and their habitats is a vital component of healthy, well-functioning ecosystems, which, in turn, sustain all life on the planet. These ecosystems and the biodiversity that is part of them provide much of what we need and want, from clean water to the air we breathe and the food we eat. Biodiversity is responsible for our food; either directly or via the pollinators, the seed dispersers and the web of organisms and habitats that relate to aspects of our diet. Our health is linked to biodiversity in several ways; for example, new drugs and treatments are developed from the natural world around us, and access to nature helps both our physical and our mental health. Indeed, studies have shown that psychological benefits of exposure to urban green space increase with greater biodiversity (Fuller *et al.*, 2007). Native biodiversity can contribute to a sense of place and belonging, and a lack of biodiversity can negatively affect both well-being and community identity (Horowitz *et al.*, 2001). Of course, there are also direct resources from nature, such as timber, and a host of natural fibres and fuels.

'Ecosystem services' is a term widely used when talking about what nature and biodiversity provide us with. For example, it refers to natural processes that clean our air and water, provide protection to our coasts from erosion, and provide defence against flooding and soil erosion. The need for these services grows ever greater as we enter a period of uncertainty and a shift in climate patterns. Research from the Millennium Ecosystem Assessment (2005) and the European Commission (EC, 2008) highlights how 'the well-being of every human population in the world is fundamentally and directly dependent on ecosystem services'.

This is a global outlook, but what is the state of biodiversity in the UK and how much do we value it? The findings reported by the UK National Ecosystem Assessment (2011) show that the economic value of nature now runs to billions of pounds in the UK alone. But the picture of the state of biodiversity is one that does give cause for some concern:

- 44% of 'priority habitats' and 33% of 'priority species' are in decline, with some showing accelerated deterioration (Defra, 2012a);
- the UK's total wild bird population has declined by 13.7% since 1977, with numbers of some specialist species falling by two-thirds (Defra, 2012b);
- butterflies associated strongly with semi-natural habitats (specialists) and those found in the wider countryside show declines of 67% and 27% respectively since 1976 (Defra, 2012a); and
- major declines in bees, arable plants and amphibians have also been recorded (Margerison, 2008).

Our built environment has the potential to have major negative impacts on biodiversity. However, if done sensitively, the development and refurbishment of buildings can, in fact, increase the ecological value of the site.

There is a growing body of research that suggests that access to biodiversity and green spaces is valuable to individuals, businesses and communities (Forest Research, 2010). Research by the former Commission for Architecture and the Built Environment (CABE) concluded that property values increase near green spaces, with houses close to parks averaging 8% higher prices than similar properties further away (CABE, 2005a). A report by Natural Economy Northwest (NEN) found that businesses located in greener settings attract and retain more motivated staff, and that green spaces near work places lead to reduced sickness and increased productivity (NEN, 2008). A government-led project on the economic valuation of the benefits of the UK Biodiversity Action Plan (Christie *et al.*, 2011) showed that the value of the benefits derived from protecting biodiversity significantly exceed the costs of delivering them, illustrating the importance of valuing the benefits of nature's services.

Bird species and, more recently, bats have been recognised as indicators of biodiversity by the Government and as such are used as a sign of the general state of biodiversity in the UK. With a number of bat and bird species relying on built structures, the impact of the building and construction industry can be significant.

Despite this, much of the information about wildlife and the built environment is largely concerned with wildlife that has become established in existing buildings, rather than when new buildings are being planned or designed. The potential for biodiversity in built structures in new developments has been given virtually no consideration at all. The likely reason for this is that traditional building styles have often had the potential for wildlife. Some species have become associated with buildings over many centuries, such as owls in barns or bats in belfries.

However, the very real need for low or zero carbon buildings has led to an acceleration in the development of building techniques, materials and designs. The one thing that all of these innovative advances have in common is the need for an 'airtight' barrier that encompasses the utilised part of the building. The result of this is that, while striving to reduce the carbon footprint of our buildings, for the first time since humans made shelters for themselves, the species that have adapted to share these buildings with us, such as swifts, house sparrows and bats, will no longer find a potential resting, nesting or roosting place.

The wildlife that has historically shared our built structures includes some of the most valued and vulnerable in Britain; whether it is our migratory birds, which fly thousands of miles across hazardous terrain to reach our shores; or our own populations of sparrow and starling, now in sharp decline; or the enigmatic barn owl, swooping majestically and silently through the adjacent countryside. Bats are so important in our ecosystems that they are now recognised by the Government as indicators of biodiversity and yet their numbers have plummeted.

So is the situation hopeless? Does the need to reduce the carbon footprint of buildings mean that these species – which are a vital part of our ecosystem, keep that important balance in nature and give joy to so many – are destined to suffer even greater threats as new buildings become barren deserts to them? Thankfully, the answer is no. It is entirely possible to continue to see these building-reliant species

thrive in low and zero carbon buildings, but the difference is that we need to consider biodiversity early on in the design process and to incorporate measures, which generally incur little extra expense, into buildings.

This book takes what we know of the needs of our building-reliant species and, at the same time, reviews the build types that are likely to be in use over the next decade. With due consideration for the Building Regulations, a series of architect's drawings are presented that are suitable for the enhancement of biodiversity in both new and existing low or zero carbon buildings.

As well as helping to maintain and enhance the populations of these species, there can actually be benefits to incorporating these bespoke roosting and nesting places. In traditional styles of building, the bats and birds could utilise any number of opportunities within a building. Sometimes this could lead to conflict with the residents, or could conflict with other uses or future plans for the building. The need for bespoke roosting and nesting places means that the species in question will be contained in those areas and conflicts with the human residents can be avoided in the vast majority of cases.

Although this book concentrates on building-reliant species, particularly birds and bats, it is recognised that buildings and developments are an opportunity for a greater range of wildlife. Green roofs and living walls are becoming ever more popular and with very good reason. Standard roofs (non-living) cover a huge area and, for the most part, are without merit, either to look at or for biodiversity. A green roof is not only visually appealing, but is good for wildlife, important in the reduction of the likelihood of flood events (by retaining rainwater to later evaporate and also by modifying the effects of rainfall), and acts as a buffer against the extremes of temperature.

It is acknowledged that the inclusion of roosting and nesting potential in low and zero carbon buildings is an evolving practice. Therefore, while the designs given are informed by best current knowledge, it is vital that the uptake of these opportunities is monitored. It is only by this sort of feedback that we can learn the relative success of designs and products, and adjust future advice on provision accordingly. The expected delay in uptake by some species will be taken into account during this process.

In the future, it would be a positive step indeed if we could see our new built environments reflecting the rich wildlife heritage that we have inherited in the UK.

CHAPTER ONE

Biodiversity and the importance of buildings

1.1 Building-reliant biodiversity

As our buildings and developments have crept over the landscape, some animal species have adapted to share our built structures with us in order to survive, and have done so for a very long time. Some of these animals have come to depend on buildings for their survival. We term them 'building-reliant species'. This book focuses on how to maintain and enhance our buildings for building-reliant species, such as some bat and bird species. However, there are a large number of other organisms, such as some insects and plants, that make use of our built structures and we can easily enhance buildings to meet their needs.

As our landscape is set to become increasingly urbanised over the next 50 years it is more important than ever to ensure there is provision for wildlife in our built environment; for building-reliant species, their very survival depends on it.

This chapter gives a general introduction to the ecology of bats, birds, invertebrates and plants and the ways in which they use buildings.

1.2 About bats and buildings

1.2.1 Bats worldwide

There are over 1,200 species of bats worldwide, which make up a fifth of all mammal species. Bats can be as small as a bumble bee or as large as a small dog. On a global scale, bats are one of the most widely distributed groups of mammals. They are found across every land mass, apart from the Arctic, the Antarctic and a few isolated oceanic islands. There are bats in the far north of Scandinavia, as well as in the deserts of south-west USA.

Bats are most numerous in the tropics. The majority eat insects, but some feed on pollen and nectar, while others eat fruit. A few highly specialised species feed on fish, frogs and even on other bats. There are also the three species of vampire bats, found in Central and South America, that feed on blood. Globally, bats play a vital role in our environment, being responsible for seed dispersal, pollination and pest control in forests, in agriculture and in the wider landscape.

Approximately 25% of the world's bats are threatened with extinction.

Natterer's bat in brickwork

1.2.2 Bats in the UK

Seventeen species of bat breed in the UK. They are all small, nocturnal and eat insects, although the habitats in which they find their insect food and the types of insect they eat vary between species. All the UK bats have reasonable eyesight, but when flying and looking for insect prey in darkness it is their ears that are most important. To navigate and hunt for insects they use echolocation; by shouting at a high pitch (above our hearing range) and listening for the returning echoes, the bats create a very clear picture of their surroundings and of the location and direction of movement of insects.

The insects on which British bats feed cover a wide range, depending on the size of the bat species and the habitats in which they feed. The hunting methods of UK bat species therefore vary depending on the habitats in which they specialise. The larger UK bats can feed on beetles as big as May bugs and dung beetles, while the smaller bats are likely to feed on smaller insects, such as gnats, crane flies and midges, of which a single bat can consume around 3,000 in one night. Unsurprisingly, bats are most likely to be found feeding over habitats that support a good number of insects, such as any body of water, native woodland, hedgerows, unimproved meadows and grassland, mature gardens and grazed pasture, where dung fauna are important. Table 1.1 gives a summary of the annual cycle of UK bats.

Table 1.1: Annual cycle of UK bats

Season	Activity
Autumn	The young born this summer are feeding independently All bats are feeding to put on weight for the winter Mating begins
Winter	Hibernation (consisting of prolonged bouts of torpor) Bats (particularly small species) feed during mild spells
Spring	Hibernation ends and females become pregnant In late spring females gather in maternity roosts, which need to be warm Non-breeding adults are found as individuals or in small numbers in cooler roosts
Summer	The young are born Each mother has a single baby, which suckles for four to five weeks

Bats do not make nests but use existing spaces to roost. These roosts must have the right climatic conditions, they must be dark and they must be free from disturbance. Bats use roosts to shelter during the day, to hibernate, to raise young and for mating. Roosts vary in size; some are used by a single bat and some by hundreds. Bats use different roosts at different times of the year, and they tend to return year after year to the same roosts in buildings, which they may have been using for generations. Bats are long lived, with some UK bats having been recorded living into their thirties in the wild. However, having only one young per year means that bat populations are very slow to recover from any changes to the environment that adversely impact them, such as the loss of prey species or the loss of roosts, which threaten their ability to survive or breed.

All UK bat populations have declined considerably during the past century. In recent years some species have shown small increases in population, but more sustained increases are needed before any populations recover. The declines were largely due to human factors – such as the loss of feeding habitats; the use of pesticides and intensive farming practices, which reduce the abundance of insects; and building and development work, which affects roosts – and these declines are the reason why all UK bats and their roosts (even when bats are not present) are now protected by law (see Chapter 2).

Brown long-eared bat

1.2.3 Importance of buildings for bats

All UK bat species will make use of buildings on occasions, but for some species buildings are essential as roost sites. This situation has arisen over a long period of time, as tree cover and the availability of caves, which would have provided natural roost sites, have become scarce. Hundreds of years ago bat species adapted to share our built structures with us.

One of the factors that make buildings suitable for bats is the ability of built structures to provide a stable microclimate. Temperature plays a key role in roosting ecology and selection. That need differs based on the time of year and the sex and species of the bat. For several weeks in the summer, female bats choose somewhere warm to gather in maternity roosts, such as in a roof space heated by

Lesser horseshoe bats in roof void

the sun or in features in a wall that is south-facing. At the same time, non-breeding adults find cooler roosts, such as north-facing features, where bats are found in small numbers or singly. In the winter, bats of both sexes choose somewhere cool with high humidity to hibernate. This is generally in underground sites, such as caves and tunnels but also cellars and ice houses.

Bats are often found roosting in buildings. Both new and old buildings are used by bats, although a greater number of roosts and wider range of species are found in older structures. Some species will roost in internal spaces, such as within the roof void or within a cavity wall, but others will tend to use external features, such as hanging tiles, weather boarding, fascias, soffits and barge boards. Bats do not take any material into the roost with them, nor do they chew wires.

When considering the roosting habits of bats in buildings, it is useful to make an arbitrary division between those crevice-dwelling species that roost in external features or that only require a small crevice type of provision within the structure, and those bats that require flying space within the building. A further distinction is needed within the group of bats that require flight space, based on access to the roost: this is because horseshoe bats have different needs to all other UK bat species.

The greater and lesser horseshoe bats are the only two species of bat in the UK that have adapted to hanging free by their feet when roosting. These two bat species, which have a very close association with buildings, are among our rarest species – whose numbers have suffered the steepest decline, although both species have shown signs of a reverse of that trend in very recent years (see Bat Conservation Trust, 2012). Their range within the UK has also been constricted and they are currently only found in Wales and south-west England. Horseshoe bats' adaptation to hanging free by their feet has resulted in a specialisation of their leg structure, which means that they are unable to crawl very effectively – unlike all other UK species of bat. This means that, where other bat species can access their roost through a small gap, horseshoe bats prefer to be able to fly into their roosts. This requirement has increased the pressure on the population – prior to the time when bats were legally protected (1981), many large manor houses, barns and other outbuildings were converted, resulting in the loss of the bats' access points.

Table 1.2 lists the categories within which the UK bat species fall, but it is important to note that this is only an arbitrary grouping: the type of roost (maternity, non-breeding adults, transitory, mating, hibernacula, night or feeding roosts) and the part of the country it is located in will both make a difference to what bats require of a roost. The finer details of bat roosting ecology are beyond the scope of this book – an experienced bat ecologist should be consulted over this level of detail.

Table 1.2: The roosting preferences of UK bat species

Category	Bat species
Crevice-dwelling bats (that tend to be hidden from view)	Common pipistrelle, soprano pipistrelle, Nathusius' pipistrelle, Brandt's, whiskered
Crevice-dwelling bats found in roof-void (that may be visible on roof timbers)	Noctule, serotine, Leisler's, Daubenton's, Alcathoe, barbastelle and Bechstein's
Crevice-dwelling bats found in roof-void (require flight space in certain types of roost)	Natterer's, and brown and grey long-eared
Bats that need flight space and flying access	Greater horseshoe, lesser horseshoe

Roosts in existing building stock are vitally important and this book will briefly look at the issues surrounding the refurbishment and retrofitting of our current housing stock to achieve low carbon buildings (Chapter 4). But this book is mostly concerned with looking to the future and the requirement for low and zero carbon homes, and incorporating provision as enhancement (Chapter 3). In more traditional designs, some potential for crevice-dwelling bat species may remain, and also where weather boarding/wood cladding is used. However, without positive, proactive measures, the fact is that future housing stock will hold no potential roosts for the majority of bat species.

1.3 About birds and buildings
(by John Day, RSPB)

Some birds, just like some bats, have developed such close associations with buildings that they have become almost entirely reliant on them. We concentrate within this book on these species which are also undergoing declines in their populations, including swift, house martin, swallow, house sparrow and black redstart. Other birds, such as starling, barn owl, peregrine and kestrel, less dependent but frequently associated with using buildings to nest, are also considered.

Barn owl

There are many localised instances of other birds using buildings on which to nest, often as a result of loss, damage or disturbance to their nearby natural habitat or through opportunism. The most common are various species of gull, jackdaw and pied wagtail, but others have included birds as unlikely as oystercatcher, ringed plover, lapwing and skylark.

1.3.1 Why building for birds matters

Although a lack of nest sites has yet to be identified as a direct cause of decline for building-dependent birds, protection of exiting nests and appropriate provision of new nests makes a valuable contribution to alleviating the pressures faced by those species.

With the exception of peregrine, each bird species considered here is widely distributed but mostly declining and is listed as a Bird of Conservation Concern (BoCC) (see Table 1.3).

Table 1.3: Conservation status of birds referred to in this text

Species	Notes
Kestrel	Having recovered during the 1970s after the withdrawal of organochlorine pesticides, they have since declined, particularly in Scotland since 1994
Peregrine	After withdrawal of organochlorine pesticides numbers have gradually increased and birds are now a familiar sight in our cities
Barn owl	Appears to be undergoing a distribution decline
Swift	Steep declines in recent years
Swallow	Possible increasing trend
House martin	Gradual recent decline
Black redstart	Small, localised populations in a handful of major cities
Starling	Declines in most regions, with some of the largest being in Wales and the south-west
House sparrow	Decline in cities and across much of the south-east, eastern and the Midlands region of Britain

NB: Colours indicate BoCC status – see Jargon buster

1.3.2 Causes of decline

For the most part, the causes of decline in bird populations have been difficult to establish. In the case of aerial feeders such as swift, swallow and house martin, establishing the causes of decline is made more difficult by their migratory lifestyle. They spend the majority of their time on the wing, ranging over large distances to forage. They are long-distance, trans-Saharan migrants, wintering in various parts of southern Africa.

We know swifts often lose traditional nest sites and modern building design provides them with few or no nesting opportunities. Similarly, for the barn owl, swallow and house sparrow, access to farm stores is now restricted and old farm outbuildings either demolished or converted into living accommodation. Despite declines in Scotland and south-west England, the kestrel breeds at high densities across mixed farmland and frequently occurs in our towns and cities, where it often breeds on buildings.

Rural populations of house sparrow have seemingly declined due to lack of seed availability in winter. In towns, the cause is unknown but may be linked to lack of invertebrate food for chicks or to increased predation pressure.

House sparrow

The starling appears to be suffering poor survival of first-year birds, possibly caused by a lack of soil invertebrates due to drying and compaction of soils, thus inhibiting their ability to forage.

It is anecdotally recognised that refurbishments in older properties, such as soffit and fascia board replacement, can have localised impacts on populations of at least three species reliant on old buildings for nesting. In addition, large-scale regeneration programmes covering whole housing estates can potentially oust entire populations of house sparrow, swift and starling.

1.3.3   What birds need

Ensuring somewhere safe to nest, year-round food and shelter is important for birds. Depending on the species and its foraging range, our influence can vary. For house sparrow and starling, which forage close to the nest, ensuring the right habitat of thick native deciduous shrubs and mosaics of short and long grasses are available is something achievable.

Tall buildings with green roofs (see Section 3.14.1), gantries, walkways and other complex structures, and or mosaics of stony waste ground with sparse ruderal vegetation (brownfield) are favoured by the black redstart.

For kestrel and barn owl, suitable rough grassland and field margins over an area of 10 sq km should help provide habitats for enough small mammals and invertebrates to meet their requirements.

For birds that feed in flight and forage over much wider areas, protection of existing nests and provision of new nesting sites are important as there is often little direct influence in meeting habitat requirements far away from the nest. Creating local wetlands, with shallows to promote insect abundance, will provide valuable feeding sites.

Peregrine over city

1.3.4   Further reading

- www.blackredstarts.org.uk
- www.bto.org/about-birds/birdfacts
- *Building Space for Wildlife*, Kier-RSPB advisory sheet
- Ramsden, D. and Twiggs, M. (2009) *Barn Owls and Rural Planning Applications*. Ashburton: Barn Owl Trust. www.naturalengland.org.uk/Images/barnowl-rpa_tcm6-12652.pdf
- www.rspb.org.uk/wildlife/birdguide/name/index.aspx
- www.rspb.org.uk/wildlife/birdguide/status_explained.aspx

1.4   About invertebrates and buildings
(by Steven Falk, Buglife)

Buildings and built environments have considerable potential to support the activities of insects and other invertebrates and may quickly acquire good populations of species that are often much scarcer in the wider environment. This can include bees, such as the hairy-footed flower-bee and leafcutter bees, slugs, assorted beetles and spiders, such as lace-weavers and even the familiar garden spider, which can attain impressive population densities in urban settings and gardens, all of which have a vital place in the food chain.

Bee hotel and leafcutter bees. Leafcutter bees are some of the main exploiters of bee hotels in the built environment.

However, what one would ideally wish for is a built environment that is deliberately designed to promote invertebrate diversity beyond the norm, for any of the following reasons:

- to compensate for or mitigate any habitat losses associated with development, in the spirit of biodiversity offsetting;
- to provide people with the chance to see interesting and attractive species, such as butterflies, bees and hoverflies, at close quarters;
- to promote 'ecosystem services' by supporting invertebrates that act as pollinators, pest predators, decomposers and soil aerators and contribute to food chains; and
- to contribute to larger landscape-scale habitats with increased potential for rich, varied and interesting invertebrate assemblages, i.e. built environments that complement and interact with their surrounding landscape and provide corridors and stepping stones for invertebrate movement at a landscape scale.

1.4.1 How invertebrates can use the built environment

External walls
Older walls with soft mortar often support a variety of bees, wasps, spiders, beetles and other invertebrates that require holes and crevices. It is possible to incorporate features in new buildings that can replicate these microhabitats. On sunny walls, 'bee hotels' (blocks of tubes of different dimension with one end facing outwards) can be attached or even incorporated directly into the brickwork and will usually attract nesting mason bees, leafcutter bees and mason wasps plus various parasites and lodgers such as ruby-tailed wasps within a few years, especially if flowery habitats are present nearby. Bumblebees require larger nesting boxes, but these can also be attached to walls and may be colonised by aerial-nesting species such as the tree bumblebee. Walls provide a good opportunity for promoting key pollinators such as bees.

Inside a building
Humidity, darkness and shelter are requirements for many invertebrates living inside buildings, including a variety of building-reliant 'synanthropic' species. For the most part, these will be common species that do not require active conservation, and some, such as clothes moths and carpet beetles, are pests. Outhouses tend to be cooler, damper and less airtight. As such, they can support a far larger potential fauna and interact more strongly with gardens and surrounding green space.

Living walls
Training appropriate climbing plants up walls is a particularly easy way of creating diverse opportunities for invertebrates in new developments, especially if the climbers provide both shelter and flowers. Evergreen species such as ivy make the best option as they provide year-round shelter and the flowers attract a good variety of insects, especially if grown on the sunny sides of buildings. Pyracantha and cotoneaster are often used and have great wildlife value, but beware as a number of varieties are highly invasive within semi-natural habitats, and there are parts of Britain where Natural England strongly advises against the planting of these. Roses, honeysuckles and clematis species are generally deciduous, with flowers that appeal to fewer insects, though they can add diversity, and honeysuckle flowers are much used by bumblebees and moths. The foliage of climbers can support further invertebrates, such as spiders, and any accumulating leaf litter can attract woodlice, snails, etc.

Peacock caterpillar and butterfly. Tolerating nettle beds in the corner of a garden or elsewhere within urban greenspace will benefit several butterflies including the Peacock

Bumblebees will seek nectar from a wide range of plants. Ensuring something is in flower for much of the year is invaluable

Careful selection of plant species can ensure that living walls are in flower from spring until autumn. Climbing plants on north-facing walls are also valuable for invertebrates that like shade, shelter and greater humidity. They have the potential to be valuable overwintering sites. North-facing walls are also ideal for ferns, which have some associated invertebrates.

More information is provided in Chapters 3 and 5.

1.5 About plants and buildings

In the built environment, vegetation usually occupies specific spaces for which it has been assigned, such as gardens, parks and landscape design features. However, certain plants that are adapted to shallow, nutrient-poor substrates, such as stone and gravel, can grow on our buildings without invitation. In some cases the growth can enhance the appearance and character of buildings. But some plant species can cause damage, direct and indirect, to materials and elements of construction. Managing such growth requires consideration of various factors and the undertaking of a risk assessment weighing the potential damage against the ecological and aesthetic benefits. Legislative protection may restrict or remove treatment options.

Deliberate growth of vegetation on buildings using green roof and living-wall systems provides a way to harness the benefits while reducing the risk of damage to the structure. See Chapter 3 for more information.

Cable trellises with climbing plants are a simple way to create a living wall

1.5.1 Why buildings are important for plants

Buildings present habitats for species from all plant groups. In lowland Britain and Ireland they are especially important for lower plants, ferns, mosses and liverworts, for which they provide the firm, rocky substrate that would otherwise be absent. The flora of buildings varies greatly around the country, depending on climate, degree of pollution, age of the structure and the building materials used.

Restoration and maintenance of buildings needs to be adapted to maintain and enhance this flora. Most plants are found rooted in mortar joints – many species require the alkaline conditions provided by lime mortar, although the stonework itself may be of acidic rock, such as granite. The wall base, face and top each support a different suite of species.

Spectacular vegetation can be associated with the vertical faces of buildings. Walls provide ecologically demanding conditions so may in places support a highly specialist flora – these are usually species of nature conservation value which have minimal impact on the wall structure. Opportunist species, such as bramble, sycamore and buddleia, will grow anywhere and are usually problematic – they have little conservation importance except as habitats for other species.

The presence of biological growth on buildings often provides a useful indicator of excess moisture. Investigation of the nature and extent of growth can highlight defects in the fabric or rainwater, overflows or plumbing drainage systems. It might also indicate the exposed nature of the location, a south-western elevation facing a coast, prevailing precipitation from sea mists, river valley fog, etc. and the absence of local atmospheric pollution.

Honeysuckle is a valuable source of nectar for day and night flying insects. Birds will also use it to forage for fruits and insects, and also to nest in

Ivy is important for late summer nectar and late winter fruits. It also provides invertebrates with cover and shelter throughout the year

1.5.2 Herbaceous and woody plants, climbers and creepers

Small herbaceous species with soft stems – such as ivy-leaved toadflax, ferns, hawkweeds, yellow corydalis, stonecrops, bellflowers, winter annuals, purple toadflax, Oxford ragwort and many others – do not break down walls. Many are considered attractive and can be left to decorate walls, providing local character and softening otherwise hard landscape features. Ivy-leaved toadflax can become locally so dense that it obscures stonework and needs controlling.

Climbing plants should never be allowed to grow into the roof space or in and out of the gutters. They can lift entire roof timbers and misalign the surfaces and also break slates and tiles.

Aim to use climbing plants that do not have suckers. The suckers can break through the outer painted surface or into the stone or pointing and are often difficult to remove.

The best way to make use of climbing plants is by using a trellis, or a series of wires or other structure which provides a frame for climbing, with the plant being attached to the frame and not to the wall. This will also, if cleverly designed, enable redecoration of the wall behind the plant.

Ivy is one of the most common, and most potentially structurally damaging, woody plants found on walls. It does not necessarily pose a threat; if growing on good brickwork it simply grows over the surface and will not cause damage. On older walls the stems can enter cracks and expand, loosening the blocks. However, a really dense growth of old stems can also hold a wall together – in this case its removal can both be unsightly and lead to severe damage. A build-up of dense growth at a wall head can also increase the 'wall area' exposed to the wind. This imposes additional stresses in the wall structure which, in extreme conditions, can lead to premature failure or wall collapse. Therefore, if the decision is taken to leave the ivy in situ, it will be necessary to control its growth at the wall head.

Ivy is also important for other wildlife. It provides a home and food source for some invertebrates, but it can shade out lichens. If important lichen species are present it may be preferable to remove some of the ivy.

Oxford ragwort and ivy-leaved toadflax
on a Warwick wall

Climbing plants

1.5.3 Lichens and mosses

The presence of lichen and mosses on roof coverings and wall surfaces often has aesthetic appeal and can contribute to the appearance of the building. A new concrete or rendered building can often be a glaring eyesore. It might be more rapidly toned down and given an older, more muted appearance via the colonisation of lichens, algae and mosses.

Lichens, needing only an attachment, can colonise almost any surface, even sheet metals (such as copper and lead flashings and roof coverings) and other inorganic materials, and assist in the colonisation of surfaces by mosses and other plants. Some lichens have a preference for specific types of surfaces, e.g. basic concrete or acidic rock. While lichens cause virtually no deterioration of a substrate, their removal can be damaging to the substrate.

Mosses and liverworts present little threat to a building – their root-like rhizoids can do no damage. They do absorb and hold moisture, which means they can keep the surfaces of tiles and slates damp, which can then speed up the process of weathering. If the retained water freezes, roof tiles/slates can be damaged. In addition, colonies that dry out can become detached from the roof and block gutters and flumes.

If it is believed that moss/liverwort growth on a certain roof slope needs to be controlled, care must be taken to ensure that the plants are not completely removed if any are rare. A number of moss and liverwort species are protected under Schedule 8 of the Wildlife and Countryside Act 1981 (see Table 2.2). It is an offence to destroy these species, wherever they are found, if it can be reasonably avoided.

The microhabitat of the building will have a profound effect on which species will grow at a particular site. A low-pitched, north-facing roof will be colonised most readily by mosses. A steep-pitched, north-facing roof will frequently be covered in grey *Physcia* lichen species as well as the mosses. A south-facing roof is better illuminated and also drier and would favour the yellow *Xanthoria* and other sun-loving species of lichen, such as *Lecanora muralis*. Any shading from other buildings or trees will also affect the range of species that colonise the site. Overhanging trees may, however, increase the amount of nutrient that falls on the roof, from bird droppings, pollen, dust and also the 'honeydew' secreted by aphids. Damp retained in cracks on roofs, or between tiles, will help the colonisation of mosses and lichens. If soft mortar is used in walls, this will retain the moisture for longer periods. Soft or cement mortars will, over a period, leach out and make the surrounding brickwork more alkaline and therefore more suitable for the species that need an alkaline situation. Shaded damp sites will also encourage the growth of green algae.

1.5.4 Green roofs and living walls

Purpose-built solutions for plants on buildings, such as green roofs and living walls, minimise the potential problems for the building structure while maximising gains for biodiversity (if designed correctly). More information is provided in Chapters 3 and 5.

1.5.5 Further reading

- *When Nature Moves In: A Guide to Managing Wildlife on Buildings*, National Trust (2013)
- Watt, David (2006) *Managing Biological Growth on Buildings*. Available at: www.buildingconservation.com/article/bio/bio.htm
- British Lichen Society (1996) *Lichens on Man-made Surfaces*. www.thebls.org.uk/content/mmade.html

Lichens are incredibly useful because they tell us about the health of our environment. Lichens are very sensitive to air pollution; the type and size of lichen can tell us how polluted the area is. Lichens are also useful to their neighbours, recycling nutrients used by other plants and providing homes for spiders, mites, lice and other insects. Humans use them for extracting an incredible range of wool dyes and also eat some of the edible species, while drug companies use lichens to make antibiotics or sunscreen cream. (source: http://www.nhm.ac.uk/nature-online/life/plants-fungi/lichens).

Wall with moss and ferns

Lichens growing on a mortered grit stone wall

CHAPTER TWO

Legislation, policy and regulations

This chapter provides an overview of wildlife and planning legislation, the current policy surrounding the superseded Biodiversity Action Plan and the Building Regulations. The intention is to illustrate the processes and common areas that link legislation, policy and regulations together, and then view the whole picture in the context of the theme of this book. It is, however, natural that some readers may wish to explore certain aspects in more depth and so alongside the key facts there are links to further sources of information.

2.1 Wildlife legislation and what it means

There is a range of wildlife legislation that applies to species that use buildings. This legislation falls into two types:

1. To protect those species that have been deemed sufficiently vulnerable to require either protection under national legislation or from European Directives which have subsequently been implemented into UK law. Some species, including all bat species, are protected by both and are commonly referred to as European Protected Species (EPS).
2. There is also legislation that emphasises the need to maintain and enhance biodiversity.

Importantly, this book deals with enhancing biodiversity by providing potential roosting and nesting sites that low or zero carbon buildings are otherwise unlikely to support. Before we concentrate on enhancement for biodiversity, it is important that we outline the role of the legislation that protects the species in question when they are already present and likely to be adversely affected by development proposals. Table 2.1 provides a list of the legislation most likely to apply to species associated with buildings. Table 2.2 explores, in uncomplicated terms, the most common application of this key legislation as it relates to wildlife and buildings.

Table 2.1: UK wildlife legislation relevant to biodiversity in buildings

England	Wales	Scotland	Northern Ireland
Wildlife and Countryside Act 1981 (as amended)			Wildlife NI Order 1985 (as amended)
Conservation of Habitats and Species Regulations 2010 and Amendments (2012)			Nature Conservation and Amenity Lands (NI) Order 1985 (as amended)
Countryside and Rights of Way Act 2000		The Nature Conservation (Scotland) Act 2004	The Conservation (Natural Habitats etc.) Regulations (NI) 1995 (as amended)
Natural Environment and Rural Communities Act 2006			Environment (Northern Ireland) Order 2002

Table 2.2: The UK's main wildlife legislation in practical terms

Legislation	Application
Wildlife and Countryside Act 1981 (as amended)	This is the principal wildlife legislation in Great Britain for birds and includes the protection of certain species and the places they use for shelter and protection. All wild birds, their nests and eggs are, with few exceptions, fully protected by law. In addition, over 80 species or groups of species are listed under Schedule 1 of the Wildlife and Countryside Act 1981 (as amended).
	The Act makes it an offence to intentionally kill, injure or take any wild bird or their eggs or to take, damage or destroy the nest while that nest is in use or being built (with the exception of a small number of birds listed under Schedule 2).
	Special penalties may be awarded for any offences related to birds listed on Schedule 1 of the Act. These include the peregrine falcon and barn owl, for which there are additional offences of disturbing while at their nests, or their dependent young.
	The maximum penalty that can be imposed for an offence in respect of a single bird, nest or egg is a fine of up to £5,000 and/or six months' imprisonment.
	The Act does also give some protection for bats and roosts in England and Wales, such as for intentional or reckless obstruction of access to a roost, but for practical purposes the protection of bats and their roosts now falls mostly under the Conservation of Habitats and Species Regulations 2010 (see below).
Conservation of Habitats and Species Regulations 2010 and Amendments (2012)	The Conservation of Habitats and Species Regulations 2010 (and Amendments 2012) acts to consolidate all the amendments made to the Conservation (Natural Habitats &c.) Regulations 1994 in respect to England and Wales. The 1994 Regulations derived from the EU Directive 92/43/EEC on the Conservation of Natural Habitats and of Wild Fauna and Flora 1992 and Council Directive 79/409/EEC on the conservation of wild birds. The Habitats Regulations implemented these Directives into National law. This legislation affords protection to a range of species termed 'European Protected Species' (EPS). EPS include all species of bats found in the UK.
	Under Regulation 39 it is an offence for anyone to intentionally kill, injure or take any wild bat, or sell, offer or expose for sale any live or dead bat. It is also an offence to damage or destroy any place used by bats for shelter or as a breeding site, whether they are present or not. A further offence is to deliberately or recklessly disturb a bat in a way that would affect its ability to survive, breed or rear young or affect the local distribution or abundance of the species.
	The maximum sentences for offences relating to bats are a £5,000 fine and/or six months' imprisonment. The forfeiture of any bat or other thing by the court is mandatory on conviction, and items used to commit the offence – vehicles, for example – may be forfeited.
Countryside and Rights of Way Act 2000	For protected species, this Act strengthens the existing wildlife legislation by clarifying the wording of what constitutes an offence and the severity of penalties.
Natural Environment and Rural Communities Act 2006	This legislation places a statutory duty on all public bodies in England and Wales that each must, in exercising its functions, have regard, so far as is consistent with the proper exercise of those functions, to the purpose of conserving biodiversity (Section 40).
	Section 41 of the Act requires the Secretary of State to publish a list of habitats and species which are of principal importance for the conservation of biodiversity. The list has been drawn up in consultation with Natural England, as required by the Act.
	The Section 41 list (UK List of Priority Species and Habitats) is used to guide decision makers such as public bodies, including local and regional authorities, in implementing their duty under Section 40 of the Act, to have regard to the conservation of biodiversity in England, when carrying out their normal functions.
	There are 944 species of principal importance included on the Section 41 list. These are the species which have been identified as requiring action under the UK Biodiversity Action Plan (now superseded) and which continue to be regarded as conservation priorities under the UK Post 2010 Biodiversity Framework. Species listed include the house sparrow, starling and seven species of bat – of which four are particularly reliant on buildings for roosts (greater and lesser horseshoe bats, soprano pipistrelle and brown long-eared bats).
The Nature Conservation (Scotland) Act 2004	In Scotland, it is the duty of every public body and office holder, in exercising any functions, to further the conservation of biodiversity so far as is consistent with the proper exercise of those functions.

For activities that would otherwise be illegal, but where a valid justification exists, European Protected Species (EPS) licences can be issued. However, these can only be granted if the licensing authority is satisfied that the activity is preserving public health or public safety, or if there are other imperative reasons of overriding public interest. It must also be satisfied that there is no satisfactory alternative, and that the action authorised will not be detrimental to the maintenance of the population of the species concerned at a favourable conservation status in their natural range (i.e. affect the long-term distribution and abundance of its populations within the area). These licences are issued by Natural England in England, Natural Resources Wales in Wales, the Scottish Government Rural Directorate in Scotland, and the Environment and Heritage Service Northern Ireland.

For further details on species legislation, please refer to the following websites:

- Joint Nature Conservation Committee www.jncc.gov.uk
- Department for Environment, Food and Rural Affairs www.defra.gov.uk
- Natural England www.naturalengland.org.uk
- Natural Resources Wales http://naturalresourceswales.gov.uk
- Scottish Government www.scotland.gov.uk
- Northern Ireland Environment Agency www.ehsni.gov.uk
- Bat Conservation Trust www.bats.org.uk
- Royal Society for the Protection of Birds www.rspb.org.uk

2.2 The planning process and biodiversity

The planning process is guided by its own set of legislation and regulations, and the most prominent of these are shown in Table 2.3.

Table 2.3: Planning legislation and policy in the UK

	England	Wales	Scotland	Northern Ireland
Planning legislation	Town and Country Planning Act 1990		Town and Country Planning (Scotland) Act 1997	The Planning (Northern Ireland) Order 1991 (as amended)
Planning regulations	The Town and Country Planning (Environmental Impact Assessment) (England and Wales) Regulations 2011 (SI 2011 No. 1824)		The Environmental Impact Assessment (Scotland) Regulations 1999 (Scottish SI 1999 No. 1)	Planning (Environmental Impact Assessment) Regulations (Northern Ireland) 1999 (SR 1999 No. 73)
	The Environmental Assessment of Plans and Programmes Regulations 2004 (SI 2004 No. 1633)	The Environmental Assessment of Plans and Programmes (Wales) Regulations 2004 Welsh Statutory Instrument No.1656 (W.170)	The Environmental Assessment of Plans and Programmes (Scotland) Regulations 2004 (Scottish Statutory Instrument No. 258) Circular 2/2004: Strategic Environmental Assessment for Development Planning; The Environmental Assessment of Plans and Programmes (Scotland) Regulations 2004	The Environmental Assessment of Plans and Programmes Regulations (Northern Ireland) 2004 (Statutory Rule 2004 No. 280)

Guidance from the Government on the implementation of this legislation is given in a series of planning policy guidance. In the UK we have the following guidance on how planning officers should take nature conservation matters into account:

- In England, National Planning Policy Framework NPPF 2012; Circular 06/2005 Biodiversity and Geological Conservation — Statutory Obligations and their Impact within the Planning System (ODPM, 2005a); Planning for Biodiversity and Geological Conservation: A Good Practice Guide (ODPM, 2006) (see www.communities.gov.uk).
- In Wales, TAN5 Nature Conservation and Planning 2009 (http://new.wales.gov.uk).
- In Scotland, National Planning Framework for Scotland 2 (2009); Scottish Planning Policy 2010 (SPP); the Scottish Biodiversity Strategy – Scotland's biodiversity: it's in your hands 2004 (www.scotland.gov.uk).
- In Northern Ireland, PPS2 Planning and Nature Conservation (www.ni-environment.gov.uk).

The planning legislation and terminology differ slightly in each country, but the principles are similar.

The important link between wildlife legislation and planning policy from the point of view of the biodiversity enhancements detailed in this book are those legislative requirements for the conservation and enhancement of biodiversity by local authorities.

Guidance exists on carrying out this function for local authorities in the form of the publication *Guidance for Local Authorities on Implementing the Biodiversity Duty* (Defra, 2007a; www.defra.gov.uk), although the most specific guidance is given in the legislation and regulations documents detailed above for each of the UK countries.

The Biodiversity Planning Toolkit provides a one-stop service for all matters related to biodiversity in the planning process. (www.biodiversityplanningtoolkit.com).

In order to give a picture of how the planning application process works with regard to the consideration of biodiversity, Table 2.4 maps the development process, biodiversity consideration and the planning process onto the stages of the RIBA Outline Plan of Work.

Table 2.4: RIBA Outline Plan of Work, showing at which stages biodiversity must be considered during a traditional procurement process. Please note that there is a Green Overlay to the RIBA Plan of Work that provides sustainability checkpoints for all the stages

RIBA work stages		
Stage 0 Strategic Definition	**Stage 1** Preparation & Brief	**Stage 2** Concept Design
Development Process		
Appraisals		**Design**
• Establish objectives • Design team selection • Initial feasibility studies • Land identification • Secure land purchase option • Produce Masterplan • Complete land purchase		• Identify opportunities and constraints • Prepare Section 106 agreement and Community Infrastructure Levy • Detailed planning application (note 1)
Biodiversity consideration		
Consultation and/or scoping study		
		Detailed survey and impact assessment
		Design of development to incorporate biodiversity objectives
Planning Process		
Pre-application guidance and advice on application type		Guidance and advice on application type
Procurement Process		
		Timescale for tendering will depend on the level of detail required and the form of procurement being used. Refer to Project Programme.

Stage 3 Developed Design	Stage 4 Technical Design	Stage 5 Construction	Stage 6 Handover & Close Out	Stage 7 In Use
	Pre-construction • Preparation of detailed production information (drawings, specifications, etc.) • Application for statutory approvals	**Construction** • Construction works • Divestiture of development		**Use** • Ongoing monitoring and maintenance by management company • Review of project performance in review
Prepare and agree enhancement, mitigation and compensation				
		Implement agreed enhancement, mitigation and compensation		
		Management, monitoring and aftercare		
Validation and registration Pre-decision assessment Formal determination of Planning application (note 1)		Compliance monitoring		Annual monitoring report, which includes reporting the effects of development consents on priority habitats and species
• Award contract • Tender returns and appraisal				

Note 1 Planning may also take place at the end of stage 2 – Refer to specific Project Programme

As Table 2.4 illustrates, information showing how well or how adversely a development has impacted on priority species and habitats is reported by the local authority in their Annual Monitoring Report. A brief explanation of priority habitats and species, and the Biodiversity Action Plan reporting that they are a part of, now follows.

2.3 National biodiversity reporting

In 1992, 153 nations signed the Convention on Biological Diversity (CBD) at the Rio Earth Summit. As a result, the UK Biodiversity Action Plan (UK BAP) for the protection of the UK's priority habitats and species was published in 1994. Individual Biodiversity Action Plans (BAPs) for the most threatened species set the targets and actions required to aid their recovery. Each plan also identified the partners who were needed to make it happen. These BAPs for priority species and habitats were produced at the national, regional and local levels. National reporting on the progress of biodiversity action in line with the CBD was to be delivered every three to five years. The local-level plans translated the national targets into local actions. Additional local plans were also produced for any species or habitats that were considered important at a local level.

In 1998, devolution led the four countries of the UK (England, Northern Ireland, Scotland and Wales) to develop their own country-specific strategies for biodiversity, allowing conservation approaches to differ depending on the priorities within each country. In 2007, however, a shared vision for UK biodiversity conservation was adopted by the devolved administrations and the UK Government, and is described in *Conserving Biodiversity – The UK Approach* (Defra, 2007b).

In 2011 the Government published *Biodiversity 2020: A Strategy for England's Wildlife and Ecosystem Services* which set out a strategic direction for biodiversity policy. The *UK Post-2010 Biodiversity Framework* (JNCC and Defra, 2012), published in July 2012, is the Government's response to a change in strategic thinking following the publication of the CBD's *Strategic Plan for Biodiversity 2011–2020* (CBD, 2010), and the launch of the new *EU Biodiversity Strategy* (EUBS) in May 2011 (European Commission, 2011). The framework now replaces the UK-level BAP and its associated processes and demonstrates how the work of the four countries and the UK contributes to achieving the specific targets detailed within the framework. It also identifies the activities required to complement the country biodiversity strategies in achieving the targets.

Following the publication of the outputs of the new Framework, the UK BAP partnership no longer operates, but many of the outputs originally developed under the UK BAP remain valid and of use. For example, background information on UK BAP priority habitats and species still informs much of the biodiversity work at country level and remains a point of reference for targeted conservation efforts.

It is biodiversity at the local level that public bodies have a duty to conserve and enhance. Within the Local Development Framework (LDF) guidance there is a requirement for local authorities to report annually against a series of Core Output Indicators. One such indicator is entitled 'Ways of assessing biodiversity change'. So losses and gains to biodiversity that are anticipated as a result of a proposed development must be reported on in detail as part of a planning application which the Local Planning Authority will consider when reaching its decision. If consented, the information on losses or gains to biodiversity is fed through the reporting system and will inform a feedback mechanism (see Figure 2.1) on the impact of the construction industry on biodiversity.

Figure 2.1 illustrates the feedback loop. This was produced by a project working group, hosted by the Royal Town Planning Institute (RTPI) and involved representatives from industry, government advisory bodies and non-government wildlife organisations, working towards making this complex reporting system easier to use, more effective and, potentially, more widely used than it is currently.

This section has illustrated the connection between wildlife legislation, planning policy and process and biodiversity reporting that are relevant to the enhancement measures made to buildings. This is shown diagrammatically in Figure 2.2.

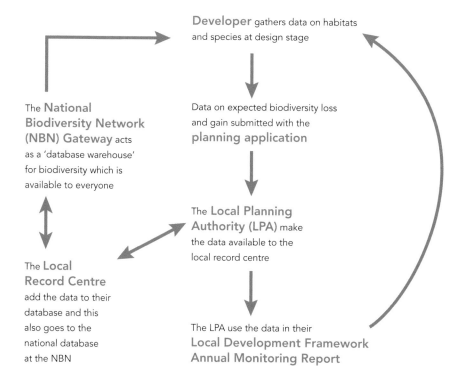

Developer gathers data on habitats and species at design stage

The National Biodiversity Network (NBN) Gateway acts as a 'database warehouse' for biodiversity which is available to everyone

Data on expected biodiversity loss and gain submitted with the planning application

The Local Planning Authority (LPA) make the data available to the local record centre

The Local Record Centre add the data to their database and this also goes to the national database at the NBN

The LPA use the data in their Local Development Framework Annual Monitoring Report

2.1: Reporting between the developer, the Local Planning Authority and Local Record Centres should act as a feedback loop to measure the impact of construction on biodiversity

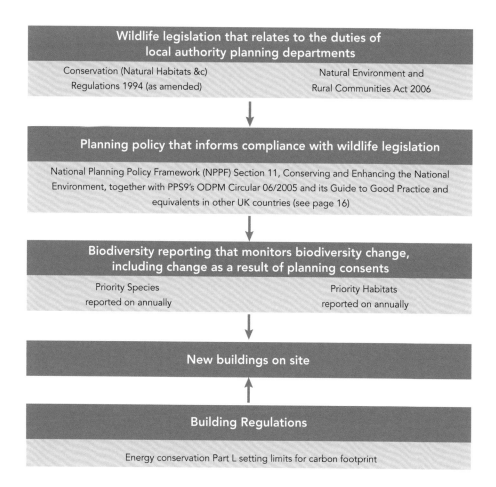

Wildlife legislation that relates to the duties of local authority planning departments

Conservation (Natural Habitats &c) Regulations 1994 (as amended)

Natural Environment and Rural Communities Act 2006

Planning policy that informs compliance with wildlife legislation

National Planning Policy Framework (NPPF) Section 11, Conserving and Enhancing the National Environment, together with PPS9's ODPM Circular 06/2005 and its Guide to Good Practice and equivalents in other UK countries (see page 16)

Biodiversity reporting that monitors biodiversity change, including change as a result of planning consents

Priority Species reported on annually

Priority Habitats reported on annually

New buildings on site

Building Regulations

Energy conservation Part L setting limits for carbon footprint

2.2: Connection between wildlife legislation, planning policy and process, and biodiversity in England

The part of the diagram in Figure 2.2 yet to be covered, but of great importance, concerns the Building Regulations.

2.4 Building Regulations

The Building Regulations set standards for the design and construction of buildings in order to ensure the safety and health of people in or about those buildings. They also include requirements to ensure that fuel and power are conserved and that facilities are provided for people, including those with disabilities, to access and move around inside buildings. The relevant Acts and regulations for the UK are shown in Table 2.5.

Table 2.5: Acts and regulations for the UK

	Act	Regulations	Part relating to Energy	Date last updated
England and Wales	Building Act 1984	Building Regulations 2010	Part L	2013
Scotland	Building (Scotland) Act 2003	Building (Scotland) Regulations 2011	Section 6	2011
Northern Ireland	Building Regulations (Northern Ireland) Order 1979	Building Regulations (Northern Ireland) 2012	Sections F1 and F2	2012

The Building Regulations for England and Wales are made under powers provided in the Building Act 1984. The current (2010) edition of the regulations are the Building Regulations 2000 (as amended) and The Building (Approved Inspectors etc.) Regulations 2000 (as amended), and the majority of building projects are required to comply with them.

The requirements with which building work should comply are contained in Schedule 1 to the Building Regulations and are grouped under 14 'parts', which include subjects such as fire safety, access, toxic substances, ventilation and, most importantly for this book, the conservation of fuel and power.

The Approved Documents (ADs) are produced by the Government and give guidance on how the requirements of the Building Regulations can be satisfied. The guidance given in these ADs does not have to be followed, but if it is not, then it has to be demonstrated that by other means the requirements have been satisfied. The ADs are updated more often than the regulations themselves.

The ADs are published by NBS and paper versions can be purchased from the RIBA (www.ribabookshops.com) or they can be downloaded for free from the Planning Portal website (www.planningportal.gov.uk).

There are four Approved Documents to Part L on the conservation of fuel and power:

Dwellings:
- Approved Document L1A: Conservation of fuel and power (New dwellings) (2010 edition).
- Approved Document L1B: Conservation of fuel and power (Existing dwellings) (2010 edition).

Buildings other than dwellings:
- Approved Document L2A: Conservation of fuel and power (New buildings other than dwellings) (2010 edition).
- Approved Document L2B: Conservation of fuel and power (Existing buildings other than dwellings) (2010 edition).

Part L underwent a major revision in 2010, and the drivers for the change included the Government's Energy White Paper commitment to raise the energy performance of buildings and the introduction of European legislation — the Energy Performance of Buildings Directive. Further revisions to Part L demanding increased energy efficiency are expected in 2013 and 2016. By 2016, all homes must be zero carbon and all buildings must be zero carbon by 2019.

In order to reach these energy targets, buildings must have sufficient thermal insulation to slow down the flow of heat from inside to outside. Ideally this insulation is continuous, with no gaps for heat loss, thermal bridging or thermal flanking. U values give a measure of heat loss; the lower the U value, the smaller the loss of heat — so a low U value is a good U value. There is also a need for an 'airtightness layer' to stop heat loss through warm air leakage occurring. This can be achieved in a number of ways depending on the design of the building and the materials used. So the difference between a low or zero carbon energy building and a conventional building will be the presence of a very good U value, thermal bridge-free and airtightness minimising the need for heating ventilation and/or cooling. In practice, all new buildings and refurbishments should be low energy. Turning low to zero energy buildings into low to zero carbon buildings relies on adopting an appropriate combination of the following options; building fabric being the priority for new build and low carbon energy for conservation quality refurbishment projects:

- Decarbonising the grid-supplied energy by reducing the number of fossil fuel power stations and increasing renewable energy input.
- Choosing from lower carbon fuel options and power options.
- Project producing its own renewable energy (any surplus to requirements to top up the grid supply)
- Decarbonising the building fabric:
  - replacing fossil carbon-based or carbon generating materials (e.g. cement, hydro-carbons (plastics))
  - increasing renewable-carbon materials (plant-fibre and timber-based materials)

In July 2009 the UK Government published *The UK Low Carbon Transition Plan: National Strategy for Climate and Energy*. This confirmed the Government's policy that all new homes will be zero carbon from 2016. This was reconfirmed by the *Carbon Plan: Delivering our low carbon future* published by the Department of Energy and Climate Change in 2011. In July 2013 HM Government announced amendments to The Building Regulations 2010 affecting Approved Documents L1A, L1B, L2A, L2B coming into force in April 2014 and indicated that the 2016 targets are now delayed to 2019.

Unless biodiversity is considered early on in the design process, these ever more stringent demands for increased energy efficiency of buildings will lead to losses for the biodiversity that has shared our built environment for centuries. This book addresses this issue because if we do not, there will be very few, if any, future roosting opportunities for bats or nesting opportunities for birds in our buildings. Without these measures, key species will be adversely affected by new developments and low carbon refurbishments, meaning not only a failure to achieve truly sustainable building, but also an erosion of the quality of life we all hope to experience in our working and home environments.

CHAPTER THREE

Designing for biodiversity in new buildings

This chapter highlights some general principles about nesting and roosting that should be considered when designing for biodiversity enhancement. It then considers some of the ready-made products for roosting and nesting that are on the market, before going on to explain how these, and bespoke roosting and nesting spaces, can be incorporated into new building design.

As this book is about biodiversity enhancement, the importance of other environmental sustainability issues is recognised and this is reflected in the comments on a range of other associated topics that will be referred to in this chapter.

3.1 General principles

There are certain details about nesting and roosting that need to be considered. These will be related to the size of the provision, the size and location of the access to it, the aspect and height at which it is placed, the spacing between each, the materials it is made of, and its location in the context of features of the surrounding environment. In addition, the presence or absence of target bird and bat species should be considered.

Looking at the needs of building-reliant species in a slightly wider context, it will always be important that they are able to find sufficient food within the range they can travel from the building in which they have their nesting/roosting provision. The range will vary between species, but it is worth noting that many of the species in question are insectivorous and so any habitat features nearby that host insects, such as rivers, ponds, unimproved grasslands, ancient semi-natural woodland and hedgerows planted with native vegetation, will all prove valuable if close at hand. Even species that can travel many kilometres will benefit from saving their energy and being able to feed closer to home.

Information on landscape and connectivity is covered in more detail in Chapter 5.

This book is not intended to take the place of an ecologist and it is expected that the choice of provision for enhancing the biodiversity of built structures, and how that is accommodated within any development, will be guided by an experienced ecologist (website details for ecologist organisations are given at the end of this book). It is always preferable to get a recommendation for similar work undertaken.

Table 3.1 takes principles about the dimensions, internal conditions and location of roost and nest provision, and gives some general indications of requirements.

Legend to Table 3.1:
(w) external width of body or box across the front shown face
(h) external height of body or box from top to bottom
(d) external depth of body or box from front shown front face to hidden back

Bat/bird species	Access dimensions	Roost/nesting dimensions	Height of entry	
Crevice-dwelling bats	20–50 mm (w) x 15–20 mm (h)	Any size as long as some components of the area are crevices in the region of 20–30 mm Greater total areas of about 1 sq m would be useful for nursery (summer) roosts Male roosts contain smaller numbers of bats or even individual bats Roof void-dwelling bats need timber joists or beams on which to roost	2–7 m	
Bats needing a flying area	20–50 mm (w) x 15–20 mm (h)	5 m (w) x 2.8 m (h) x 5 m (d) Not trussed, to allow flight Ideally 2.8 m height, but a height of 2 m may be acceptable in some circumstances To incorporate roost crevices, dimensions as above for crevice-dwelling bats	Over 2 m	
Horseshoe bats	Lesser horseshoes: 300 mm (w) x 200 mm (h) Greater horseshoes: 400 mm (w) x 300 mm (h)	5 m (w) x 2.8 m (h) x 5 m (d) Not trussed, to allow flight A height of 2 m may be acceptable in some circumstances	Over 2 m	
Swift	At least 65 mm (w) x 33 mm (h) This excludes starlings The bottom of the hole should be no more than 5 cm above the floor of the nest	Floor area at least 350 sq cm, e.g.: 12 cm x 30 cm 17.5 cm x 20 cm 15 cm x 25 cm Preferably larger where space is available, e.g. 400 mm (w) x 175 mm (h) Headroom possibly as low as 75 mm when space is constrained; recommend greater than 100 mm where space is available, e.g. 150 mm or 200 mm	At least 5 m above ground and away from obstructions and creepers Preferably integral to the building, but where this is not possible external, e.g. under the eaves	
House sparrow	32 mm diameter round hole Bottom of the hole must be no less than 150 mm from base of box	150 mm (w) x 250 mm (h) x 150 mm (d)	Ideally within the structure at soffit/eaves level, but otherwise as an external box at this same location At least 3 m high for starlings and 2 m for sparrows	
Starling	45 mm diameter round hole Bottom of the hole must be no less than 180 mm from base of box	180 mm (w) x 300 mm (h) x 180 mm (d)		
House martin	60–65 mm (w) x 25 mm (h)	180 mm diameter	Precast nests are available and should be placed at least 3 m above the ground underneath the eaves, but not directly above windows or doors	
Swallow	To access the interior of a building, swallows require a gap of 70 mm (w) x 50 mm (h)	Nesting platform 260 mm (w) x 100 mm (d)	Precast nests are available or nesting platforms can be made These should be placed on a ledge inside a building at least 2 m above the ground where droppings will not be a nuisance	
Black redstart	Open-fronted box 75 mm high at front	150 mm (w) x 260 mm (h) x 150 mm (d)	Locate in sheltered ledges or beneath the eaves of a service entrance on top of a roof	
Barn owl	130 mm (w) x 250 mm (h) into building 130 mm (w) x 130 mm (h) into internal box where these are provided	400 mm (w) x 600 (h) x 400 mm (d)	Over 3 m	
Peregrine falcon	Open air	A shallow tray with raised edges, optionally containing substrate such as gravel or pea shingle and compost or woodchips, is secured to a sheltered ledge on the structure 600 mm (w) x 40 mm (h) x 450 mm (d) Alternatively, a box 600 mm (w) x 900 mm (h) x 450 mm (d) can be provided	Over 20 m	
Kestrel	300 mm (w) x 300 mm (h) 500 mm (d) with a minimum 100 mm overhanging roof above entrance	300 mm (w) x 300 (h) x 500 mm (d)	Over 3 m	

Aspect of roost	Temperature °C		Materials and other comments
	Summer	Winter	
Summer nursery roosts on most southerly or westerly aspect for solar heating. However, the risk of overheating should be considered. A location that provides a stable microclimate/regime may work better than one that heats up quickly and loses heat quickly Male roosts and winter hibernation roosts on northerly aspect	30–40 (daytime)	0–6	Rough (for grip) Natural materials such as untreated timber, stone or masonry is preferred Not toxic or corrosive No risk of entanglement Suitable thermal properties (reducing 24-hour fluctuations), but allowing suitable thermal gain for summer roosts
The crevice-roosting provision within the roost to be located on the south or west side for solar heating, or in the most thermally stable location The location of the flight area is not as important	30–40	0–6	North facing boxes used for hibernating will benefit from using insulating materials Larger crevice spaces (particularly in the vertical dimension) can provide a range of temperatures, which will allow the bats to move according to their temperature needs Access not lit by artificial lighting
The roost is most likely to be in a roof space; this should have an orientation that allows a south-facing solar gain or, better still, an L-shape to allow temperature-range choice	30–40	6–10	
In shade, out of direct sunlight and away from windows	Avoid direct sun that would lead to overheating		Boxes made from concrete, masonry or marine ply or else compartments created within a suitable part of the building It is important to have several potential nest sites for swifts in one area For establishing a new colony, playing recorded swift calls is extremely useful to aid their finding the site
Out of direct sun; preferably east-facing			It is important to have several potential nest sites in one area Can be as close as 150 mm apart
Out of direct sunlight; preferably east-facing Not over the main living area as the birds can be noisy			It is important to have several potential nest sites in one area Can be as close as 1.5 m apart
North- or east-facing Avoid positioning where droppings will be an issue			Swallows and house martins require a source of damp mud in order to construct their nests Swallow nests should not be placed close together
No requirement			House martins are colonial in their nesting, so several nests together will prove attractive to them
Out of direct sun, wind and rain			Brownfield sites with patchy, sparse vegetation growing on stony shale with ephemeral artificial pools provide suitable foraging areas
Facing away from prevailing winds and towards open countryside	No requirement		Internal boxes: softwood shuttering ply or similar No sharp edges Where access is through a vertical structure, a ledge on which to land to gain access to the roof space and/or roost is important unless the gap is large enough for flight Protected Schedule 1 species and must not be disturbed while breeding
Not located on a part of the building that would face full sun, to prevent overheating of eggs and young North or north-east aspect is best Away from human disturbance and prevailing winds	No requirement, except avoiding full sun		Solid surface An awning or overhang to provide protection from rain can be beneficial for brood nests Protected Schedule 1 species and must not be disturbed while breeding
Facing away from prevailing winds and towards open countryside	No requirement, except avoiding full sun		Internal boxes: softwood shuttering ply or similar No sharp edges Requires a landing perch at entrance

Ready-made products – general principles

There are a number of products available that provide roosting or nesting potential either as features to be incorporated into the building or as attachments to it. This book concentrates on those that are designed to be an integral part of the building. These range in price from under £15 to over £120 each, with most in the region of £30 to £80. The market for ready-made products has greatly expanded in the past few years. The products reviewed represent only a selection of the products available on the market, but some of the most popular and well-known products are featured.

Ready-made products are available for some, but not all, of the species discussed in this chapter. Where relevant, a critique of these products is supplied from a construction point of view. Unfortunately, it is not yet possible to make an evaluation based on the extent of use of these products by the wildlife for which they were intended, as often the data on the degree of uptake have not been collected or not enough time has elapsed to give a verdict. The importance of monitoring uptake cannot be overstated. It is only by feedback on success, or otherwise, that future designs and recommendations can be effective.

There are some general points that relate to the size of the product and the ease with which it can be incorporated within any construction. For example, if made in the UK by a brick or stone manufacturer, then it is likely to fit either UK brick or stone measurements. Products from outside the UK will fit the standard construction sizes for the country in question, which differ from those in the UK and so work is required to accommodate them. If designed by species specialists, these may not be to a UK standard construction size.

Solutions to some common problems regarding dimensions and ready-made products are given in Table 3.2. Table 3.3 outlines the advantages of and considerations for materials used in ready-made products.

Register the location of your integrated bat box with the Bat Conservation Trust at www.bats.org.uk/boxplot.

Table 3.2: Solutions to common problems regarding dimensions and ready-made products

Problem	Solution
Width out of coordination	Increase widths of perpend joint in brickwork either side and/or above and below to fit, or add fired clay tile to maintain 10 mm joints
Height out of coordination	Turn bricks on edge underneath or on end and cut soldier course to length
Depth out of coordination	No easy solution – likely to cause thermal bridge through the U value envelope
Width and height out of coordination	Do not use brickwork, but instead use blockwork and render or insulated render so it is possible to conceal the necessary correction measures under render
Width, height and depth out of coordination	No easy solution – consider a different product or method of construction

Tables 3.4 and 3.5 (page 28) explain the advantages and considerations regarding thermal insulation and the airtightness of ready-made products.

To support manufacturers, designers and DIY bat box and bird box makers, GreenSpec Download (www.greenspecdownload.co.uk) has developed a spreadsheet to help determine the sizes of boxes to coordinate with masonry sizes. The aim is to try to work with masonry sizes to avoid disruptive working, to maintain the aesthetics of fair-faced masonry, and to avoid cutting and material waste. Numerous issues are addressed, such as: coordinating with brick, block and stone;

Material		Advantages	Considerations
Clay facing brick		Frost resistant Strong Thermal mass Durable	Absorbent of moisture including urine High embodied energy
Cement-based concrete		Cement is impervious to moisture Strong Durable Thermal mass	High embodied energy High embodied carbon Alkali – do not use aluminium fasteners OPC replacement to reduce embodied carbon
Cement and wood chip fibre concrete		Thermal mass Added moisture mass Medium carbon sequestration Vapour permeable Easy to mould to any shape 50-year track record	Wood will absorb moisture and urine Medium embodied energy Medium embodied carbon Alkali – do not use aluminium fasteners OPC replacement to reduce embodied carbon
Plywood	INT – internal plywood	Carbon sequestration during growth INT suitable for internal construction	INT not suitable for damp, humid conditions Unsuitable in the presence of urine (EN314-1, EN 636-1)
	WBP – weather and boil proof (exterior)	Carbon sequestration during growth External – suitable for external construction WBP suitable for damp, humid conditions Likely to be suitable in the presence of urine	(EN314-3, EN 636-3)
	Marine grade ply	Carbon sequestration during growth Made for yacht making Much more than required for building applications Check for the BSI Kitemark to ensure product is as specified	(BS 1080, EN 350-2, EN 314 class 3)
Cement and wood particle board		Standard building product Fire protection High thermal mass Medium carbon sequestration (wood particles) Tough Durable Low moisture permeable (cement) Uncut cement surfaces will resist water absorption	Wood particles on cut edges may absorb moisture Tough on carpentry tools Alkali – do not use aluminium fasteners Surface hard and smooth – needs roughening for climbing and hanging OPC replacement to reduce embodied carbon
Softwood		Carbon sequestration during growth Readily available locally Reclaimed and reused scraps can be used UKWAS or FSC Easy to work Easy on tools Douglas fir is naturally durable	Most not durable and wood preservatives cannot be used Choose reclaimed, locally grown UKWAS or FSC temperate durable species (avoid preservatives)
Hardwood		Carbon sequestration during growth Readily available locally Reclaimed and reused scraps can be used Easy to work (old oak is hard work) Easy on tools (old oak is hard on tools) Most English hardwoods are naturally durable Most English hardwoods do not require preservatives UKWAS or FSC	New acidic timber will stain a building with tannin New acidic timber will stain steel fasteners and vice versa Ideally need stainless steel fasteners (not as cheap as steel) Bright polished surface may cause reflections that may disturb wildlife: dull surface or add plastic cap Details of box need to be self-draining (roof and floor) away from a building Choose reclaimed, locally grown or UKWAS or FSC temperate durable species (avoid preservatives)

Table 3.4: Thermal insulation and ready-made products

	Advantages	Considerations
None of the pre-made boxes considered are insulated, so if they breach the U value envelop of low or zero carbon buildings they need to be wrapped in thermal insulation* and linked to the U value envelope to maintain its integrity	This can be allowed for during the design process	This has to be done in such a way as to preserve the integrity of the U value envelope

* Features of thermal insulation materials:
  Foamed cellular glass has high thermal mass, high decrement and water/vapour resistance
  Rock mineral fibre has low thermal/acoustic mass, low decrement and is air/vapour permeable – performance is diminished if moist, hydrophobic (rejects water)
  Slag mineral fibre has low thermal/acoustic mass, low decrement and is air/vapour permeable – performance is diminished if moist, hydrophobic (rejects water)
  Glass mineral fibre has low thermal/acoustic mass, low decrement and is air/vapour permeable – performance is diminished if moist, hydrophobic (rejects water)
  Expanded polystyrene has low thermal/acoustic mass, low decrement and can reject moisture
  Cellulose fibre is hygroscopic and will absorb moisture into fibres without loss of performance
  Dense wood fibre is hygroscopic and will absorb moisture into fibres without loss of performance, and the high thermal/acoustic mass decrement delay will protect from solar radiation and noise, but hold heat longer
  Wood has poor k value but good decrement delay
  Plastics – avoid the risk of off-gassing, low thermal/acoustic mass, low decrement, not hygroscopic, hydrophobic, not normally breathing
  A more comprehensive comparison is available on the GreenSpec Download website (www.greenspecdownload.co.uk)

Table 3.5: Airtightness of ready-made products

	Advantages	Considerations
Airtightness is unlikely to have been a high priority in the design and manufacture of these products, so if they breach the U value envelope of low to zero carbon buildings they need to be wrapped in an airtightness layer (ATL) and linked to the U value envelope's ATL in order to maintain its integrity.	This can be allowed for during the design process. Bat box joints can be taped over. Natural paper-based ATLs are available. Natural adhesives are available.	This has to be done in such a way as to preserve the integrity of the U value envelope.

accounting for the fact that UK and EU masonry block dimensions differ; the fact that UK was imperial, has been modular and now uses metric bricks; jointing may be imperial, 10 mm or thin joint; building in, or installing into, built openings requires different sizes; and insulation may need to be accommodated around the box.

The spreadsheet gives instant sizes and provides guidance on the space left inside for bat/bird accommodation. The spreadsheet is on GreenSpec Download (www.greenspecdownload.co.uk). GreenSpec Download has also created specifications for the products mentioned in this book.

Having looked at the general principles that apply to ready-made products, this book now examines the provision for each species or species group in turn. For each, any ready-made products (where these are available) will be reviewed. Section 3.12 (page 63) then illustrates the integration of these products or bespoke spaces for roosting or nesting into a range of building types.

3.2   Crevice-dwelling bats

'Crevice-dwelling bats' is an arbitrary category that covers a wide range of species that tend to select roosts which could be described as a crevices or narrow gaps. This might be the area in traditional houses that is found between the roofing felt and tiles, or under hanging tiles or the weather boarding on the exterior of a building, or in gaps in the woodwork within a roof space, such as mortise joints. The expanse of the crevice might be small or cover a large area, but what these bats have in common is the preference to roost somewhere where they can retreat from open spaces. The species in question are: common pipistrelle, soprano pipistrelle, Nathusius' pipistrelle, Brandt's bat, whiskered bat, noctule, serotine, Leisler's bat, Daubenton's bat, barbastelle and Bechstein's bat. Table 3.6 lists some considerations for crevice-dwelling bats.

Table 3.6: Considerations and key requirements for crevice-dwelling bats

Consideration	Solution
Where in a development	Anywhere that the access is not illuminated by artificial lighting
Where in a building	Summer nursery roosts in most southerly or westerly aspect for solar heating, or in a location that provides thermal stability Male roosts and winter hibernation roosts on northerly aspect
Height	2–7 m
Dimensions	Any size as long as some components of the area are crevices in the region of 20–30 mm wide Greater total area of this crevice provision of something like 1 sq m would be useful for nursery (summer) roosts Male roosts contain a smaller number of bats or even individual bats
Access dimensions	20–50 mm (w) x 15–20 mm (h)
Other considerations	Rough (for grip) Non-toxic and non-corrosive No risk of entanglement (see Section 4.3.2, *Roofing membranes*) Suitable thermal properties (reducing 24-hour fluctuations), but allowing maximum thermal gain for summer roosts The use of thermal insulation materials for nursery roosts should be carefully considered and appropriate properties selected (see Table 3.4). Some thermal insulation materials can help reduce thermal fluctuations, providing stability, but will also reduce thermal gain Use of thermal insulation in transitional or winter roosts may be of value Access not lit by artificial lighting

BAT ACCESS TILE SET
Tudor Roof Tile Co. Limited

FAMILIAR MATERIAL	Yes
EASY TO INSTALL	Yes
DURABLE	Yes
LOW OR NO MAINTENANCE	Yes
FROST RESISTANT	Yes
THERMAL MASS	Medium or high
FITS UK CONSTRUCTION SIZES	Yes
UNFAMILIAR MATERIAL; UNSURE HOW TO PROTECT	N/A
THERMAL BRIDGES	N/A (but does create an opening into an unheated roof space)
EXPOSED WOOD PARTICLES ON CUT OR DAMAGED EDGES MAY ABSORB MOISTURE	N/A
MUST BE MAINTAINED WITH 'SPECIAL' UNFAMILIAR PAINT	N/A
EMBODIED ENERGY	Medium
EMBODIED CARBON	Depends on fuel used
DEGREE OF FIT TO UK CONSTRUCTION SIZES	Fits all 3 dimensions
PRODUCT UPTAKE	Unknown

OTHER

→ Could be used scattered across a roof slope or on different roof slopes
→ Ridge entry tile available – this may form a roost area too or provide access to one
→ Will act as roof vents if used in uninsulated roof slopes
→ Standard tile set is designed for roof slopes and can be placed above, at or below eaves triangles, over the roof slope generally or at the ridge triangle
→ Supported lapped underlay and aperture through the underlay give access to the roof space
→ Add and support an extra layer of underlay below the entrance to collect any rainwater, with a shallower slope back up to overlap with the main underlay
→ Limit insect access to the roof beyond the bat roost using insect-resistant metal mesh/perforated metal

TYPE OF PRODUCT:
Bat access tiles

WEBSITE:
www.tudorrooftiles.co.uk

WHERE USED:
On a roof slope in place of standard tiles

PRODUCT INFORMATION:
Texture – Natural Clay (without sand face) or Sandface
Five Tudor colours and natural clay

PRODUCT USE:
For use within the roof tiles – the top 'tunnel' tile offers the bat a 165 mm (l) x 18 mm (h) (approx.) tunnel to an entrance hole in the undertiles. This allows the bat to crawl into the roost area

(see Drawings Nos 1, 3, 5, 8, 9, 10, 11 and 19
pp. 44, 60, 66, 72, 74, 76, 78 and 112, respectively)

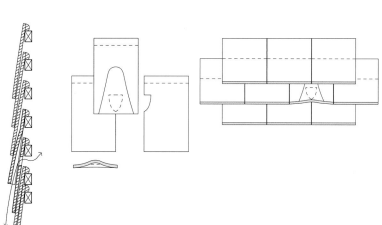

HABIBAT CLAY BAT ACCESS TILE
Habibat

TYPE OF PRODUCT:
Bat access roof tile

WEBSITE:
www.habibat.co.uk

WHERE USED:
Replaces clay roof tile

PRODUCT INFORMATION:
Five-piece set fits seamlessly on any roof with plain clay tiles. Available in a full range of colours, from red and brindle colours to Staffordshire blue

PRODUCT USE:
Provides a means for bats to crawl behind the tiles and, if an aperture is created in the underlay, to the roof space

(see Drawings Nos 1, 3, 5, 8, 9, 10, 11 and 19 pp. 44, 60, 66, 72, 74, 76, 78 and 112, respectively)

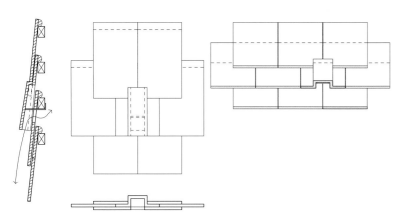

FAMILIAR MATERIAL	Yes
EASY TO INSTALL	Yes
DURABLE	Yes
LOW OR NO MAINTENANCE	Yes
FROST RESISTANT	Yes
THERMAL MASS	Yes
FITS UK CONSTRUCTION SIZES	Yes
UNFAMILIAR MATERIAL; UNSURE HOW TO PROTECT	N/A
THERMAL BRIDGES	N/A (but does create an opening into an unheated roof space)
EXPOSED WOOD PARTICLES ON CUT OR DAMAGED EDGES MAY ABSORB MOISTURE	N/A
MUST BE MAINTAINED WITH 'SPECIAL' UNFAMILIAR PAINT	N/A
EMBODIED ENERGY	Medium
EMBODIED CARBON	Depends on fuel used
DEGREE OF FIT TO UK CONSTRUCTION SIZES	Fits all 3 dimensions
PRODUCT UPTAKE	Unknown

OTHER

→ Could be used scattered across a roof slope or on different roof slopes

→ Will act as roof vents if used in uninsulated roof slopes

→ Where access to the roof space is needed for bats, an aperture in the underlay may be required

→ Offsetting this aperture to one side of the bat access tile and limiting the cut in the horizontal direction, as shown in the drawing, will reduce any potential ingress of water

→ Follow manufacturer's instruction to maintain guarantee

→ Take necessary precautions to collect rainwater below the entrance by providing a second layer of supported underlay to collect water, with a shallow slope overlapping the main underlay

→ Limit insect access to roof beyond bat roost using insect resistant metal mesh/perforated metal

HABIBAT BAT ACCESS TILE

Habibat

FAMILIAR MATERIAL	Yes
EASY TO INSTALL	Yes
DURABLE	Yes
LOW OR NO MAINTENANCE	Yes
FROST RESISTANT	Yes
THERMAL MASS	Varies with choice of material
FITS UK CONSTRUCTION SIZES	Yes
UNFAMILIAR MATERIAL; UNSURE HOW TO PROTECT	N/A
THERMAL BRIDGES	N/A (but does create an opening into an unheated roof space)
EXPOSED WOOD PARTICLES ON CUT OR DAMAGED EDGES MAY ABSORB MOISTURE	N/A
MUST BE MAINTAINED WITH 'SPECIAL' UNFAMILIAR PAINT	N/A
EMBODIED ENERGY	High
EMBODIED CARBON	High
DEGREE OF FIT TO UK CONSTRUCTION SIZES	Cut through slate/tile and two parts connected through hole
PRODUCT UPTAKE	Unknown

OTHER

→ Size of access can be large or small
→ Will last for the lifetime of the roof covering
→ The under-base is shaped to ensure gravity plays its part in trapping wind-driven rain in the entrance, not allowing it to enter the roof space, and draining it on to the tiles

TYPE OF PRODUCT:
Bat roof access

WEBSITE:
www.habibat.co.uk

WHERE USED:
Replaces roofing slate or tile on pitched roof (ridge tile also available)

PRODUCT INFORMATION:
Provides a discreet and uninterrupted path from the roof exterior to the batten cavity or interior of the roof
Available in a number of materials, sizes, plain and profiles; to suit slate, clay, concrete and resin tiles
The bat access tile comprises an exterior weathering cowl to allow bat entry into the body of the roof covering, combined with a plastic under-base unit
Factory-applied non-slip surface to the tile/slate facilitates easy landing and access for the bat

PRODUCT USE:
For access into the batten cavity or roof space

(see Drawings Nos 1, 3, 5, 8, 9, 10, 11 and 19 pp. 44, 60, 66, 72, 74, 76, 78 and 112, respectively)

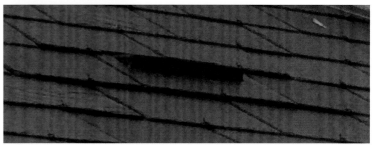

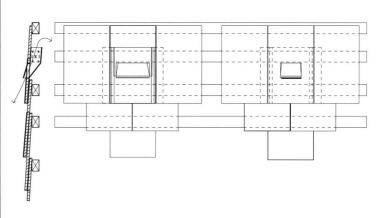

IBSTOCK BAT ROOST ENTRANCE ARCH BRICK

Ibstock Ltd

TYPE OF PRODUCT:
Bat roost entrance brick

WEBSITE:
www.ibstock.com

WHERE USED:
In place of a normal single brick–bed joint omitted for middle two-thirds of brick

PRODUCT INFORMATION:
Fired clay brick – size 215 mm (w) x 65 mm (h) 102 mm (d)

PRODUCT USE:
Allows bats to pass through the outer leaf to the cavity of the wall or to spaces provided beyond

(see Drawings Nos 2, 5 and 20, pp. 58, 66 and 114, respectively)

FAMILIAR MATERIAL	Yes
EASY TO INSTALL	Yes
DURABLE	Yes
LOW OR NO MAINTENANCE	N/A
FROST RESISTANT	Yes
THERMAL MASS	Medium or high
FITS UK CONSTRUCTION SIZES	Yes
UNFAMILIAR MATERIAL; UNSURE HOW TO PROTECT	N/A
THERMAL BRIDGES	N/A but does create opening
EXPOSED WOOD PARTICLES ON CUT OR DAMAGED EDGES MAY ABSORB MOISTURE	N/A
MUST BE MAINTAINED WITH 'SPECIAL' UNFAMILIAR PAINT	N/A
EMBODIED ENERGY	Medium
EMBODIED CARBON	Depends on fuel used
DEGREE OF FIT TO UK CONSTRUCTION SIZES	Fits all 3 dimensions
PRODUCT UPTAKE	Unknown

OTHER

→ Can be used as an access via eaves into the roof voids
→ Fair-faced, no need for rendering over
→ Versatile: can be used singularly, in opposed pairs (for small bird access) or in multiples (creating larger bird openings) (see Drawings Nos 2 and 5, pages 58 and 65)
→ Only a passage, not a roost
→ Only suitable for uninsulated cavity walls, which will not feature in future low and zero carbon buildings except to unoccupied, uninsulated attic spaces or outbuildings

ROOFBLOCK
RoofBLOCK

FAMILIAR MATERIAL	Yes
EASY TO INSTALL	Must be designed in
DURABLE	Yes
LOW OR NO MAINTENANCE	Yes
FROST RESISTANT	Yes
THERMAL MASS	High
FITS UK CONSTRUCTION SIZES	Yes
UNFAMILIAR MATERIAL; UNSURE HOW TO PROTECT	N/A
THERMAL BRIDGES	Risk of thermal bridge through thin cavity wall construction – can be improved with wider insulated cavity (see below)
EXPOSED WOOD PARTICLES ON CUT OR DAMAGED EDGES MAY ABSORB MOISTURE	N/A
MUST BE MAINTAINED WITH 'SPECIAL' UNFAMILIAR PAINT	N/A
EMBODIED ENERGY	Medium to low
EMBODIED CARBON	Low (eco-cement)
DEGREE OF FIT TO UK CONSTRUCTION SIZES	Fits 2 dimensions (see Table 3.2)
PRODUCT UPTAKE	Unknown

OTHER

→ Numerous endorsements and accolades as an eco-product (not as a bat roost)
→ Roosts can be positioned on any elevation unobtrusively
→ Adjacent blocks can be linked
→ Made for cavity walls but will fit on half-brick upstand of 1B solid wall
→ Fair-faced – no need for rendering over
→ Reduces U value locally in wider cavity wall construction with full fill cavity insulation
→ Profile may need to be modified with thicker walls and thicker roof and wall insulation (see Drawing No. 6, page 68)
→ Eco-cement should have less embodied carbon
→ Recycled aggregates are likely to have less embodied energy and/or carbon

TYPE OF PRODUCT:

Bat roost – concrete eaves/verge system

WEBSITE:

www.roofblock.co.uk

WHERE USED:

Flat, hipped or any pitch roof
Outer leaf of cavity wall or half-brick uninsulated walls to outbuildings

PRODUCT INFORMATION:

Made from recycled aggregates and eco-cement

PRODUCT USE:

Block with bat access slit in bottom into interior chamber

(see Drawings No. 6, p. 68)

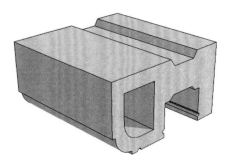

HABIBAT BAT BOX

Habibat

TYPE OF PRODUCT:
Bat roost

WEBSITE:
www.habibat.co.uk

WHERE USED:
Replaces six bricks in stackbond in cavity wall construction, or tooth bonded into adjacent walls

PRODUCT INFORMATION:
Fired clay brick slip face – available for all brick types
Alternative facing materials can be included, such as stone, masonry, tile hanging, timber and render
Multiple units can be connected in series horizontally or vertically to create a much larger roosting space
Dense aggregate or lightweight options are available
Size: 215 mm (w) x 440 mm (h) x 103 mm (d)

PRODUCT USE:
Roost contained within product
Inside chamber has inverted V wedges for different temperature zones and to create different roosting surfaces

(see Drawings Nos 7, 8 and 20,
pp. 70, 72 and 114, respectively)

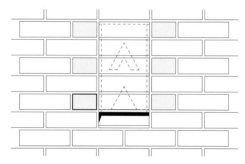

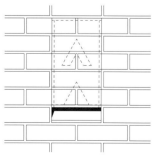

FAMILIAR MATERIAL	Yes
EASY TO INSTALL	Yes
DURABLE	Yes
LOW OR NO MAINTENANCE	Yes
FROST RESISTANT	Yes
THERMAL MASS	Low to medium
FITS UK CONSTRUCTION SIZES	Yes
UNFAMILIAR MATERIAL; UNSURE HOW TO PROTECT	N/A
THERMAL BRIDGES	Yes, but in outer leaf, outside of cavity insulation, so little effect Access version should only access unheated roof spaces
EXPOSED WOOD PARTICLES ON CUT OR DAMAGED EDGES MAY ABSORB MOISTURE	N/A
MUST BE MAINTAINED WITH 'SPECIAL' UNFAMILIAR PAINT	N/A
EMBODIED ENERGY	Medium
EMBODIED CARBON	Medium to high
DEGREE OF FIT TO UK CONSTRUCTION SIZES	Fits 2–3 dimensions Stack bond version requires half-cut bricks either side
PRODUCT UPTAKE	Unknown

OTHER

→ Can be used in multiples (but lintel required if side by side)
→ The stack bond model can be side by side or one on top of another
→ The tooth bond model will be spaced apart
→ Access versions are available to allow bat entry into roof space
→ May absorb urine, which in time may result in localised odour

IBSTOCK ENCLOSED BAT BOX

Ibstock Ltd

FAMILIAR MATERIAL	Yes
EASY TO INSTALL	Yes
DURABLE	Yes
LOW OR NO MAINTENANCE	Yes
FROST RESISTANT	Yes
THERMAL MASS	Medium or high
FITS UK CONSTRUCTION SIZES	Yes
UNFAMILIAR MATERIAL: UNSURE HOW TO PROTECT	N/A
THERMAL BRIDGES	N/A
EXPOSED WOOD PARTICLES ON CUT OR DAMAGED EDGES MAY ABSORB MOISTURE	N/A
MUST BE MAINTAINED WITH 'SPECIAL' UNFAMILIAR PAINT	N/A
EMBODIED ENERGY	High
EMBODIED CARBON	High
DEGREE OF FIT TO UK CONSTRUCTION SIZES	Fits all three dimensions Stack bond requires half-cut bricks either side
PRODUCT UPTAKE	Unknown

OTHER

→ Can be used in unconnected multiples (but lintel required if side by side)
→ May absorb urine, which in time may result in localised odour

TYPE OF PRODUCT:
Bat roost

WEBSITE:
www.ibstock.com

WHERE USED:
Replaces three or four bricks in stack bond in outer leaf of external cavity wall construction.

PRODUCT INFORMATION:
Fired clay brick slip face – available for all brick types and with option of bat design. Bat motif: durable metallic, set in face of brick Sizes: 215 mm (w) x 215 mm (h) x 102 mm (d), or 215 mm (w) x 290 mm (h) x 102 mm (d)

PRODUCT USE:
Roost contained within product – creates several roosting zones inside the box

(see Drawings Nos 7 and 20,
pp. 70 and 114, respectively)

FORTICRETE BAT BOX

Forticrete Ltd

TYPE OF PRODUCT:
Bat roost

WEBSITE:
www.forticrete.co.uk

WHERE USED:
In outer wall construction

PRODUCT INFORMATION:
Cast stone front face
Bat silhouette plaque cast into face
Backing – high-grade plywood that is sawn and roughened internally for bat use
Maintenance free
Size: 440 mm (w) x 215 mm (h) x 100 mm (d) overall (depth comprises 65 mm cast stone and 35 mm plywood)
Bespoke sizes and designs available to special order

PRODUCT USE:
Roost contained within product

(see Drawing No. 7, p. 70
if brick replaced with blockwork or stonework)

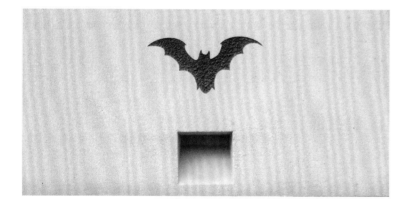

FAMILIAR MATERIAL	Yes
EASY TO INSTALL	Yes
DURABLE	Yes
LOW OR NO MAINTENANCE	See Other below
FROST RESISTANT	Yes
THERMAL MASS	Medium or high
FITS UK CONSTRUCTION SIZES	Yes
UNFAMILIAR MATERIAL; UNSURE HOW TO PROTECT	N/A
THERMAL BRIDGES	N/A
EXPOSED WOOD PARTICLES ON CUT OR DAMAGED EDGES MAY ABSORB MOISTURE	N/A
MUST BE MAINTAINED WITH 'SPECIAL' UNFAMILIAR PAINT	N/A
EMBODIED ENERGY	High
EMBODIED CARBON	High
DEGREE OF FIT TO UK CONSTRUCTION SIZES	Fits all 3 dimensions
PRODUCT UPTAKE	Unknown

OTHER

→ Can be used in a multiple arrangement with mortared perpend between (but lintel required if side by side)
→ Fair-faced so no need for rendering over
→ High thermal mass and decrement delay outer face
→ Narrow entrance makes maintenance difficult and traps droppings at sides

FAMILIAR MATERIAL	Yes
EASY TO INSTALL	Yes
DURABLE	Yes
LOW OR NO MAINTENANCE	Yes
FROST RESISTANT	Yes
THERMAL MASS	Medium or high
FITS UK CONSTRUCTION SIZES	Yes
UNFAMILIAR MATERIAL: UNSURE HOW TO PROTECT	N/A
THERMAL BRIDGES	N/A
EXPOSED WOOD PARTICLES ON CUT OR DAMAGED EDGES MAY ABSORB MOISTURE	N/A
MUST BE MAINTAINED WITH 'SPECIAL' UNFAMILIAR PAINT	N/A
EMBODIED ENERGY	High
EMBODIED CARBON	Depends on fuel used
DEGREE OF FIT TO UK CONSTRUCTION SIZES	Approximate fit all 3 dimensions
PRODUCT UPTAKE	Known to be well-used by bats Recommended for structures such as arches, tunnels and bridges where crevices are in short supply

OTHER

→ Could be used in multiples (but lintel required if side by side)
→ Not designed for, and generally not suitable for, low and zero carbon buildings
→ These are not designed as access bricks

THE NORFOLK BAT BRICK
These are *only* produced by the Norfolk Bat Group

TYPE OF PRODUCT:
Bat roost

WEBSITE:
www.norfolk-bat-group.org.uk

WHERE USED:
In bridges, tunnels and similar structures

PRODUCT INFORMATION:
Size: brick-sized, approximately 200 mm (w) x 70 mm (h) x 100 mm (d)
Handmade using absorbent clay, roughened with sand and fired to about 1,100 °C to make them frost proof. They have a series of appropriately sized slits on the face for bat crevices

PRODUCT USE:
Provides the right conditions for hibernating bats, such as Daubenton's bat, Natterer's bat, brown long-eared bat, Brandt's bat, whiskered bat and barbastelle

(see Drawings Nos 1, 3, 5 (internal face on wall) and 9 (inner face of outer leaf), pp. 44, 60, 66 and 74, respectively)

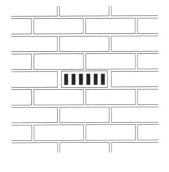

SCHWEGLER BAT ROOST RANGE

Schwegler GmbH

TYPE OF PRODUCT:
Bat roost

WEBSITE:
www.schwegler-nature.com

WHERE USED:
In outer wall construction

PRODUCT INFORMATION:
Durable, weather resistant and air permeable Schwegler wood-concrete

(see Drawings Nos 7, 8, 9, 10, 11, 14, 15, 16, 17, 18 and 19,
pp. 70, 72, 74, 76, 78, 86, 90, 92, 94, 110 and 112, respectively)

- -

BAT ACCESS PANEL 1FE
Can be used to create access or as a
roost space by the use of the optional
back plate
300 mm (w) x 300 mm (h) x 80 mm (d)
With an overall depth of just 8 cm, it
is easily integrated within masonry or
insulation

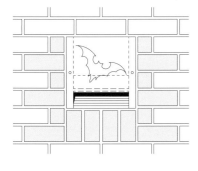

- -

BAT TUBE 1FR
Roosting space with wooden roosting
panel at rear
200 mm (w) x 475 mm (h) x 125 mm (d)

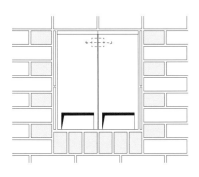

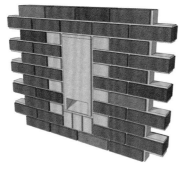

continued overleaf

FAMILIAR MATERIAL	N/A
EASY TO INSTALL	Depends on context and surrounding materials
DURABLE	Yes
LOW OR NO MAINTENANCE	Some access hatches permit internal cleaning
FROST RESISTANT	Yes
THERMAL MASS	Medium or high
FITS UK CONSTRUCTION SIZES	No
UNFAMILIAR MATERIAL: UNSURE HOW TO PROTECT	Yes
THERMAL BRIDGES	Where cavity walls bridged will need cavity tray damp proof course
EXPOSED WOOD PARTICLES ON CUT OR DAMAGED EDGES MAY ABSORB MOISTURE	Yes
MUST BE MAINTAINED WITH 'SPECIAL' UNFAMILIAR PAINT	Some
EMBODIED ENERGY	High
EMBODIED CARBON	High to medium
DEGREE OF FIT TO UK CONSTRUCTION SIZES	Do not coordinate with UK brick construction in two or three dimensions (see Table 3.2 on dimensions)
PRODUCT UPTAKE	The use of Schwegler 1FE and 1FR by bats has been confirmed in some mitigation scenarios, but as yet unconfirmed for enhancement

OTHER

→ 2FR allows a larger roost area to be provided
→ 1FE, 1FR, 2FR and type 27 can either be set flush or be set into masonry and rendered so that only the entrance or front access panels is visible
→ 1FE and 2FR have the capacity to lead to other roosting areas from the rear of the product
→ 1FE is the most versatile of the range and can be incorporated into a number of construction types
→ Avoid using aluminium nails
→ Non-loadbearing wall will need lintel if used in multiples, side by side

BAT TUBE 2FR

For the creation of spaces for larger bat colonies, with optional access to other roosting areas from the rear of the product

Dimensions as 1FR, but possible to link as multiple units, as shown below, due to transverse connecting holes at the top of the tube. It is recommended to connect at least three of the tubes together

An additional feature is an optional passage through the rear panel to link horizontally through the back to other deeper cavities

Creates a thermal bridge if access is to a heated space, but is suitable if accessing an unheated roof space

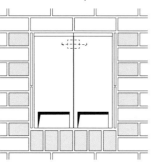
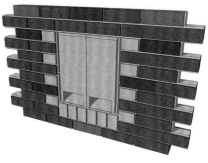

SUMMER AND WINTER BATBOX 1WI

For installation into the walls of buildings and structures. This design is for hibernation in winter as well as summer use. The interior is designed with different surface textures and areas with changing hanging depths. Uses Schwegler light-concrete.

Dimensions: 350 mm (w) x 550 mm (h) x 95 mm (d)

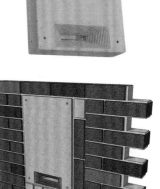
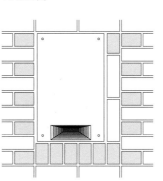

BRICK BOX FOR BATS TYPE 27

For installation into the walls of buildings and structures
Front access panel is removable.
Dimensions: 180 mm (w) x 265 mm (h) x 240 mm (d)

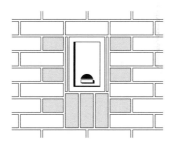
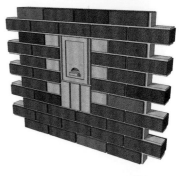

3.3   Bats needing a flying area

These bat species (brown long-eared, grey long-eared and Natterer's) can, in the same way as crevice-dwelling bats, gain access to their roost spaces by crawling through a small gap, but they need a roost in which they can fly. This fact will necessitate the use of a cold roof space in most instances as their need to gain access to a flight area would breach the airtightness of that part of the structure. Inside the roof space, bats will roost within crevices, see Drawings Nos 1, 3, 5, 6, 8, 9, 10, pages 44, 60, 66, 68, 72, 74, 76, but they require the additional space for flying and dimensions of 5 m (w) x 2.8 m (h) x 5 m (d) are optimal. It is also important that this space is dark and not trussed to ensure sufficient flight space. Table 3.7 lists some considerations for these bat species.

Table 3.7 Considerations and key requirements for bats needing flying space

Consideration	Solution
Where in a development	Anywhere where the access is not illuminated by artificial lighting
Where in a building	The crevice roosting provision within the roost is to be located on the south or west side for solar heating, or a suitable location that ensures thermal stability. The location of the flight area is not as important
Height	Over 2 m
Flight area	5 m (w) x 2.8 m (h) x 5 m (d), not trussed. Ideally 2.8 m height, but a height of 2 m may be acceptable
Roost dimensions	To incorporate roost crevices with dimensions of any size as long as some components of the area are crevices in the region of 20–30 mm Greater total areas of in the region of 1 m² would be useful for nursery (summer) roosts
Access dimensions	20–50 mm (w) x 15–20 mm (h)
Other considerations	Rough (for grip) Non-toxic and non-corrosive No risk of entanglement Suitable thermal properties (reducing 24-hour fluctuations), but allowing maximum thermal gain Access not lit by artificial lighting

3.4   Horseshoe bats

Horseshoe bats are among the species that have suffered the greatest decline in numbers in recent decades and their range in the UK has also shrunk. Currently their range is restricted predominantly to Wales and south-west England, although it is possible that climate change, along with a hoped for recovery in numbers, could see this range expanded north and east again, assuming suitable foraging habitats and roosting opportunities exist.

Greater and lesser horseshoe bats fall into the category of bats that need to fly within their roost and, as such, the details of the needs of these bats are largely covered by Section 3.3. However, horseshoe bats have adapted to hang vertically from their roosting places and, as such, have lost the ability to crawl with ease, a capacity common to other bat species. This means that, in addition to the needs of bats that require a flying area, horseshoe bats need access through which they can fly, and this must be taken into consideration early on in the design process. Table 3.8 (overleaf) lists some considerations for horseshoe bats.

Lesser horseshoe bats

Table 3.8 Considerations and key requirements for horseshoe bats

Consideration	Solution
Where in a development	Anywhere where the access and flight paths are not illuminated by artificial lighting
Where in a building	The roost is most likely to be in a roof space and this should have an orientation that allows a south-facing solar gain or, better still, an L-shape to allow temperature-range choice
Height	Over 2 m
Dimensions	5 m (w) x 2 - 2.8 m (h) x 5 m (d), not trussed to allow flight. Ideally 2.8 m height, but a height of 2 m may be acceptable in certain circumstances
Access dimensions	Lesser horseshoes: 300 mm (w) x 200 mm (h) Greater horseshoes: 400 mm (w) x 300 mm (h)
Other considerations	Rough (for grip) Non-toxic and non-corrosive No risk of entanglement Suitable thermal properties (reducing 24-hour fluctuations), but allowing maximum thermal gain Access not lit by artificial lighting

Ideally the access to the roost area should be a simple opening with a canopy above and with the top and bottom of the entrance sloped down and outwards. However, there are a range of considerations and if vandals are likely to be a problem one or two horizontal bars may be added, ensuring that a sufficient gap for flight into the roost is retained.

If there is concern about the use of the roof space by less desirable species, such as jackdaws, then Drawing No. 1, page 44, shows a design that will prevent their entry as well as protecting against weather. This has been shown to be successful for lesser horseshoe bats in particular.

This drawing illustrates the incorporation of a sloped tunnel that matches the entry gap for the species in question. For greater horseshoes this is 400 mm (w) x 300 mm (h) and for lesser horseshoes it is 300 mm (w) x 200 mm (h). The length of the tunnel with the overshot top section prevents the entry of weather, while the steepness of the tunnel (with the lower surface being smooth) prevents jackdaws, pigeons, etc., from either flying or scrabbling their way in. The access should be positioned so that the bats can fly into cover nearby. As with all bat access, it should not be illuminated by artificial light (see Section 5.2).

For greater horseshoe bats there is some evidence that these measures to prevent the entry of other species could detract from the likelihood of the use of the roost by this species. Other alternative measures, such as a an internal 'hopper', and further details for consideration can be found in the Vincent Wildlife Trust publication *The Lesser Horseshoe Bat* (Schofield, 2008; www.vwt.org.uk) and the Natural England *Bat Mitigation Guidelines* (Mitchell-Jones, 2004; www.naturalengland.org.uk). It is recommended that the advice of an experienced ecologist is utilised to discuss the best option.

While the other bats species that need a flying space also need to have somewhere within the roost where they can access a more enclosed area, for horseshoe bats this does not apply. What is important is the roughness of the surfaces from which the bats can hang. While it is often surprising to see horseshoe bats clinging to surfaces that appear to give little purchase, if the surface is very smooth, like some roofing membranes can be, then suitable netting or some rough timber would need to be added.

3.5 Swifts

In order to breed, swifts need access to a space in buildings where they can construct their simple nest. As swifts like to nest within a space or cavity, their presence as a nesting bird is not generally visible. It is therefore important to ensure that anyone involved in the future maintenance of the building is aware of their use of the building. Table 3.9 lists some considerations for swifts.

Extensive information about swifts and, in particular, about how to design and site swift boxes can be found at the Swift Conservation website (www.swift-conservation.org).

Table 3.9 Considerations and key requirements for swifts

Consideration	Solution
Where in a development	Anywhere high, shaded and away from disturbance and obstructions to their flight paths
Where in a building	Out of direct sunlight, such as under deep eaves or an aspect of the building that does not receive much direct sunlight Not adjacent to climbing plants that may give predators, such as rats, access to the nest Where the swifts will have clear airspace into which they can fly from their nests Preferably integral to the building, but where this is not possible, external under the eaves, under roof edges and gables It is important to have several potential nest sites for swifts in one area
Height	At least 5 m
Dimensions	400 mm (w) x 200 mm (d) x 175 mm (h) ideally, but can be smaller
Access dimensions	65 mm (w) x 33 mm (h) oval or rectangle. The bottom of the hole should be no more than 5 cm from base of box
Other considerations	Swifts are colonial nesters so, where room allows, it is preferable to have more than one swift nest incorporated into a building. As a starting guide: 1 to 4 nest provisions on a house 4 to 10 on a small block of flats 10 to 20 on a larger building, e.g. offices or industrial site These figures may vary on a site-by-site basis, dependent on site-specific constraints and criteria In establishing a new colony, playing recorded swift calls is advised to bring birds in to find the nest places

Swifts in nest boxes

3.5.1 Further reading:

http://actionforswifts.blogspot.co.uk/
http://www.swift-conservation.org/

Drawing No.
01

Horseshoe bat access
– uninsulated pitched roof gable wall with access tunnel

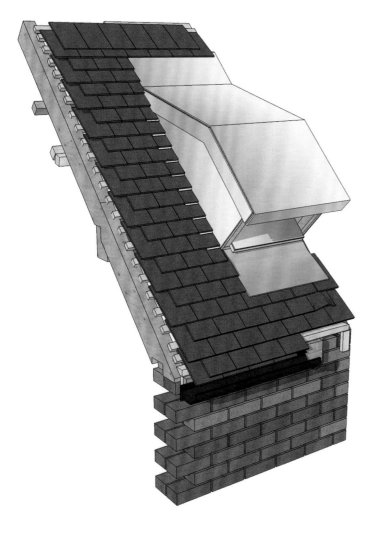

1 FSC WBP weather and boil proof plywood lining, 6 mm

2 Reclaimed, locally grown UKWAS or FSC temperate softwood framing, 50 x 50 mm

3 FSC WBP weather and boil proof plywood, 25 mm

4 Malleable metal standing seam roof cladding. See Lead or Zinc Development Association or manufacturer's guidance on details

5 Clay plain tile roofing

6 Reclaimed, locally grown UKWAS or temperate durable hardwood

7 Reclaimed, locally grown UKWAS or FSC temperate softwood roofing battens

8 Reclaimed, locally grown UKWAS or FSC temperate softwood rafters

9 Malleable metal apron flashing. See Lead or Zinc Development Association or manufacturer's guidance on details

10 FSC WBP weather and boil proof plywood, 25 mm

11 Reclaimed, locally grown UKWAS or FSC temperate durable hardwood wall plate

12 Clay brick solid wall, 1B, 215 mm

13 'Lindab Rainline' rainwater gutter (galvanized steel, half round)

14 Bat access tile set, 18 mm gap x 165 mm long

15 FSC WBP weather and boil proof plywood, 25 mm

16 Anti-bird-slope slip plain, Perspex, 6 mm

17 Access hole size: see Table 3.8 on page 42

18 Malleable metal cheek cladding. See Lead or Zinc Development Association or manufacturer's guidance on details

19 Malleable metal soakers/flashings to roof tiling. See Lead or Zinc Development Association or manufacturer's guidance on details

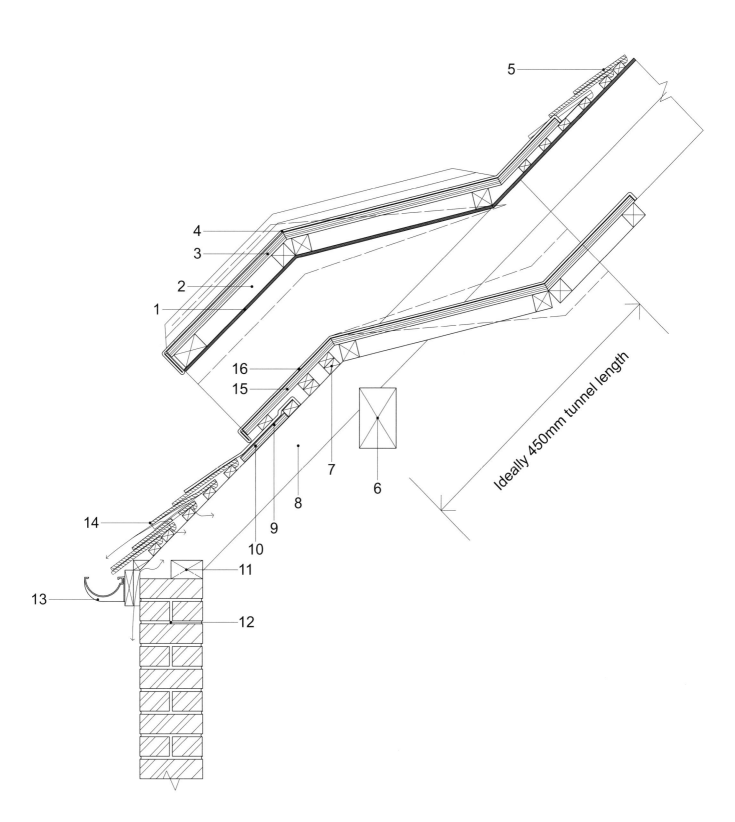

5

4

3

2

1

16

15

10

9

8

7

6

14

13

11

12

Ideally 450mm tunnel length

FAMILIAR MATERIAL	Yes
EASY TO INSTALL	Yes
DURABLE	Yes
LOW OR NO MAINTENANCE	Yes
FROST RESISTANT	Yes
THERMAL MASS	Medium
FITS UK CONSTRUCTION SIZES	Yes
UNFAMILIAR MATERIAL: UNSURE HOW TO PROTECT	N/A
THERMAL BRIDGES	N/A
EXPOSED WOOD PARTICLES ON CUT OR DAMAGED EDGES MAY ABSORB MOISTURE	N/A
MUST BE MAINTAINED WITH 'SPECIAL' UNFAMILIAR PAINT	N/A
EMBODIED ENERGY	Medium
EMBODIED CARBON	Depends on fuel used
DEGREE OF FIT TO UK CONSTRUCTION SIZES	Approximate fit all 3 dimensions Some cut bricks either side
PRODUCT UPTAKE	Unknown

OTHER

→ Products can be faced or coloured to suit the building. Finishes include brick, stone, masonry or render
→ Can be used in multiple arrangements with mortared perpend between (but lintel required)
→ Fair-faced, no need for rendering
→ The product can be supplied in different sizes and formats to suit design needs and relevant building regulations

ECOSURV SWIFT BOX
Ecosurv Ltd

TYPE OF PRODUCT:
Swift box

WEBSITE:
www.ecosurv.co.uk

WHERE USED:
External elevations of buildings. Discreet nesting box for location near the eaves. Replaces two whole and two half bricks in single leaf of cavity wall construction

PRODUCT INFORMATION:
Facings can match any type of façade
Dimensions (external): 328 mm (w) x 140 mm (h) x 200 mm (d)

PRODUCT USE:
Nest contained within product
Swift nesting – ensure it is fitted with the entrance hole towards the bottom edge of the front panel

(see Drawings Nos 7, 8, 9 (below eaves), 10 and 11, pp. 70, 72, 74, 76 and 78, respectively)

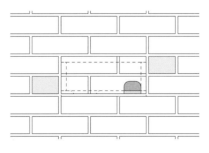

SWIFT AND BAT BOX 1MF

Schwegler GmbH

TYPE OF PRODUCT:
Swift and bat box

WEBSITE:
www.schwegler-nature.com

WHERE USED:
The box is hung from a galvanized mild steel mounting plate
Using the Bat Slope, the 1MF can be built directly into the brickwork of a wall, with the box flush with the face of the wall and access to the rear space for bats

PRODUCT INFORMATION:
Schwegler wood-concrete
1MF with Bat Slope: 430 mm (w) x 700 mm (h) x 225 mm (d)
Bat Slope: 430 mm (w) x 250 mm (h) x 225 mm (d)
Combined height: 700 mm

PRODUCT USE:
The 1MF contains two nesting chambers for swifts, each with its own entrance. A recess in the rear panel creates a space between the wall of the building and box for use by bats

(see Drawings Nos 9 (in outer leaf below cavity tray DPC), 12 and 13, pp. 74, 82 and 84, respectively)

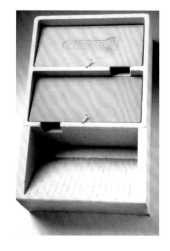

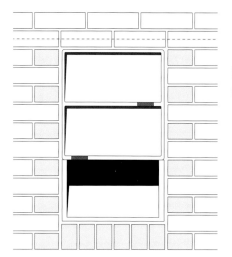

FAMILIAR MATERIAL	N/A
EASY TO INSTALL	Depends on context and surrounding materials
DURABLE	Yes
LOW OR NO MAINTENANCE	Access hatches permit internal cleaning
FROST RESISTANT	Yes
THERMAL MASS	Medium or high
FITS UK CONSTRUCTION SIZES	No
UNFAMILIAR MATERIAL; UNSURE HOW TO PROTECT	Yes
THERMAL BRIDGES	Where cavity walls bridged will need cavity tray damp proof course
EXPOSED WOOD PARTICLES ON CUT OR DAMAGED EDGES MAY ABSORB MOISTURE	N/A
MUST BE MAINTAINED WITH 'SPECIAL' UNFAMILIAR PAINT	Some
EMBODIED ENERGY	High
EMBODIED CARBON	High to medium
DEGREE OF FIT TO UK CONSTRUCTION SIZES	Not good in 2 or 3 dimensions
PRODUCT UPTAKE	Unknown

OTHER

→ Thicker walls needed to accommodate
→ Avoid using aluminium nails
→ Compromises U value of wall
→ Birds and bats have very different temperature needs so location of box may need to be a compromise for both

SWIFT BOX TYPE 25

Schwegler GmbH, Germany

FAMILIAR MATERIAL	N/A
EASY TO INSTALL	Depends on context and surrounding materials
DURABLE	Yes
LOW OR NO MAINTENANCE	Some – no access hatches to permit internal cleaning
FROST RESISTANT	Yes
THERMAL MASS	Medium or high
FITS UK CONSTRUCTION SIZES	No
UNFAMILIAR MATERIAL; UNSURE HOW TO PROTECT	Yes
THERMAL BRIDGES	Where cavity walls bridged will need cavity tray damp proof course
EXPOSED WOOD PARTICLES ON CUT OR DAMAGED EDGES MAY ABSORB MOISTURE	N/A
MUST BE MAINTAINED WITH 'SPECIAL' UNFAMILIAR PAINT	N/A
EMBODIED ENERGY	High
EMBODIED CARBON	High to medium
DEGREE OF FIT TO UK CONSTRUCTION SIZES	Not good in 3 dimensions
PRODUCT UPTAKE	Unknown

OTHER

→ Impairs U value if bridging cavity
→ Thicker walls needed to accommodate
→ Avoid using aluminium nails

TYPE OF PRODUCT:
Swift box

WEBSITE:
www.schwegler-nature.com

WHERE USED:
For installation into walls of buildings and structures

PRODUCT INFORMATION:
Schwegler wood-concrete: 265 mm (w) x 180 mm (h) x 220 mm (d)
Entrance hole: 55 mm (w) x 33 mm (h)

PRODUCT USE:
Swift nesting

(see Drawings Nos 5 (inside face of wall) and 9 (outer leaf),
pp. 66 and 74, respectively)

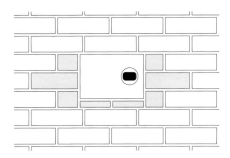

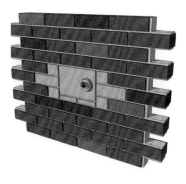

SWIFT BOX TYPE 16

Schwegler GmbH

TYPE OF PRODUCT:
Swift box

WEBSITE:
www.schwegler-nature.com

WHERE USED:
For installation into the walls of buildings and structures

PRODUCT INFORMATION:
Schwegler wood-concrete
430 mm (w) x 240mm (h) x 220 mm (d)

PRODUCT USE:
Swift nesting

(see Drawings Nos 9 (outer leaf below cavity tray DPC), 12 and 13, pp. 74, 82 and 84, respectively)

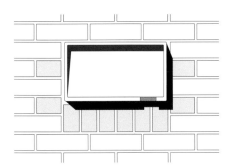

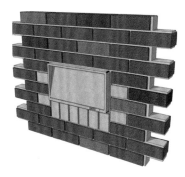

FAMILIAR MATERIAL	N/A
EASY TO INSTALL	Depends on context and surrounding materials
DURABLE	Yes
LOW OR NO MAINTENANCE	Some – no access hatches to permit cleaning
FROST RESISTANT	Yes
THERMAL MASS	Medium or high
FITS UK CONSTRUCTION SIZES	No
UNFAMILIAR MATERIAL: UNSURE HOW TO PROTECT	Yes
THERMAL BRIDGES	Where cavity walls bridged will need cavity tray damp proof course
EXPOSED WOOD PARTICLES ON CUT OR DAMAGED EDGES MAY ABSORB MOISTURE	N/A
MUST BE MAINTAINED WITH 'SPECIAL' UNFAMILIAR PAINT	N/A
EMBODIED ENERGY	High
EMBODIED CARBON	High to medium
DEGREE OF FIT TO UK CONSTRUCTION SIZES	Not good in 3 dimensions
PRODUCT UPTAKE	There has been some success recorded with this box

OTHER

→ Reduces U value if bridging cavity
→ Thicker walls needed to accommodate
→ Avoid using aluminium nails

HOUGHTON PRIMARY SCHOOL (HUNTINGDON)
– SWIFT, STARLING AND SPARROW BRICKS

Kier Eastern worked in partnership with Mouchel (architects), the RSPB and Houghton Primary School to change the detail design of a new school in Huntingdon to enable five bird bricks to be incorporated into the outer walls of the building. A number of swift, starling and sparrow bricks were carefully installed. Kier confirms that one of the bricks has been utilised by a family of house sparrows.

Kier says: 'We learnt how easy it is to incorporate bird bricks into new structures, which was straightforward, inexpensive and effective. We will now review all future builds for further opportunities.'

The project won a silver in the Green Apple Awards.

Installation of the Schwegler type 25 into the brick work

The sparrow box in situ

When rendered over only a small access hole is visible

3.6 Swallows

When swallows construct their nests they use around 1,000 pellets of mud taken from the edges of ponds, puddles and rivers. The nest is built by both sexes, and the pair mate for life. Suitable ledges or ready-made nests can be provided. Table 3.10 lists some considerations for swallows.

Table 3.10 Considerations and key requirements for swallows

Consideration	Solution
Where in a development	Inside a cold roof space or other unheated structure not requiring thermal insulation nor included in airtightness testing, such as garages and outbuildings. Possibly under very deep eaves
Where in a building	Swallows prefer outbuildings that provide dark ledges and nooks and crannies for nesting. These are protected from the worst of the cold weather and remain cool when it is hot. There needs to be permanent access
Height	It needs to be at least 2 m high and out of the reach of predators, such as cats
Dimensions	Fix a nest platform or ready-made nest where it would be suitable for them to nest. This needs to be 260 mm (w) x 100 mm (d)
Access dimensions	Minimum 70 mm (w) and 50 mm (h)
Other considerations	Droppings will occur below the nest, so locate the nest wisely or provide a ledge to catch the droppings The nesting area only needs to receive a minimal amount of daylight Nesting is only likely in suitable rural areas. Target provision in proximity of suitable wetland habitats and areas of livestock grazing, from which birds can obtain sufficient insects

Swallows

3.7   House martins

Various ready-made house martin nests are available. They do not guarantee that martins will nest, but often encourage them to build their own. As well as ready-made nests, it is possible to make nests that mimic these from exterior fillers or a mixture of cement and sawdust. These should measure about 180 mm in diameter, with a semi-circular entrance hole measuring 60–65 mm wide and 25 mm high. The nest can be mounted on a board or fixed directly to the building. Table 3.11 lists some considerations for house martins.

House martin's ready-made nest

Table 3.11 Considerations and key requirements for house martins

Consideration	Solution
Where in a development	Under overhanging eaves with unobstructed access
Where on a building	These are usually mounted on a board and can be fixed easily under the eaves. Nests are best placed in groups and there is some evidence that martins prefer to nest on north- and east-facing walls
Height	At least 3 m
Dimensions	180 mm in diameter
Access dimensions	A semi-circular hole 60–65 mm wide and 25 mm high
Other considerations	Ensure that the nest is under an overhang to protect it from the weather Nests can be fixed in groups to increase the likelihood of use Place nests away from areas where droppings may be a nuisance Nesting is only likely in suitable suburban and rural areas. Target provision in proximity of suitable wetland habitats and areas of livestock grazing from which birds can obtain sufficient insects

3.8   House sparrows

Pairs are faithful to their nest site and to each other for life, although a lost mate of either sex is normally replaced within days. Sparrows prefer to nest in holes in an occupied building, but they regularly use other kinds of holes, for example in trees, and nest boxes. Table 3.12 lists some considerations for house sparrows.

Table 3.12 Considerations and key requirements for house sparrows

Consideration	Solution
Where in a development	Any suitable building
Where in a building	Ideally within the structure at the soffit/eaves level, but otherwise as an external box at the same location Out of direct sunlight – the preferred aspect is easterly
Height	2 m
Dimensions	150 mm (w) x 350 mm (h) x 150 mm (d). Bottom of the hole must be no less than 150 mm from base of box
Access dimensions	A 32 mm round hole. Bottom of the hole must be no less than 150 mm from base of box
Other considerations	House sparrows nest in loose colonies of 10–20 pairs. Males will defend a territory adjacent to the nest entrance. While nests can be as little as 200–300 mm apart, spacing them at 1m reduces aggression between males vying to mate with females. Locate nests near dense deciduous shrubs which may be used for cover, roosting and feeding in, and areas of short and long grass which are also important as a source of insect and seed food.

BRICK BOX TYPE 24

Schwegler GmbH

TYPE OF PRODUCT:
House sparrow brick box

WEBSITE:
www.schwegler-nature.com

WHERE USED:
For incorporation into an outer wall as appropriate

PRODUCT INFORMATION:
Made of woodcrete
Dimensions: 180 mm (w) x 235 mm (h) x 180 mm (d)
Entrance hole: 32 mm
The brick boxes can be installed flush with the outside wall and can be rendered or covered so that only the entrance hole is visible

PRODUCT USE:
As well as sparrows, the box may be used by great, blue and coal tits, redstart and nuthatch

(see Drawings Nos 5 (inside face of wall) and 9 (in outer leaf), pp. 66 and 74, respectively)

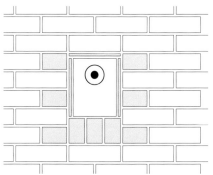

FAMILIAR MATERIAL	N/A
EASY TO INSTALL	Depends on context and surrounding materials and sizes
DURABLE	Yes
LOW OR NO MAINTENANCE	Some – access hatch permits internal cleaning
FROST RESISTANT	Yes
THERMAL MASS	Medium or high
FITS UK CONSTRUCTION SIZES	No
UNFAMILIAR MATERIAL: UNSURE HOW TO PROTECT	Yes
THERMAL BRIDGES	Where cavity walls bridged will need cavity tray damp proof course
EXPOSED WOOD PARTICLES ON CUT OR DAMAGED EDGES MAY ABSORB MOISTURE	N/A
MUST BE MAINTAINED WITH 'SPECIAL' UNFAMILIAR PAINT	N/A
EMBODIED ENERGY	High
EMBODIED CARBON	High to medium
DEGREE OF FIT TO UK CONSTRUCTION SIZES	Poor in 3 dimensions
PRODUCT UPTAKE	Unknown

OTHER

→ Impairs U value if bridging cavity wall
→ Thicker walls needed to accommodate
→ Avoid using aluminium nails

ECOSURV SPARROW BOX

Ecosurv Ltd

FAMILIAR MATERIAL	Yes
EASY TO INSTALL	Yes
DURABLE	Yes
LOW OR NO MAINTENANCE	No way to access interior for cleaning
FROST RESISTANT	Yes
THERMAL MASS	Medium
FITS UK CONSTRUCTION SIZES	Yes
UNFAMILIAR MATERIAL; UNSURE HOW TO PROTECT	N/A
THERMAL BRIDGES	Yes through cavity wall insulation; requires high-performance insulation on back and/or wider cavity; if it bridges cavity it will need cavity tray damp proof course
EXPOSED WOOD PARTICLES ON CUT OR DAMAGED EDGES MAY ABSORB MOISTURE	N/A
MUST BE MAINTAINED WITH 'SPECIAL' UNFAMILIAR PAINT	N/A
EMBODIED ENERGY	Medium
EMBODIED CARBON	Medium
DEGREE OF FIT TO UK CONSTRUCTION SIZES	Fits in 2 dimensions, with cut bricks at sides
PRODUCT UPTAKE	Unknown

OTHER

→ This product can be supplied faced to suit the building. Finishes include brick, stone, masonry and render
→ The product can be supplied in different sizes and formats to suit design needs
→ Will need a cavity tray DPC over box

TYPE OF PRODUCT:
House sparrow box

WEBSITE:
www.ecosurv.co.uk

WHERE USED:
For incorporation into outer wall as appropriate

PRODUCT INFORMATION:
Outer facing can be changed to match any façade
Dimensions: 215 mm (w) x 210 mm (h) x 135 mm (d)

PRODUCT USE:
Can be used by sparrows

(see Drawings Nos 5 (inside face of wall) and 9 (in outer leaf), pp. 66 and 74, respectively)

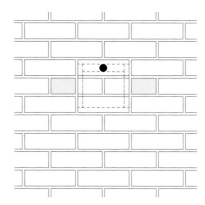

ROOFBLOCK

Roofblock

TYPE OF PRODUCT:

Bird nesting block – concrete eaves/verge system

WEBSITE:

www.roofblock.co.uk

WHERE USED:

Flat, hipped or any pitched roof. Outer leaf of cavity wall or half-brick uninsulated walls to outbuildings

PRODUCT INFORMATION:

Made from recycled aggregates and eco-cement

PRODUCT USE:

Block with 30 mm hole on front into interior chamber

(see Drawing No. 6, p. 68)

FAMILIAR MATERIAL	Yes
EASY TO INSTALL	Must be designed in
DURABLE	Yes
LOW OR NO MAINTENANCE	Yes
FROST RESISTANT	Yes
THERMAL MASS	High
FITS UK CONSTRUCTION SIZES	Yes
UNFAMILIAR MATERIAL; UNSURE HOW TO PROTECT	N/A
THERMAL BRIDGES	Risk of thermal bridge through thin cavity wall construction – can be improved with wider insulated cavity (see below); located under roof tiling and underlay, no need for cavity tray damp proof course
EXPOSED WOOD PARTICLES ON CUT OR DAMAGED EDGES MAY ABSORB MOISTURE	N/A
MUST BE MAINTAINED WITH 'SPECIAL' UNFAMILIAR PAINT	N/A
EMBODIED ENERGY	Medium to low
EMBODIED CARBON	Low (eco-cement)
DEGREE OF FIT TO UK CONSTRUCTION SIZES	Fits in 2 dimensions (see Table 3.2)
PRODUCT UPTAKE	Unknown

OTHER

→ Numerous endorsements and accolades as an eco-product (not as nesting box)
→ Can be positioned on any elevation unobtrusively
→ Potentially large nesting blocks if adjacent blocks are linked
→ Made for cavity walls but will fit on half-brick upstand of 1B solid wall
→ Fair-faced – no need for rendering over
→ Reduces U value locally in wider cavity wall construction with full fill cavity insulation
→ Profile may need to be modified with thicker walls and thicker roof and wall insulation
→ Eco-cement should have less embodied carbon
→ Recycled aggregates are likely to have less embodied energy and/or carbon

3.9 Starlings

Starlings nest in holes and cavities, especially in trees, but often use holes in buildings, including occupied houses and nest boxes. They nest in loose colonies and do not establish and defend a proper territory – only the immediate area around the nesting cavity is defended. The whole colony feeds communally in what is termed a home range.

In order to attract a mate, the male builds the base of the nest from dry grass and leaves in a hole, and sings from perches close to the nest's entrance. The female completes the nest by forming the inner cup shape of the nest and lining it with fine grasses, moss and feathers. No ready-made nest boxes for use in built structures exist, but the dimensions can be used to incorporate a bespoke space. Table 3.13 lists some considerations for starlings.

Table 3.13 Considerations and key requirements for starlings

Consideration	Solution
Where in a development	Any suitable building
Where in a building	Ideally within the structure at the soffit/eaves level, but otherwise as an external box at the same location Out of direct sunlight – the preferred aspect is easterly – and not over the main living areas as starlings can be noisy
Height	At least 3 m high
Dimensions	180 mm (w) x 400 mm (h) x 180 mm (d). Bottom of hole must be no less than 180 mm from base of box
Access dimensions	45 mm round hole – this hole needs to be located at least 125 mm above the base of the box. Bottom of hole must be no less than 180 mm from base of box
Other considerations	Nest provision can be as little as 1.5 m apart, but 3 m or more will reduce agression between pairs Locate near open grassland. In rural locations this would be close to pasture particularly with livestock. In urban areas, nests should be located close to parks and other open spaces Ensure there are plenty of dense, deciduous shrubs nearby, such as hedges which may be used for cover as well as gleaning insects, fruits and seeds

3.10 Barn owls

Although barn owls are not an urban species, any suitable new buildings in a rural development could play host to a barn owl. Table 3.14 gives details to be used when considering the potential for the provision of barn owls and their key requirements.

Drawings numbers 2 and 3 (pages 58 and 60) illustrate the incorporation of this access into a roof space. This is shown as being via the gable end wall and also via the roof itself. Within the roof space a nest box can be provided and details of these are found on the Barn Owl Trust website (www.barnowltrust.org.uk).

It is possible that the provision for barn owls could also be utilised by the little owl. This owl was introduced into Britain during the nineteenth century and is found in low numbers across much of England and parts of Wales. In order to make provision specific for little owls, information can be found on the Barn Owl Trust website (www.barnowltrust.org.uk).

Table 3.14 Considerations and key requirements for barn owls

Consideration	Solution
Type of location	The surrounding habitat needs to be open countryside (not urban or woodland) – as a general rule of thumb, no provision should be made within 1 km of a major road (dual-carriageway or motorway) or in high mountain areas
Where in a development	A suitable building would be one on the edge of the development, ideally with the access point facing open countryside One of the tallest buildings should normally be selected
Where in a building	Their requirements mean that provision for barn owls is most straightforward in buildings that have a cold roof space and for which there is not likely to be a planned conversion into a used area that would incorporate the nesting area However, it is possible to dedicate only part of a roof space to the owls, so long as a separation ensures that the owls will be hidden from view should the other part of the roof be used Alternatively, in bespoke cases, the U value envelope can be diverted to incorporate a nesting area of the dimensions given below within an exterior wall. This will need additional measures to maintain the U value envelope and early consultation between the architect and the Barn Owl Trust is recommended
Height	Access hole and nesting area no less than 3 m above ground level
Dimensions	Floor area of a nest chamber: absolute minimum 400 mm x 400 mm, ideal size is 1 sq m Minimum height: 600 mm Minimum drop from bottom of entrance hole to floor: 460 mm
Access dimensions	Access need not be by flight, but walking Entrance hole: minimum size 100 mm (w) x 200 mm (h); optimum size 130 mm (w) x 250 mm (h); maximum size 200 mm (w) x 300 mm (h) Measures aimed at reducing the chances of entry by other species (such as jackdaws) are recommended, provided that they do not significantly reduce the box's suitability for barn owls Hipped roofs, and pitched roofs where optimal siting of the access is through the roof rather than the wall/gable end, will require the use of a specially built miniature dormer or owl-hole 'tile' – NB: See Drawing No. 3 (page 60), key notes 1 and 11 for suitable materials Where the access is in a vertical structure, such as a wall or gable end, there should be an external landing platform or perch below the entrance hole to provide external exercise space for emerging nestlings/fledglings, ideally 250 x 500 mm with a grippable raised edge. Note: Where the internal depth of the nesting space (measured from hole-bottom to floor) exceeds 600 mm an external exercise platform is not required, but optional Human access via a generous-sized inspection door or removable panel is important for occasional clearing out of excess nest debris – typically 300 x 400 mm
Other considerations	Barn owls seem to prefer perching on wood, rather than metal or stone (presumably for comfort and minimum heat loss) The barn owl is a Schedule 1 species and therefore legally protected from any disturbance. Nest inspections should only be undertaken by a Schedule 1 licence holder Barn owls can easily become accustomed to almost any type of regular human activity or noise provided they can remain out of sight However, bear in mind the above note about its Schedule 1 status. Barn owls, like kestrels, need sufficient areas of prey-rich habitat. Typically, 1.1–3.7% of land within 2 km of the site should be rough grassland. For more information see section 5.2 of the Barn Owl Conservation Handbook

Further advice and information can be obtained in the *Barn Owl Conservation Handbook* in *Barn Owls and Rural Planning Applications – A Guide*, and also on the Barn Owl Trust website (www.barnowltrust.org.uk).

Drawing No.

02

Barn owl wall entrance – uninsulated pitched roof gable wall (above insulated wall)

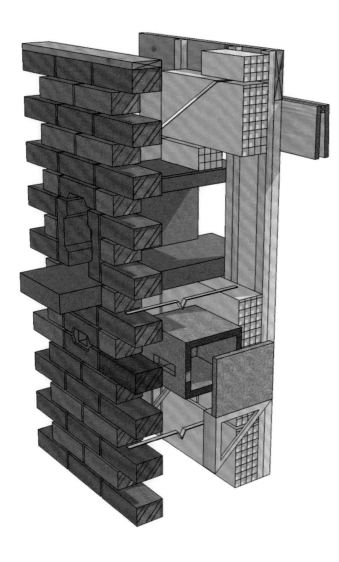

Top

1   Reclaimed, locally grown UKWAS or FSC temperate softwood roofing battens

2   Reclaimed, locally grown UKWAS or FSC temperate softwood rafters

3   Extruded cellular fired clay tunnel to cross cavity with landing and take-off areas outside of wall thickness

3a Option: Eco-concrete tunnel to cross cavity to provide external exercise platform, see Table 3.14

3b Option: Precast concrete tunnel to cross cavity

4   Uninsulated cavity above occupied floors

5   Concrete block inner leaf, 100 mm

6   Support brackets, galvanized mild steel or austenitic stainless steel

7   DIY swift box, using cement and wood fibre board, 25 mm. Size: 265 (w) x 180 (h) x 220 (d) mm

8   'Ibstock bat brick' 2 No. brick size, bottom to bottom to form larger opening

9   Fired clay facing brick outer leaf, 102 (w) x 65 (h) x 215 (l) mm

10 'Ibstock bat brick' 3 No. to form sides and top of opening, brick size

11 Metal tie for tunnel, stainless steel

12 2 courses of clay verge tiles bedded in lime mortar on outer leaf of cavity brick wall, cantilevering over gable wall face 1/3 overhang 2/3 bearing, supporting clay roof tiling at verge

13 Clay plain tile roofing

14 Option: 2 part long wall tie, austenitic stainless steel (304 equivalent), 400 mm

14a Option: 'MagmaTech TeploTie Type 4', extruded basalt and fibre long wall tie, 425 x 6.5 dia. mm

15 Cavity tray DPC damp proof course (stepped)

16 'Pro clima Solitex Plus' WTL wind-tightness layer and VPU vapour permeable underlay

Barn owl's entrance in wall

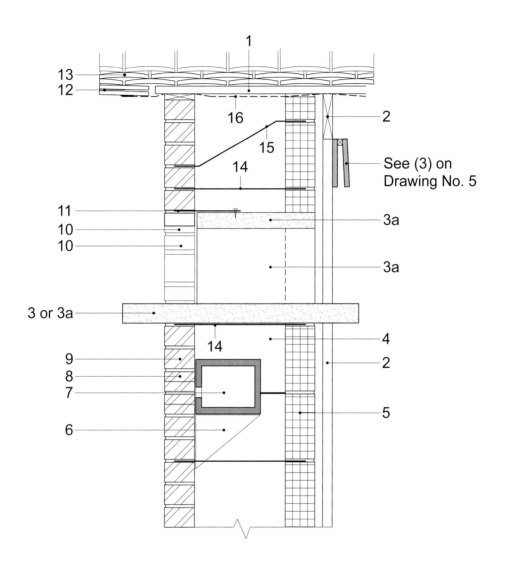

1

13

12

16

2

15

See (3) on
Drawing No. 5

14

11

10

10

3a

3a

3 or 3a

14

4

2

9

8

7

5

6

Drawing No.

03 Barn owl wall entrance – uninsulated hip or pitched roof dormer (above an uninsulated wall)

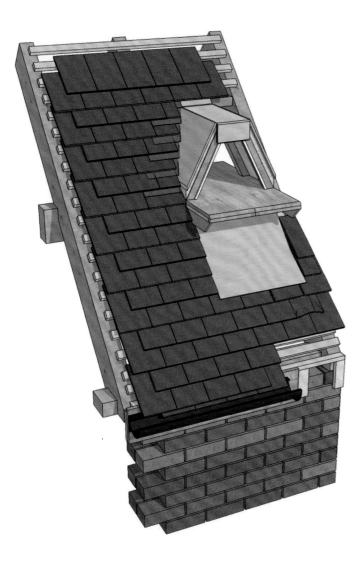

1 Reclaimed, locally grown UKWAS or FSC temperate durable hardwood frame, 38 mm x 38 mm – 50 mm x 50 mm

2 FSC WBP weather boil proof plywood, 6 mm

3 Reclaimed, locally grown UKWAS or FSC temperate softwood framing, 50 mm x 50 mm

4 FSC WBP weather boil proof plywood, 25 mm

5 Malleable metal standing seam roof cladding. See Lead or Zinc Development Association or manufacturer's guidance on details

6 Reclaimed, locally grown UKWAS or FSC temperate softwood roof tiling battens

7 Clay plain tile roofing

8 Reclaimed, locally grown UKWAS or FSC temperate softwood rafters

9 Reclaimed, locally grown UKWAS or FSC temperate hardwood framing, 50 mm x 50 mm to support 1 & 11

10 Reclaimed, locally grown UKWAS or FSC temperate durable hardwood purlin

11 FSC WBP weather and boil proof plywood, 25 mm, installed to fall to external drain hole

12 Malleable metal apron flashing, lead or zinc, etc. See Lead or Zinc Development Association or manufacturer's guidance on details

13 FSC WBP weather and boil proof plywood, 25 mm

14 Reclaimed, locally grown UKWAS or FSC temperate durable hardwood wall plate

15 Clay brick solid wall, 1B, 215 mm

16 Lindab Rainline Rainwater gutter (galvanized steel, half round)

17 Bat access tile set, 18 mm gap x 165 mm long

Bottom

1 Clay plain tile roofing

2 Malleable metal flashings to clay roof tiles

3 Malleable metal standing seam roof cladding

4 Barn owl entrance

5 Bat access tile set, 18 mm gap x 165 mm long

Barn owl's entrance in sloping roof

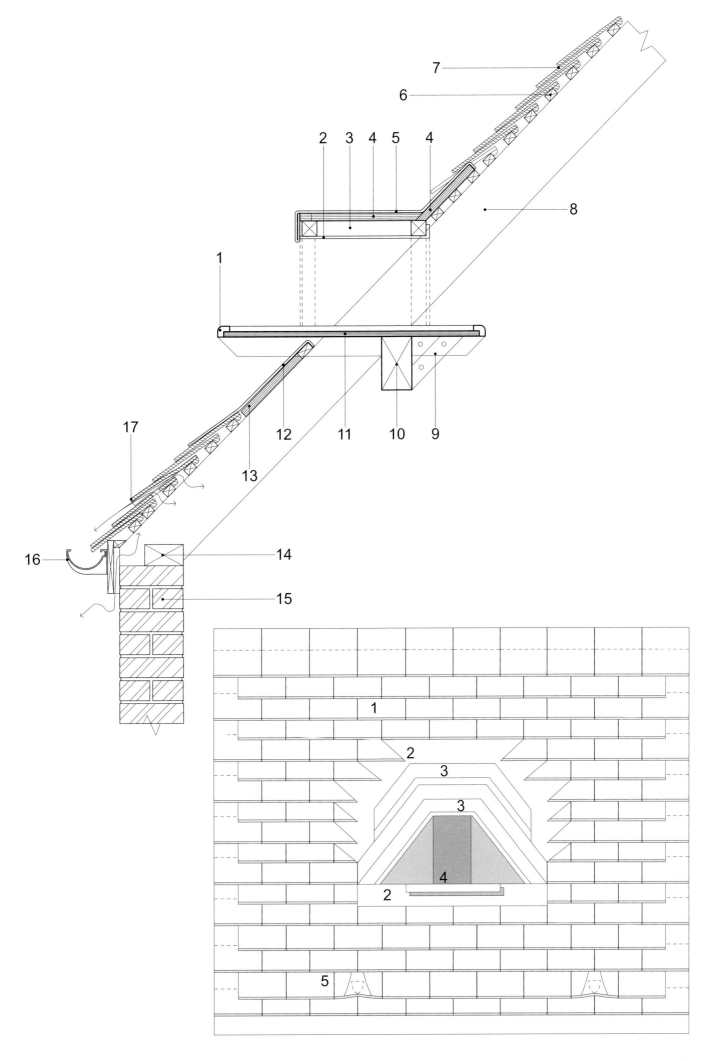

3.11 Peregrine falcons

The nest site, known as an eyrie, is usually on a cliff ledge, quarry or other inaccessible and undisturbed location, although, buildings and other constructions are increasingly being used. Old nests of other species, such as ravens, are used elsewhere in the world, but rarely in the UK. The nest itself is a slight scrape in any earth or old debris on the nest ledge. No material is brought in to build a nest. Table 3.15 lists some considerations for peregrine falcons.

See page 119 for a case study of peregrine provision retrofitted to a building.

Table 3.15 Considerations and key requirements for peregrine falcons

Consideration	Solution
Where in a development	On a wide ledge, free from disturbance and as high as possible
Where on a building	Avoid full sun and prevailing winds North or north-east preferable
Height	Over 20 m
Dimensions	Ledge: 600 mm (w) x 40 mm (h) x 450 mm (d) Box: 600 mm (w) x 900 mm (h) x 450 mm (d) (see www.raptorresource.org/build.htm or ready-made Schwegler products)
Access dimensions	N/A for ledge
Other considerations	Place the provision where routine maintenance is least likely to disturb peregrines using the ledge The Peregrine is a Schedule 1 species and legally protected from any disturbance. Maintenance should only be undertaken outside of the breeding season when the birds are not in attendance of the nest For essential, emergency maintenance it would have to be demonstrated as a lawful unavoidable operation. Ideally it would be safer to obtain a disturbance licence from a statutory agency (e.g. Natural England) Place the provision where the discarded remains of prey and pellets will not inconvenience the users of the building Peregrines are vocal when on the nest so consider the location of the provision with this in mind Secure metal tray(s) to face of or below and behind wall protection upstand, to prevent removal by bird or wind Extend tray beyond canopy, both sides to create exercise areas and to protect waterproofing from talons and beak Asphalt is assumed to be the only roof waterproofing material robust enough for this application if exposed Add gravel to fill tray Consider closing the sides and lowering the roof but seek specialist guidance if not adhering to 'Dimensions' above

3.12 Bespoke roost and nesting provision in low and zero carbon building types

Having reviewed each species, the products that can be bought ready-made and how these relate to standard building dimensions, consideration is now given to how they can be incorporated into a new build. This section discusses each of the major sorts of new build likely to be most widely used in low and zero carbon buildings and the opportunities for provision that arise in each.

It is important to note that where a ready-made product is shown as an example, other products with suitable dimensions or bespoke designs can be made to utilise the available space.

All of the suggestions made are based on what is known of the requirements of the species in question and finding ways to incorporate these into each build style, without compromising the integrity of the building and its compliance with energy standards. The success of these measures cannot be guaranteed, but any resultant monitoring of uptake will aid our development and understanding to help ensure increasing success in the future.

3.12.1 Roof space

Drawings Nos 5 and 6 (pages 66–69) make provision for crevice-dwelling bats in a roof design that uses tiles and allows access to the space between the tiles/slates and the U value envelope. Included in these figures are examples of the placement of some of the ready-made products, as well as bespoke bat roosting areas.

3.12.2 Cavity walls

Unfilled cavity walls in traditional methods of construction are used by a number of bat species. The term 'cavity wall' is used here to denote insulated cavity walls that, despite their seemingly inappropriate method of construction for low and zero carbon buildings, are nevertheless anticipated to continue to be built for some considerable time and do provide opportunities for bat roosting and bird nesting.

Drawings Nos 7 to 11 (pages 70–79) show ready-made products for bats and swifts (the Habibat bat box (see p. 35), the Ecosurv Swift box (see p. 46), Tudor Bat Access Tile Set (see p. 30) and the Schwegler Bat Roost 1FE (see p. 39)) as well as the bespoke provision of space for crevice bat roosting in a variety of options.

Drawing No.
04

Peregrine ledge – single leaf blockwork solid wall, externally insulated with solar shading shelf

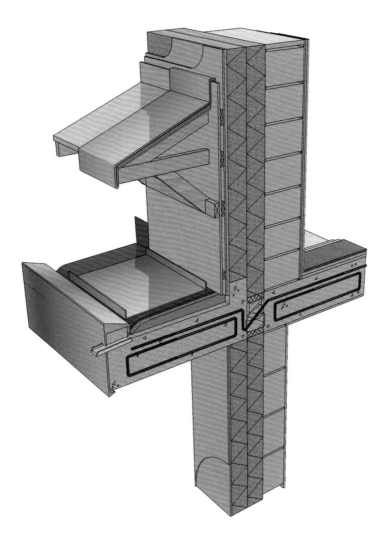

1   Dry lining board: clay board 40 mm, magnesium oxide board 12 mm, or fibre-reinforced gypsum board 12 mm

2   'Dot and dab' bonded drylining

3   Airtight parge coat: clay, lime or gypsum, 5–8 mm

4   Dense aggregate concrete block, 200 mm (w) x 215 mm (h) x 440 mm (l)

4a 215 mm (w) thick wall, 140 mm block laid on side, 150 mm (h) course height

5   'Dry screed' boards: dense desulphurisation gypsum with wood fibre reinforcement

6   In situ reinforced concrete floor, with recycled aggregates and OPC replacement GGBS cement, 200 mm (t)

7   'Schöck Isokorb Type K' thermal break with intumescent fire protection and continuity reinforcement

8   Gypsum plaster finish for airtightness with extra care to maintain integrity at skirting level

9   Lime, hemp-lime or mineral based thin render system 2 layers, reinforcement layer between (airtight and permeable) (not cement based)

10 Waterproof membrane with upstand. Asphalt is assumed to be the only roof waterproofing material robust enough for this application if exposed

11 Stainless steel tray, 600 (w) x 40 (h) x 450 (d) mm. Secure metal tray(s) to face of or below and behind wall protection upstand (11a), to prevent removal by bird or wind. Extend tray beyond canopy, both sides to create exercise areas and to protect waterproofing from talons

11a Wall protection upstand 900 (w) x 900 mm (h) with battens to support fixings for canopy. Upstand to secure the tray in place, or tray to be secured to it

12 Sand:cement screed to 1:40 fall

13 Cantilever shelf, in situ or precast concrete, 200 mm (t)

14 Drain spout

15 Pressed metal fascia/coping/drip

16 Reclaimed, locally grown, UKWAS or FSC temperate durable species softwood cantilever framing, 100 x 50 and 100 x 100 mm height and spacing to avoid conflict with standing, landing and take-off wing action and head. Consider closing the sides and lowering the roof but seek specialist guidance if not adhering to 'Dimensions' in Table 3.15

17 WBP weather and boil proof equivalent plywood sheet 12 mm lean-to roof

18 Malleable zinc standing seam roof covering to plywood with upstand and drip

19 Dense thermal insulation, 2 x 100 mm, for render to (9) above

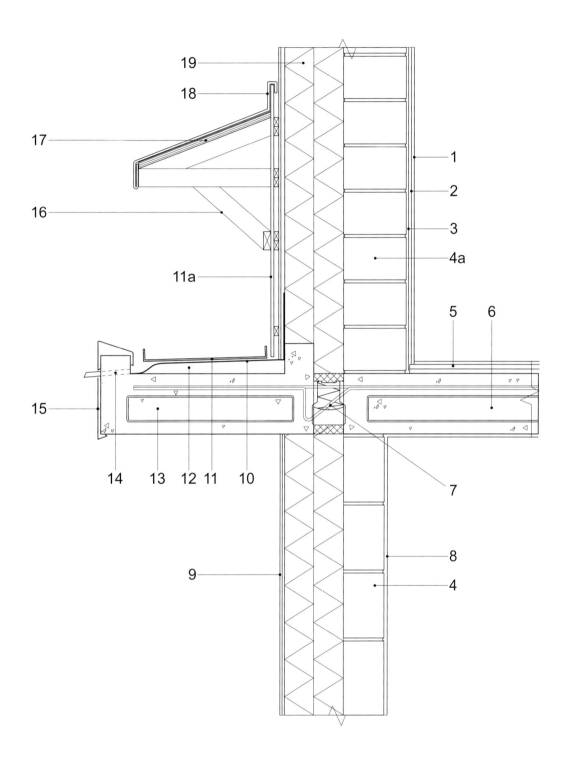

Drawing No.
05
Roofspace 1 – solid wall construction at roof eaves and ridge providing places for bats and birds (uninsulated outbuilding)

1   Ridge roost, similar materials to (3c)

1a   Option: Could be empty ridge tile space with closed ends and ways through to next ridge tile space

2   Handmade clay ridge tile with bat access

3   Bat roost fixed to side of rafters below ridge beam, 2 boards spaced apart, 15–20 mm minimum, 25–30 mm maximum 15 x 20 and 15–20 x 20 spacer battens (see section on Drawing No. 2)

3a   Option: Reclaimed, locally grown UKWAS or FSC temperate softwood scraps

3b   Option: FSC WBP weather and boil proof plywood strips

3c   Option: Cement-wood particle board, roughened/ grooved surface for climbing and hanging

4   Reclaimed, locally grown UKWAS or FSC temperate softwood rafters, 200 mm (avoid trussed rafters)

5   Reclaimed, locally grown UKWAS or FSC temperate durable hardwood wall plate

6–7   Potential roost/nest box/platform positions (not necessarily all together, along length of building) some face fixed, some open-topped, some sheltering under others to avoid predation

8   'Ibstock bat brick' 2 No. brick size, bottom to bottom to form larger opening

9   DIY swift box, using cement and wood fibreboard, 25 mm. Size: 265 (w) x 180 (h) x 220 (d) mm

10   Support brackets, galvanized mild steel or austenitic stainless steel

11   Reclaimed, locally grown or FSC UKWAS or FSC Oak or durable hardwood fascia

12   Lindab Rainline rainwater gutter (galvanized steel, half round)

13   Bat access tile set, 18 mm gap x 165 mm long

14   Reclaimed, locally grown UKWAS or FSC temperate softwood roof tiling battens

15   Not used

16   Handmade clay plain tile roofing, 160 mm (w) x 265 mm (l) x 10 mm (t)

17   Mortar bedding

18   Reclaimed, locally grown or FSC UKWAS or FSC oak or durable hardwood ridge purlin

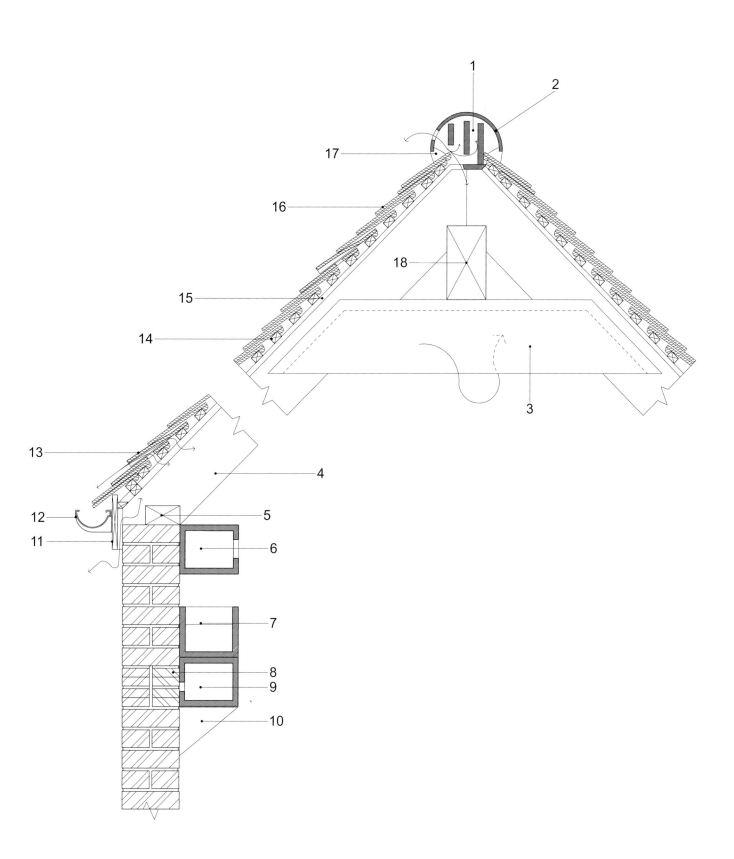

Roofspace 2 – insulated cavity wall and pitched roof providing places for bats and small birds

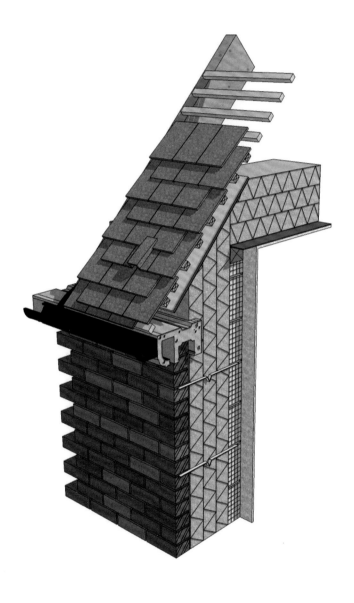

1 Reclaimed, locally grown, UKWAS or FSC temperate softwood rafters, 200 mm (avoid trussed rafters)

2 Cellulose fibre insulation, 3 x 100 mm

3 Pro clima Intello Plus' ATL Air tightness layer, polyolefine, lapped and sealed joints

4 Drylining ceiling board

5 Reclaimed, locally grown, UKWAS or FSC temperate softwood wall plate, 100 (w) x 75 (h) mm with GMS holding down straps

6 Airtight parge coat: clay, lime or gypsum, 5–8 mm or plaster

7 Cellular clay blockwork inner leaf, 100 mm

8 Not used

9 Full fill cavity wall insulation, 3 x 100 mm rock mineral fibre

10 Option: 2 part long wall tie, austenitic stainless steel (304 equivalent), 400 mm (l)

10a Option: 'MagmaTech TeploTie Type 4', extruded basalt and fibre long wall tie, 425 x 6.5 dia. mm

11 Fired clay facing brick outer leaf, 102 x 215 x 65 mm

12 'RoofBLOCK masonry roof overhang system' Hollow precast 'eco-concrete' eaves/verge system incorporating bird or bat roosts

13 Gutter galvanized mild steel (half round)

14 Locally grown, UKWAS or FSC temperate softwood tilting fillets on rafters

15 Bat access tile set, 18 mm gap x 165 long mm

16 'Pro clima Solitex Plus' WTL wind-tightness layer vapour permeable roofing underlay (breathing roof), lapped and sealed joints

16a Gap in underlay (17) below bat access tile set (15)

17 Cement-wood particle board, Roughened/grooved surface for climbing and hanging

18 50 mm ventilation sap

19 Reclaimed, locally grown, UKWAS or FSC temperate softwood roof tile battens, 25 x 38 mm

20 Dreadnought clay plain tile roofing, 160 (w) x 265 (l) x 10 (t) mm

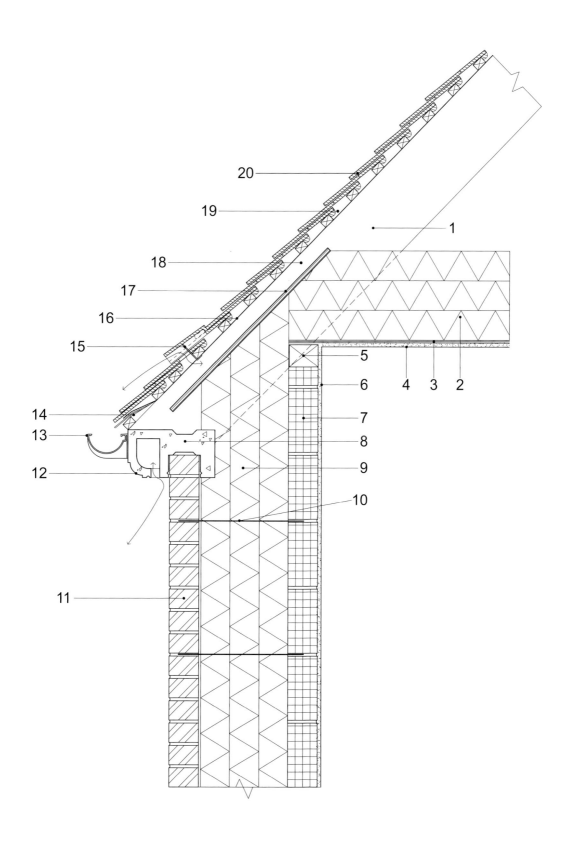

1

2
3
4
5
6
7
8
9
10
11
12
13
14
15
16
17
18
19
20

Drawing No.
07

Cavity walls
– brick/block cavity wall construction providing spaces for bats

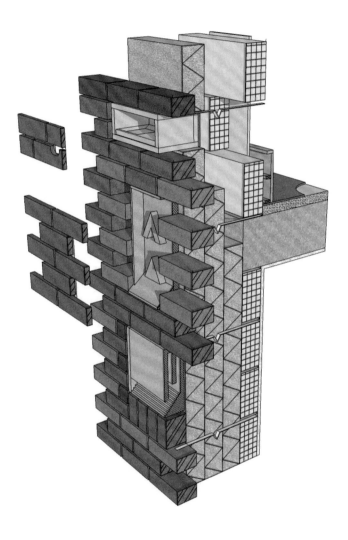

1   Hollow skirting board (and dado rails) carrying services to avoid chasing masonry walls

2   'Eco-screed': less OP cement and more GGBS 'ground granulated burst furnace slag' cement, less virgin aggregate and more recycled, secondary or manufactured aggregate, 40 mm

3   Linoleum sheet flooring, 2 mm

4   Precast concrete hollow plank floor, see (11)

5   In situ plaster for airtightness: clay, lime or gypsum

6   Locally manufactured dense recycled aggregate concrete block with lime mortar

7   2 part long wall tie, austenitic stainless steel (304 equivalent), 400 mm

8   'Schwegler Bat Box 1FE 00748/3', wood-concrete, 300 (w) x 300 (h) x 100 (d) mm. Best located at eaves level not at lower levels

8a   Option: DIY bat box using cement and wood fibre board, grooved surface for climbing and hanging, 25 mm. Best located at eaves level not at lower levels (not shown on plan)

9   Rock mineral fibre full fill cavity wall batts, 3 x 100 mm

10   'MagmaTech TeploTie Type 4', extruded basalt and fibre long wall tie, 425 x 6.5 dia. mm

11   'Pro clima Solitex Plus' WTL wind-tightness layer: top hat profile closing ends of hollow core plank floor, see (4)

12   Habibat bat box with brick slip facing and cut bricks either side

13   Reclaimed or new locally sourced facing brick, 215 (w) x 65 (h) x 102 (d) mm lime mortar

14   'Ecosurv Swift Box' 326 (w) x 140 (h) x 102 (d) mm. Best located at eaves level not at lower levels with brick slip facing

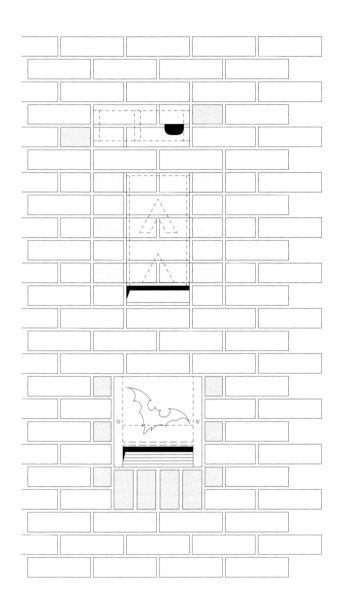

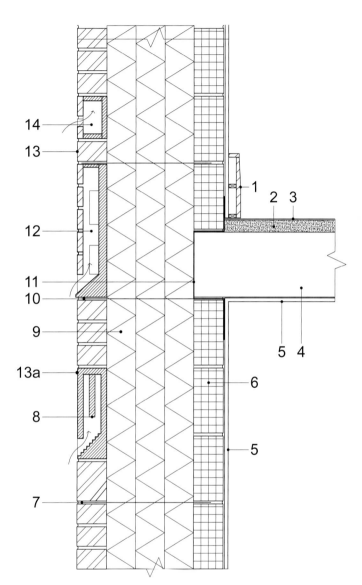

Drawing No.

08

Cavity walls – brick/block cavity wall construction eaves providing spaces for bats and birds

1   Hemp insulation, 3 x 100 (t) mm

2   Vapour barrier or intelligent airtightness layer

3   Drylining ceiling board, 12 (t) mm

4   Reclaimed, locally grown UKWAS or FSC temperate softwood wall plate, 100 (w) x 75 (h) mm with holding down straps

5   Cellular blockwork inner leaf, 100 (w) mm

6   Airtight parge coat: clay, lime or gypsum, 5–8 (t) mm or plaster

7   Full fill cavity wall insulation, 3 x 100 (w) mm rock mineral fibre

8   Wall ties option: 2 part long wall tie, austenitic stainless steel (304 equivalent), 400 mm

8a   Wall ties option: 'MagmaTech TeploTie Type 4', extruded basalt and fibre long wall tie, 425 x 6.5 dia. mm

9   Reclaimed, locally made fired clay facing brick outer leaf, 215 (w) x 65 (h) x 102 (d) mm

10   Reclaimed, locally grown or FSC UKWAS or FSC temperate durable species softwood soffit

11   Reclaimed, locally grown or FSC UKWAS or FSC temperate durable species softwood fascia

12   Gutter and brackets, galvanized steel, half round

13   Rigid HDPE flashing into gutter, laid over reclaimed, locally grown or FSC UKWAS or FSC temperate softwood tilting fillet, 50 mm x varies

14   Reclaimed, locally grown or FSC UKWAS or FSC temperate softwood tilting fillet, 50 mm x varies, gap in underlay

15   Gap in underlay below bat access tile set. 'Bat access tile set', 18 mm gap x 165 mm long

16   Reclaimed, locally grown or FSC UKWAS or FSC temperate softwood rafters (avoid trussed rafters), 50 (w) x 200 (h) x 50 mm

17   'Schwegler Bat Box 1FE 00748/3', wood-concrete, 300 (w) x 300 (h) x 100 (d) mm

18   'Pro clima Solitex Plus' roofing underlay

19   Air passage gap, 50 mm

20   FSC timber panel, 600 mm wide

21   Dreadnought clay plain tile roofing, 160 (w) x 265 (h) x 10 (t) mm

22   Reclaimed, locally grown, UKWAS or FSC temperate softwood roof tile battens, 25 x 38 mm

23   Not used

24   Not used

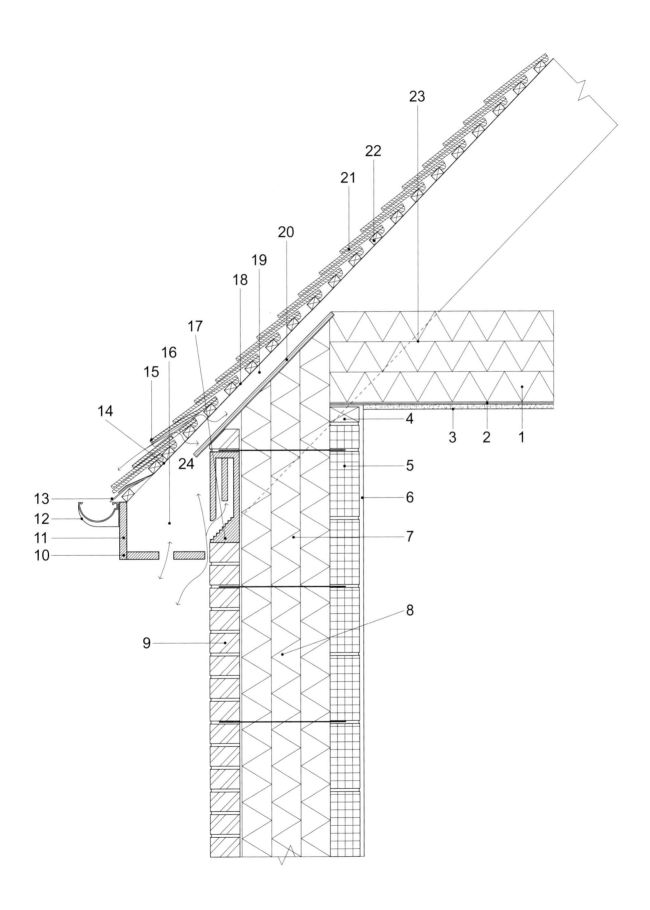

Drawing No.
09
Cavity walls – brick/block cavity gable wall construction verge providing spaces for bats and swifts

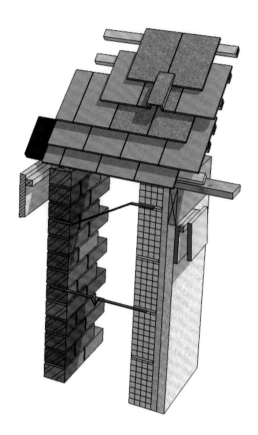

4   Cellular blockwork inner leaf, 100 (w) mm

7   Wall ties option: 2 part long wall tie, austenitic stainless steel (304 equivalent), 400 mm

7a Wall ties option: 'MagmaTech TeploTie Type 4', extruded basalt and fibre long wall tie, 425 x 6.5 dia. mm

8   Reclaimed, locally made fired clay facing brick outer leaf, 215 (w) x 65 (h) x 102 (d) mm.

15 Reclaimed, locally grown or FSC UKWAS or FSC temperate softwood rafters (avoid trussed rafters), 50 (w) x 200 (h) mm

17 'Pro clima Solitex Plus' roofing underlay

20 Reclaimed, locally sourced clay handmade plain roof tiles 160 (w) x 265 (l) x 10 (t) mm verge bedded in lime mortar

21 Reclaimed, locally grown or FSC UKWAS or FSC temperate softwood roof tile battens, 50 (h) x 25 (t) mm

24 Bat roost fixed to side of rafters below ridge beam, 2 boards spaced apart, 15–20 mm minimum, 25–30 mm maximum

24a Optional materials: reclaimed, locally grown or FSC UKWAS or FSC temperate softwood scraps

24b Optional materials: FSC WBP weather and boil proof plywood strips

24c Optional materials: cement-wood particle board, roughened/grooved surface for climbing and hanging

25 Reclaimed, locally grown or FSC UKWAS or FSC temperate durable species softwood barge board on softwood spacers, 15–30 mm gap

26 Polyethylene stepped cavity tray damp proof course

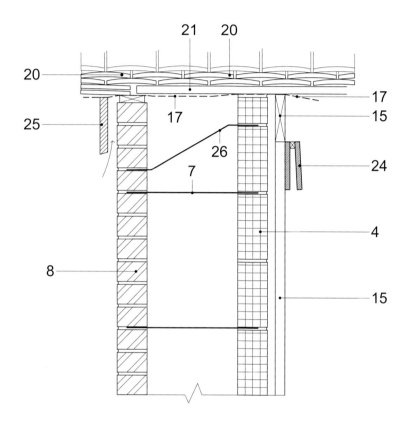

Cavity walls
– insulated brick/block cavity wall at eaves

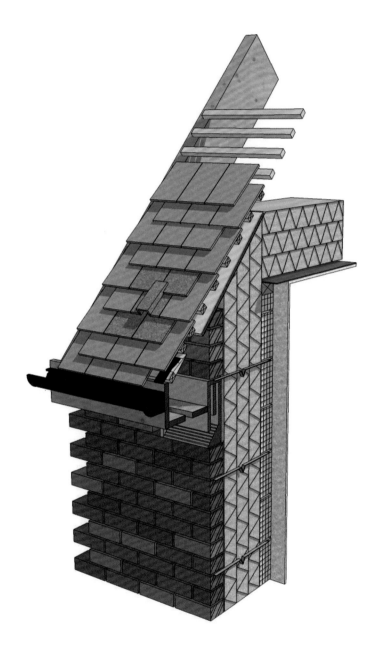

1 Hemp insulation, 3 x 100 (t) mm

2 'Pro clima DB+' ATL airtightness layer, recycled paper/cellulose, lapped and natural glued joints

3 Drylining ceiling board 12 (t) mm

4 Reclaimed, locally grown or FSC UKWAS or FSC temperate softwood wall plate, 100 (w) x 75 (h) x 100 mm with holding down straps

5 Cellular blockwork inner leaf, 100 (t) mm

6 Airtight parge coat: clay, lime or gypsum, 5–8 mm (t) or plaster

7 Full fill cavity wall insulation, 3 x 100 (t) mm rock mineral fibre

8 Wall ties option: 2 part long wall tie, austenitic stainless steel (304 equivalent), 400 mm

8a Wall ties option: 'MagmaTech TeploTie Type 4', extruded basalt and fibre long wall tie, 425 x 6.5 dia. mm

9 Reclaimed, locally made fired clay facing brick outer leaf, 102 (w) x 215 x 65 (h) x 215 (l) mm

10 Reclaimed, locally grown or FSC UKWAS or FSC temperate durable species softwood soffit

11 Reclaimed, locally grown or FSC UKWAS or FSC temperate durable species softwood fascia

12 Gutter and brackets, galvanized steel, half round

13 Rigid HDPE flashing into gutter

14 Reclaimed, locally grown or FSC UKWAS or FSC temperate softwood tilting fillet, 50 mm x varies

15 'Bat access tile-set', 18 mm gap x 165 mm long, gap in underlay below bat access tile-set

16 Reclaimed, locally grown or FSC UKWAS or FSC temperate softwood rafters (avoid trussed rafters), 200 x 50 (w) x 200 (d) mm

17 'Schwegler Bat Box 1FE 00748/3', wood-concrete, 300 (w) x 300 (h) x 100 (d) mm

18 'Pro clima Solitex Plus' roofing underlay

19 Air passage gap, 50 mm

20 FSC timber panel, 600 mm wide

21 Reclaimed, locally sourced clay handmade plain roof tiles 160 (w) x 265 (l) x 160 x 10 (t) mm

22 Reclaimed, locally grown or FSC UKWAS or FSC temperate softwood roof tile battens, 50 (h) x 25 (t) mm 25 x 50 m

23 Reclaimed, locally grown or FSC UKWAS or FSC temperate softwood ceiling joist, 50 (w) x 200 (d) x 50 mm

24 Gap in underlay below bat access tile set

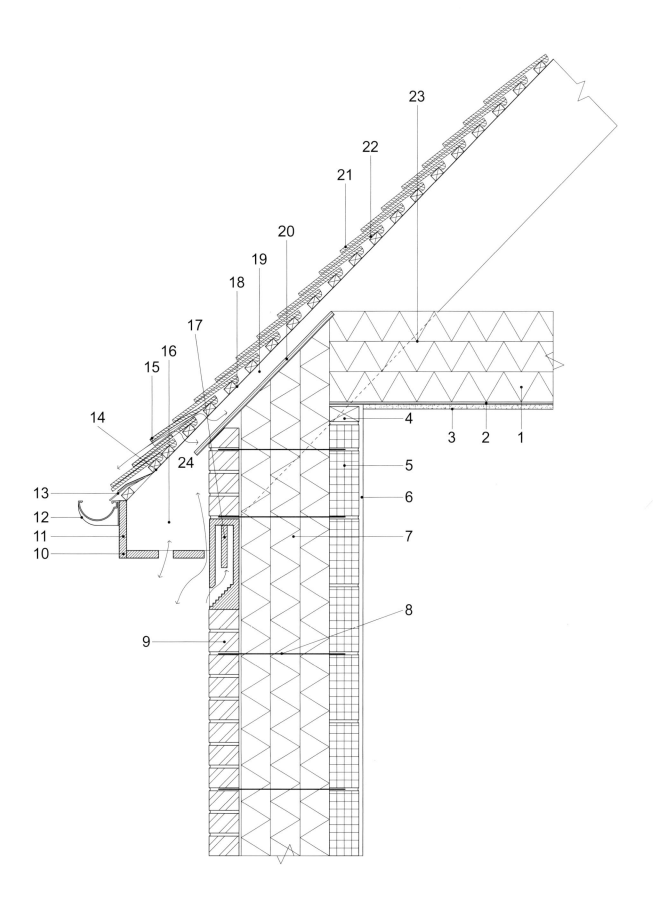

Solid in situ wall – timber framed and in situ sprayed hemp-lime infill walls providing spaces for bats and swifts

1 'Schwegler Bat Box 1FE 00748/3', wood-concrete, 300 (w) x 300 (h) x 100 (d) mm, supported by noggins

2 Reclaimed, locally grown or UKWAS or FSC temperate softwood tiling battens

3 'Pro clima Solitex Plus' WTL wind-tightness layer and VPU vapour permeable underlay

4 Reclaimed, locally grown or UKWAS or FSC temperate softwood counter battens, 50 x 25 mm with long purpose-made screws fixed to rafters

5 Reclaimed, locally sourced clay plain roof tiling

6 In situ sprayed hemp-lime mix sprayed against (8) until required thickness of wall achieved, surface flattened and keyed for (12)

6a In situ sprayed hemp-lime mix sprayed against (8) until required thickness of roof achieved, to roof between rafters, surface smoothed for (2), (3), (4), etc.

7 Reclaimed, locally grown or UKWAS or FSC temperate softwood rafter framing, 50 (w) x 300 (d) @ 600 mm centres

8 Permanent formwork, moisture tolerant, moisture permeable

9 Lime or clay plaster (internally) (not cement)

10 Reclaimed, locally grown or UKWAS or FSC temperate softwood stud framing, 38 (w) x 140 (d) @ 600 mm centres at internal face wall

10a Reclaimed, locally grown or UKWAS or FSC temperate softwood stud framing, 38 (w) x 140 (d) @ 600 mm centres at centre of wall

10b Reclaimed, locally grown or UKWAS or FSC temperate softwood stud framing, 38 (w) x 140 (d) @ 600 mm centres at external face wall

11 Reclaimed, locally grown or UKWAS or FSC temperate softwood noggins, 50 x 50 mm

12 Lime, hemp-lime or mineral based thin render system 2 layers, reinforcement layer between (airtight and permeable) (not cement)

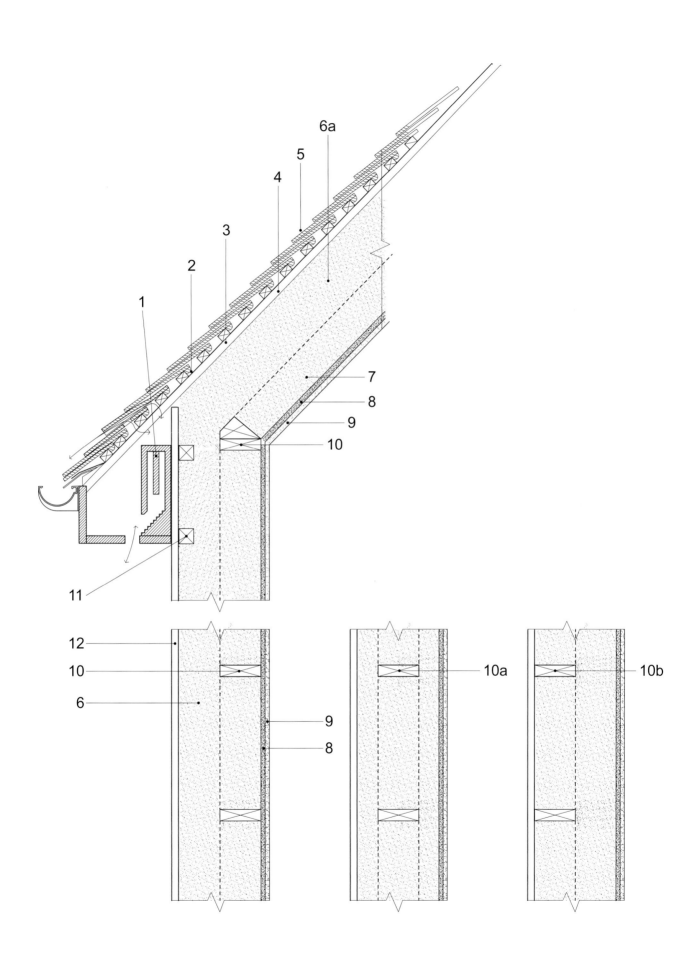

FULBOURN
(BESPOKE DESIGN OF SWIFT BOXES FOR NEW BUILD)

Built in 1966, the Windmill Estate in south Cambridgeshire required a large-scale regeneration programme. The estate boasted a sizeable swift population and the local community expressed concern for the birds during the site's re-development.

Following discussion between joint landlords South Cambridgeshire District Council (SCDC), Accent Nene Ltd (Registered Social Landlord), the contractor Kier Partnership Homes, Hunters Architects and Swift Conservation, a plan of mitigation was drawn up.

The phased re-development enabled trials of different types of boxes, starting in 2007 with external boxes. It was noted over two summers that birds seemed reluctant to take up the new accommodation. In 2009 it was decided to trial a bespoke internal box designed by Hunters.

The internal box design comprised the swift box made of ply wood (three sheets of 12 mm exterior quality) set within the timber frame wall void, above the level of the mineral wool insulation. The box was sized so that it could fit between the studs of a building's internal construction of stud work and insulation. This interior box is accessed from the exterior by a plastic drain pipe. A Schwegler cavity panel (00 618/9) was set in the wall to cover the tunnel entrance.

In total, 70 internal and 50 double chamber external boxes were provided. In addition, 10 starling boxes and 9 sparrow terraces were erected. By 2010, swifts and sparrows had begun to adopt the internal nests designed by Hunters.

The project has received widespread media coverage and won awards for its innovation. The former Windmill Estate has been re-branded as The Swifts, demonstrating how species conservation can be good for the local community and housing associations alike.

Full details can be found at: http://www.rspb.org.uk/thingstodo/surveys/swifts/casestudies/fulbournswifts.aspx

Internal box with vent holes still to be cut

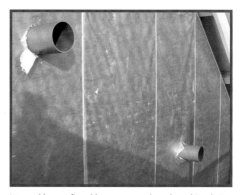

Internal boxes fitted between stud work and insulation

Internal boxes with cavity panels fitted

3.12.3 Extruded cellular fired clay block

Extruded cellular fired clay block is a method of construction that originated from mainland Europe. In the UK we have a lot of coal-fired power stations which produce a waste product called PFA (pulverised fuel ash) which is used as a cement replacement and a primary aggregate substitute. These have been used to make lower embodied energy ingredients for high embodied energy manufacturing, steam autoclaved, aerated, concrete blocks in the UK. (In mainland Europe there is a predominance of nuclear and hydro-electric power stations, so concrete blocks are not a normal part of their industry.) These cellular fired clay blocks are extruded, creating lots of air cells that trap air and create long path routes through the block for conducted heat, so offering a good U value. The blocks also have thermal mass and moisture mass, helping to moderate both the temperature and the humidity of the spaces adjacent to the blocks. Drawings Nos 12 and 13 (pages 82–85) show the incorporation of the Schwegler product Swift and Bat Box 1MF (see page 47).

3.12.4 Timber frame

Today the term 'timber frame' is used to describe timber stud framework, usually panelised (sometimes known as cassette panels), which may or may not be pre-insulated. It is usually available in kits or is produced to bespoke designs.

Drawing No. 14 (page 86) shows possibilities that allow a crevice-dwelling bat the opportunity to find a range of temperatures. This is not always easy to do in low and zero carbon builds, as the available areas are often only at one depth. The advantage of the design shown in the drawings is that, if conditions become too extreme in the outer-crevice space (extreme heat in mid-summer or very low temperatures during the winter), there is a deeper option that will provide a more stable and moderate temperature range.

3.12.5 Insulated structural panel system (ISPS)

The insulated structural panel system (ISPS) is a panelised modern method of construction developed in the UK and championed as part of a system promoted for its enhanced vapour transfer, otherwise known as breathing wall construction. Wet or dry sprayed, or blown in, cellulose fibre insulation is used as a part of the thermal insulation performance. Using a medium performance thermal insulating material means the panel is relatively thick.

Drawing No. 15 (page 90) details how the ready-made Schwegler product Bat Access Panel or roost 1FE (see page 39) could be incorporated into an ISP build. Of course it does not need to be a ready-made product and, as with all these drawings, it could incorporate a bespoke space.

3.12.6 Structural insulation panel system (SIPS)

The structural insulation panel system (SIPS) is a panelised modern method of construction developed in mainland Europe, and which has been adopted in the UK. Foamed insulation is used as a part of the structural performance, thus enabling a reduced thickness of the panel for strength. The insulation is foamed into the panel, but there may be alternative methods of making them using laminated construction.

For structural insulation panel systems there is limited space to work with, but even here it is possible to include ready-made (as illustrated by the Schwegler product Bat Access Panel or Roost 1FE (see page 39) and Drawing No. 16, page 92) or bespoke roost spaces.

Drawing No.

12

Cellular block solid wall
– extruded cellular block walling providing spaces for bats and swifts

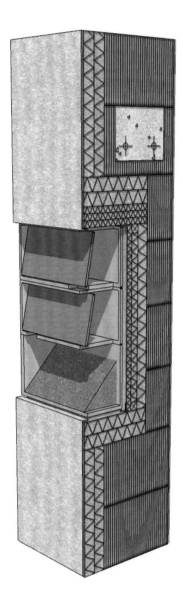

1   Option: Extruded cellular fired clay block wall, 365 (w) x 250 (h) x 248 (l) mm

1a   Option: Extruded cellular lime pumice blocks

2   'Eco-concrete': Less OP cement and more GGBS ground granulated burst furnace slag cement, less virgin aggregate and more recycled, secondary or manufactured aggregate

3   Reinforcement bars

4   Reclaimed, locally grown on UKWAS or FSC temperate softwood framing, 33 (w) x 33 (d) fixed back to blockwork with purpose-made fasterners

5   Extruded cellular fired clay block leaf, 140 (w) x 250 (h) x 300 (d) mm

6   Cement/clay/adhesive bed joint 1 mm (dry perpends)

7   Airtight parge coat: clay, lime or gypsum, 5–8 (t) mm or plaster

8   Dense wood fibre board, thermal and acoustic insulation board, T&G jointed for airtightness, (no substitution), 100 mm consisting of 4 x 25, 3 x 33 or 2 x 50 (t) mm

8a   75 mm consisting of 3 x 25 (t) mm to suit

8b   25 + 33 + 50 mm thick layers to suit

9   Lime, hemp-lime or mineral based thin render system 2 layers, reinforcement layer between (airtight and permeable) (not cement)

10   'Pro clima Tescon No. 1 & Tescon Primer RP' airtight joint taping (option)

11   'Schwegler Bat Ramp', wood-concrete, 430 (w) x 250 (h) x 430 (w) x 225 (d) mm fixed back to softwood framing

12   'Schwegler Bird/Bat Box', wood-concrete, 730 (w) x 460 (h) x 730 (w) x 225 (d) mm. Locate towards eaves. Interlocking and assembled, 430 (w) x 700 (h) x 430 (w) x 225 (d) mm (includes (11) above) fixed back to softwood framing

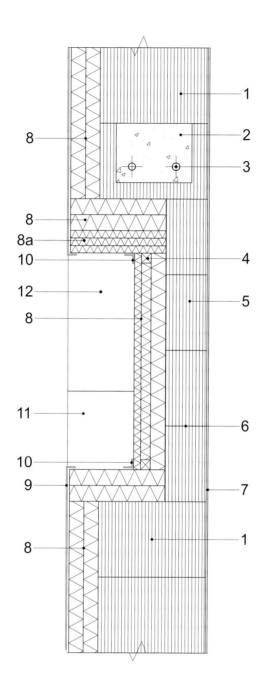

Drawing No.
13

Cellular block solid wall
– extruded cellular block walling providing spaces for bats and swifts

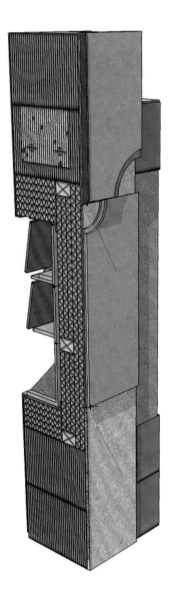

1   Option: Clay skim/finish, 2 mm

2   'Clayboard' reed reinforced clay drylining board, 40 mm

3   Tooth combed adhesive bonded drylining

4   Airtight parge coat: 5–8 mm clay, lime or gypsum plaster

5   Option: Gypsum plaster skim, 2 mm

6   Option: Plasterboard dry lining, 12.5 mm

6a   Option: Dense gypsum wood fibre-reinforced board lining, 10 mm

7   Airtight clay plaster, 20 mm

8   Bed joint: clay/cement/adhesive, 1 mm

8a   Interlocking T&G dry perpend joint, 1 mm (air leaky)

9   Option: Extruded cellular fired clay blocks walling 265 (w) x 250 (h) x 248 (l) mm

9a   Option: Extruded cellular lime pumice blocks

10   Lime, hemp-lime or mineral based thin render system 2 layers, reinforcement layer between (airtight and permeable) (not cement render)

11   Dense wood fibre board, 25 mm thermal and acoustic insulation (no substitution permitted)

11a   Same as (11) but a different assembled thickness to (11)

11b   Reclaimed, locally grown or FSC UKWAS or FSC temperate softwood 50 x 50 and 50 x 75 mm battens and cross counter battens 50 x 50 and 50 x 75 mm (to minimise thermal bridge through insulations) fixed back to extruded blocks with purpose-made fasteners

12   'Pro clima Tescon No. 1 and Tescon Primer RP' airtight joint taping (option)

13   'Schwegler Bat Ramp', wood-concrete, 430 (w) x 250 (h) x 225 (d) mm fixed back to softwood framing

14   'Schwegler Swift/Bat Box', wood-concrete, 430 (w) x 460 (h) x 225 (d) mm fixed back to softwood framing

13/14   Interlocking assembled: 430 (w) x 700 (h) x 430 (w) x 225 (d) mm fixed back to softwood framing

15   Option: Trough lintel: cellular fired clay, 50 mm wall

15a   Option: Trough lintel: cellular lime pumice, 50 mm wall

16   Reinforcement bars

17   'Eco-concrete': Less OP cement and more GGBS ground granulated burst furnace slag cement, less virgin aggregate and more recycled, secondary or manufactured aggregate

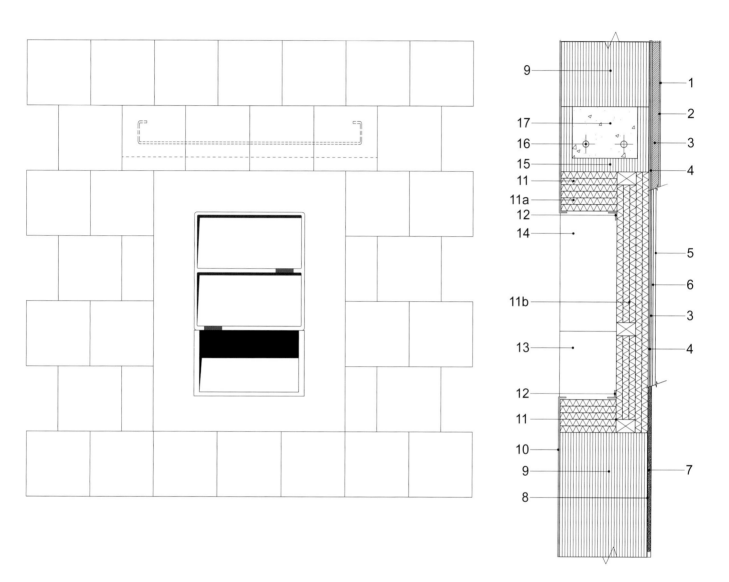

Timber frame
– timber stud framed walls (external and internal insulation) providing spaces for bats

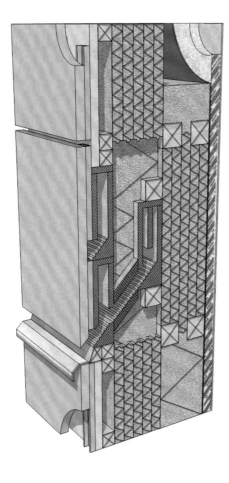

1   Dense wood fibre board, thermal and acoustic insulation board, T&G jointed for airtightness; external to stud, 200 mm consisting of 5 No. x 40 mm. Avoids thermal bridges through insulation

1a Compressible cellulose fibre thermal insulation (easy to cut to shape and to fit odd shaped cavity ensuring no gaps)

2   Noggins, durable species softwood to avoid preservative treatment, size and shape to suit

2a Noggins, durable species softwood to avoid preservative treatment, 75 x 75 mm

3   'Schwegler Bat Box/entrance 1FE 00747/6', wood-concrete, 300 (w) x 300 (h) x 80 (d) mm cut opening in back to permit access to tunnel (4)

3a 'Schwegler Bat Box 1FE 00748/3', wood-concrete, 300 (w) x 300 (h) x 100 (d) mm

4   Cement-wood particle board fabricated tunnel between roosts, roughened grooved surface for climbing and hanging

5   'Pro clima DB+' ATL airtightness layer, recycled paper/cellulose, lapped and natural glued joints

6   'Clayboard' reed reinforced clay drylining board, 40 mm

7   Clay skim finish, 2 mm

8   Cladding rails/battens, metal, UKWAS or FSC hardwood or durable species softwood to avoid preservative treatment

9   Pressed metal drip or durable FSC hardwood sloping top and drip profile bottom, use stainless steel if acidic timber species cladding or framing

10 Rainscreen cladding, open joints ventilated cavity, pressure equalised, many material choices, many systems on market

11 Cement-wood particle board, roughened/grooved surface for climbing and hanging

12 Cavity fire barrier: galvanized mild steel angle; softwood UKWAS or FSC: 50 mm x width to suit cavity or plastic sheathed rock mineral fibre

13 Battens, durable species UKWAS or FSC softwood to avoid preservative treatment, 50 x 50 mm @ 600 mm centres

14 'Pro clima Solitex WA' WTL wind-tightness layer, lapped and sealed joints

15 Reclaimed, locally grown UKWAS or FSC temperate softwood stud framing, 38 (w) x 140 (d) mm @ 600 mm centres

Plan view

1
14
13
12
3
11
4
11
10
3
2
9
8
1

1a
2
1a
3a
4
1
2
5
6
7
1a

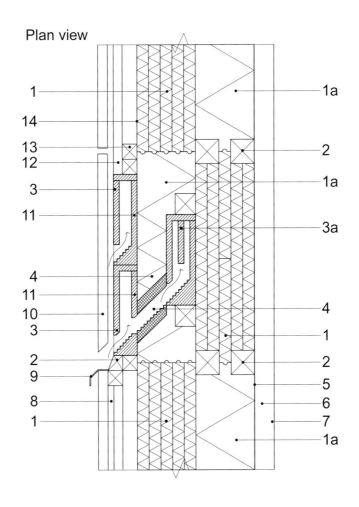

Section

1
14
13
1a
2
10
3
11
4
2
13
14

1a
15
1
2a
5
6
3a
2
15
1a

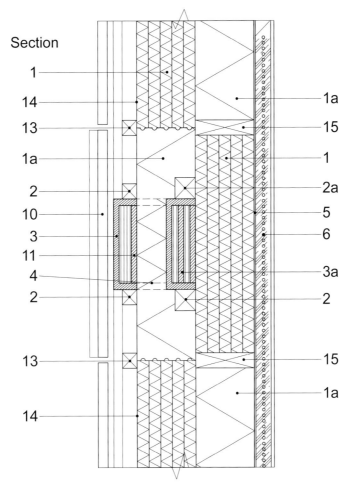

Drawing No.
14
continued

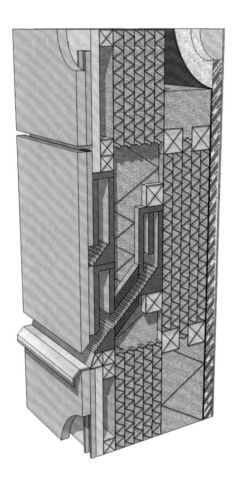

1   Rainscreen cladding, open joints ventilated cavity, pressure equalised, many material choices, many systems on market

2   Noggins, durable species softwood to avoid preservative treatment, size and shape to suit

3   Schwegler Bat Box/entrance 1FE 00747/6', wood-concrete, 300 (w) x 300 (h) x 80 (d) mm

3a Schwegler Bat Box 1FE 00748/3', wood-concrete, 300 (w) x 300 (h) x 100 (d) mm

9   Pressed metal drip or durable FSC hardwood sloping top and drip profile bottom

Elevation

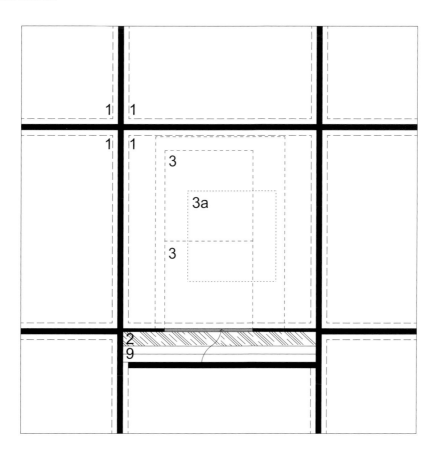

Drawing No.

15

Insulated Structural Panel Systems (ISPS)
– composite timber I-stud framed walls providing spaces for bats

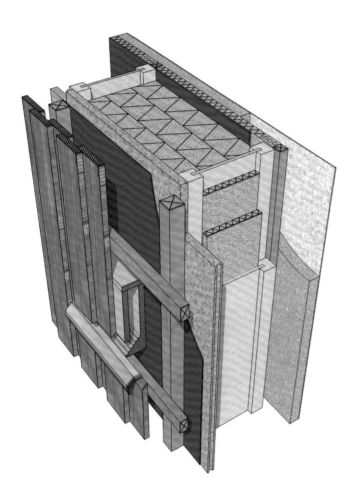

1   Reclaimed, locally grown UKWAS or FSC temperate softwood service zone battens, 30 x 30 mm services and insulation to fill voids

2   Clayboard reed reinforced clay drylining board, 40 mm

3   Clay finish, 2 mm

4   'Pro clima DB+' ATL airtightness layer, recycled paper/cellulose, lapped and natural glued joints

5   'Homatherm flexCL 400', 3 x 100 mm, dense cellulose fibre, recycled magazines, Thermal/acoustic insulation

5a Options: Alternatives: dry or damp spray or blown in insulation, can be pre or post installed

6   Reclaimed, locally grown UKWAS or FSC temperate durable hardwood weatherboarding, board on board

7   Pressed metal drip or durable FSC hardwood sloping top and drip profile bottom, use stainless steel if acidic timber species cladding or framing

8   Cement-wood particleboard, 25 mm roughened/grooved for climbing and hanging

9   'Schwegler Bat Box 1FE 00747/6', wood-concrete, 300 x 300 x 80 mm locate towards eaves

10 Breathing Sheathing Board, T&G jointed, with or without racking strength dense wood fibreboard, 25 mm

11 'Pro clima Solitex WA' WTL wind-tightness layer, lapped and sealed joints

12 Reclaimed, locally grown UKWAS or FSC temperate durable hardwood battens for weatherboarding, 25 x 50 mm

13 Services in services zone

14 'Masonite I-stud' @ 600 mm, Excel Industries in UK, 50 (w) x 300 (d) mm length to suit, many other sizes available

15 Dense wood fibreboard insulation within joint between ISPs, to suit profile or rebate

16 Reclaimed, locally grown UKWAS or FSC temperate softwood counter battens, 50 x 50 mm @ 600 centres

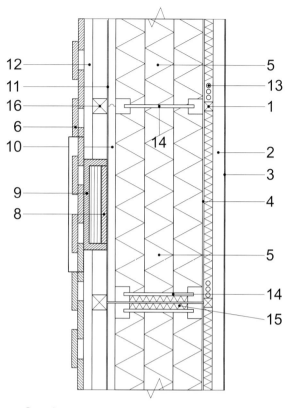

12 — 5
11 — 13
16 — 1
6 —
10 —
14
9 — 2
8 — 3
4
5
14
15

Elevation

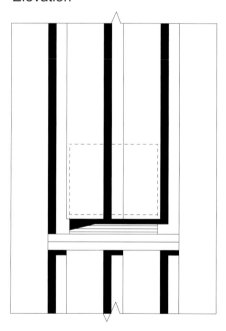

Section

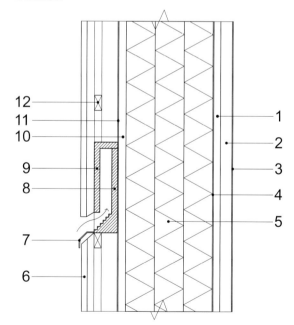

12 — 1
11 —
10 — 2
9 — 3
8 — 4
5
7 —
6 —

16
Structural Insulation Panel System (SIPS)
wall panels providing spaces for bats

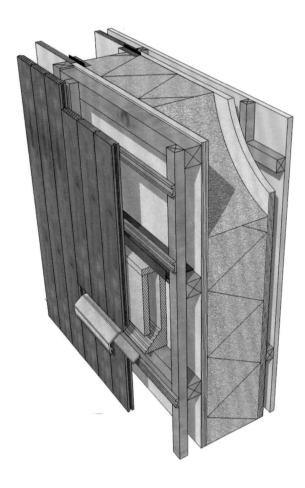

1   Drylining gypsum plasterboard, 12.5 mm and 2 mm skim or flush taped and filled joints

2   Structural insulated panel

2a   Non-renewable, foamed plastics insulation

2b   Or laminated assembly with adhesive

2c   FSC OSB or other timber panel, both sides

3   Pressed metal drip or durable FSC hardwood sloping top and drip profile bottom, use stainless steel if acidic timber species cladding or framing

4   'Schwegler Bat Box 1FE 00747/6', wood-concrete, 300 x 300 x 80 mm locate towards eaves

5   Cement-wood particle board, 12 mm roughened surface for climbing/hanging

6   Reclaimed, locally grown or FSC temperate softwood noggins, 50 x 50 mm

7   Insect resistant mesh/perforated metal

8   Durable species hardwood or softwood UKWAS or FSC timber (avoiding preservatives) vertical weatherboarding

9   Durable species hardwood or softwood UKWAS or FSC timber (avoiding preservatives) weatherboarding battens

10   'Pro clima Rapidcell' airtight jointing tape to joints

11   Reclaimed, locally grown or FSC temperate softwood pressure batten (internal), 50 x 50 mm to secure airtight seal (10 above)

12   Note, do not try to make airtight with sealant gun afterwards: little hope, unless bottomless funds and open-ended programme

13   Reclaimed, locally grown or FSC temperate softwood durable species, pressure batten, 50 x 50 mm to secure wind-tight seal (14 below)

14   'Pro clima Tescon No.1' wind-tightness tape to joints

15   SIPS panel abutment interlocking joint, with continuous runs of adhesive/sealant to achieve airtightness, or ATL & WTL strips and pressure battens inside and out. See (10), (11), (13), (14)

Section

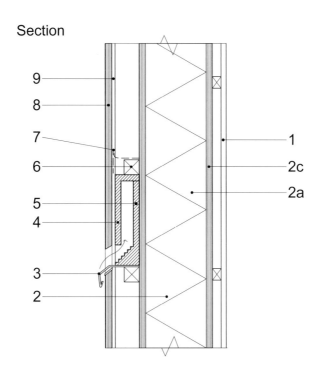

9

8

7

6

5

4

3

2

1

2c

2a

Plan view

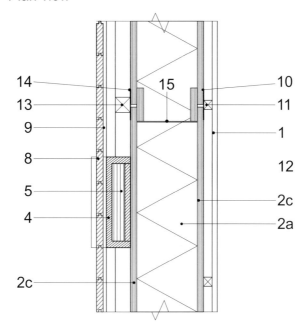

14

13

9

8

5

4

2c

15

10

11

1

12

2c

2a

Drawing No.

17

Cross-laminated timber panel (CLTP) system – accommodation over carport or passageway providing spaces for bats

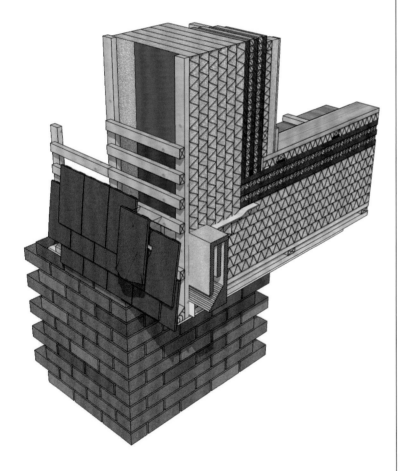

1 CLTP Cross-Laminated Timber Panel wall, consisting of 25 mm UKWAS or FSC plywood core, one or more layers each side of 25 mm layers of 25 x 25 mm UKWAS or FSC temperate plantation thinnings softwood cross laminated battens to required thickness for fire and acoustic performance

2 'Pro clima Intello Plus' ATL lapped bonded

3 Reclaimed, locally grown or UKWAS or FSC temperate softwood service batten, 30 x 30 mm services and insulation

4 Option: 'Clayboard' reed reinforced clay drylining board, 40 mm

4a Option: Plasterboard dry lining, 12.5 mm

5 Clay skim/finish, 2 mm

6 Reclaimed, locally grown or UKWAS or FSC temperate softwood or FSC ZF MDF Zero Formaldehyde Medium Density Fibreboard skirting, 20 x 100 mm

7 GMS galvanized mild steel angle cleats and screws

8 Reclaimed, locally grown or UKWAS or FSC temperate durable hardwood or softwood T&G board flooring

9 Acoustic isolation battens with compliant layer at bottom, 50 (w) mm

10 Acoustic/thermal insulation to fill floor batten zone

11 'Pro clima Intello Plus' ATL airtightness layer lapped bonded

12 CLTP Cross-Laminated Timber Panel floor, consisting of 25 mm UKWAS or FSC plywood core, two or more layers each side, of 25 mm layers of 25 x 25 mm UKWAS or FSC temperate plantation thinings softwood cross battens to required thickness for structural, fire and acoustic performance

13 Reclaimed, locally grown or UKWAS or FSC temporary durable hardwood weather-boarded soffit, 25 mm. No finish

14 Reclaimed, locally grown or UKWAS or FSC temperate softwood battens, 50 x 25 mm for weather boarding

15 Reclaimed, locally grown or UKWAS or FSC temperate softwood counter battens, 50 x 25 mm

16 'Pro clima Solitex Plus' WTL wind-tightness layer and VPU vapour permeable underlay

17 Dense wood fibre board, thermal and acoustic insulation, 6 x 50 mm

18 GMS galvanized mild steel fixing strap screwed to background and box

19 Insect-resistant mesh to isolate air spaces (locate higher to offer more space for bats within wall and soffit cladding zones)

21 Reclaimed, locally grown or UKWAS or FSC temperate softwood tilting fillet for bottom of tiling to maintain tile slope angle and bat access

22 'Bat access tile set', 18 mm gap x 165 mm long, gap in underlay below bat access tile set

23 'Schwegler Bat Box 1FE 00748/3', wood-concrete, 300 x 300 x 100 mm

24 'Compriband' pre-compressed impregnated foam, self-adhesive in 25 mm x 25 mm channel in (1)

25 Tile hanging or weather boarding (see also 20 above)

26 Reclaimed, locally grown or FSC temperate softwood battens, 50 x 25 mm

27 Reclaimed, locally grown or FSC temperate softwood counter battens, 50 x 50 mm

28 'Pro clima Solitex Plus' WTL wind-tightness layer and VPU vapour permeable underlay

29 Dense wood fibre board, thermal and acoustic insulation, 6 x 50 mm

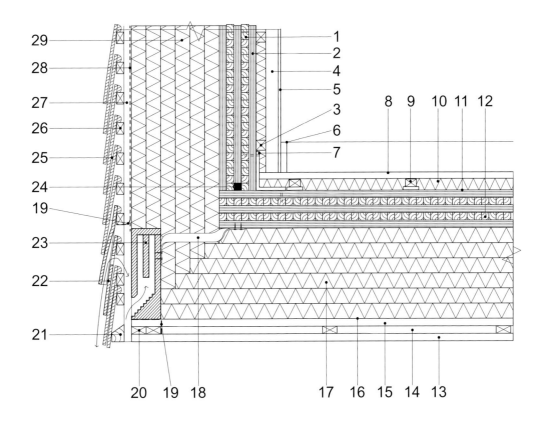

Insulating concrete formwork (ICF) is a small-scale modular formwork system that uses thermal insulation in place of plywood, and which also has a system to hold the two forms together and apart at the required distance, using a variety of different methods as diverse as reinforcement cages or plastic ties. The space in between is filled with reinforcing rods and in situ concrete to make insulated structural loadbearing walls. Some systems are restricted to straight walls and right angles; others have curves. This method of wall construction is often adopted by self-builders because it is lightweight, easy to handle, simple and fast.

Although designs for crevice-dwelling bats were developed, it was not felt that there was sufficient confidence in finding ways in which to: (a) maintain the necessary level of thermal insulation and decrement delay in a standard way; and (b) acoustically isolate the bats from the interior of the building. So, for these reasons, it has been decided not to include the drawings in this book at this time. It is recognised that construction using ICF will have a place in future low and zero energy buildings, and therefore further development of the appropriate biodiversity provision that meets all necessary considerations will be continued as a collaborative work in progress.

3.12.8 Cross-laminated timber panels (CLTP)

Cross-laminated panels is a method of construction originating from mainland Europe that makes use of tree plantation thinnings of small section. It usually consists of same-sized square battens bonded to create a sheet one batten thick. To this are added two or more layers of the same, but each layer of battens is arranged at right angles to the previous layer, and all are adhered to each other. This makes a very strong, dimensionally stable, rigid panel from which structural panels are cut to size and shape. They are used for floors, walls, roofs and partitions, and even for stairs. Holes for doors and windows are cut out at the factory and cable ways can be routed in. The panels are assembled in relation to each other and are secured to each other with galvanized steel angles and nuts and bolts. It is a rapid method of construction. From this description, it is not surprising that cross-laminated panels have few limitations. However, all provision for wildlife should occur outside of the panels' thicknesses within the cladding zones.
See Drawing No. 17 (page 94).

3.13 Invertebrates

Bug boxes and bee hotels are available in a wide range of designs, either for purchase or to be handmade. Most are placed externally to the building, either in the garden or attached to an outside wall. Since these do not impact on low-carbon design, they are not featured in this book. However, there is one product that provides an integrated solution, which is detailed on page 97. For more information on bug hotels, visit www.buglife.org.uk/getinvolved/gardening.

INTEGRATED BUG BOX

Habibat

TYPE OF PRODUCT:

Integrated Bug Box

WEBSITE:

www.ecosurv.co.uk

WHERE USED:

In the outer skin of cavity wall buildings

PRODUCT INFORMATION:

Perforated terracotta brick with a lightweight concrete block back plate
Size: 215 mm (w) x 140 mm (h) x 85 mm (d)

PRODUCT USE:

Rounded slots of different sizes provide nesting/sheltering crevices for invertebrates, including solitary bees

FAMILIAR MATERIAL	Yes
EASY TO INSTALL	Yes
DURABLE	Yes
LOW OR NO MAINTENANCE	Yes
FROST RESISTANT	No
THERMAL MASS	Yes
FITS UK CONSTRUCTION SIZES	Yes
UNFAMILIAR MATERIAL; UNSURE HOW TO PROTECT	N/A
THERMAL BRIDGES	In outer leaf outside of cavity insulation so limited effect
EXPOSED WOOD PARTICLES ON CUT OR DAMAGED EDGES MAY ABSORB MOISTURE	N/A
MUST BE MAINTAINED WITH 'SPECIAL' UNFAMILIAR PAINT	N/A
EMBODIED ENERGY	Medium
EMBODIED CARBON	Medium
DEGREE OF FIT TO UK CONSTRUCTION SIZES	Fits 2 dimensions and short on 3rd
PRODUCT UPTAKE	Unknown

OTHER

→ This product is supplied unfilled. Materials such as sawdust and circular tubes can be slotted in to provide nesting for various solitary bees and wasps if in sunny locations

→ The product can be supplied in different sizes and formats to suit design needs

3.14 Green roofs and living walls

Green or living roofs and walls have been adopted more widely in Germany and Switzerland, although major cities in the UK and elsewhere in Europe, North America and Asia are now starting to follow suit. These features can form important elements of sustainable building by reducing the risk of flooding, reducing the extremes of temperature fluctuation in a building and providing enhancement for biodiversity. Much has already been written about the benefits of these features, and so this section will only provide an overview, while directing the reader to much more extensive publications on the subject.

3.14.1 Green (living) roofs

Green roofs

The area of roofs in the urban environment is considerable and it tends to be a sterile environment, largely uninviting for biodiversity and not pleasant to look at from upstairs windows. Green roofs can support a whole range of invertebrates, depending on the type of roof grown. There will be generalist invertebrates, such as spiders, beetles and bees, but there is also a possibility of supporting more uncommon species, including moth and butterfly species not normally found in the conditions present in gardens. Information on the range of invertebrates found on green roofs and techniques for encouraging invertebrates on green roofs can be found at the Buglife website.

The array of insects and the seeds produced by the flowering plants all provide good feeding opportunities to a range of birds, from common garden birds, such as greenfinch, blackbird and wren, to goldfinch, linnet and even the rare black redstart in certain parts of the country. This proliferation of insects is also likely to be a feature that will be of benefit to foraging bats, as all the UK bats are insectivorous. A bird particularly associated with living roofs is the black redstart. This has a limited distribution in the UK, predominantly being found in London, Birmingham and the Black Country. In these urban areas it can be very beneficial for the populations of black redstart if green roofs, which meet the needs of this species, are incorporated. Details of these needs can be found on the specialist website www.blackredstarts.org.uk and www.buglife.org.uk.

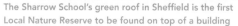
The Sharrow School's green roof in Sheffield is the first
Local Nature Reserve to be found on top of a building

In addition to these benefits for biodiversity, green roofs have other positive benefits such as moderating the temperature of the rooms beneath, helping to keep them cool in warm weather and insulating them against cold. In heavy or prolonged rainfall, living roofs reduce the likelihood of floods by acting as a sponge that absorbs water before allowing it to evaporate back into the atmosphere. Green roofs also protect the roof material from the effects of ultra-violet light and frost that shortens the life of the waterproofing.

Types of green roof

Mosses and lichens naturally colonise roofs and establish themselves in the harshest of environments without substrate or support. Roofs that have moss and lichen will host a whole range of associated invertebrates and microscopic creatures, which are, in turn, a valuable food source for birds. Besides these naturally occurring colonists, it is possible to create a living roof on a new or existing building.

A range of green roofs are available, which fall under three broad categories. Extensive green roofs tend to be shallow, self-supporting systems that are vegetated with drought tolerant plants typical of harsh environments, such as cliffs and mountains – they require little maintenance and are not irrigated. Intensive green roofs, or roof gardens, due to the deeper growing substrate, allow a greater range of plants to be grown, which in turn can support a wide range of species. However, they do need to be planted appropriately and require irrigation and regular maintenance. Very deep roofs have a depth of substrate sufficient to allow shrubs and even trees to be grown, but are less often likely to be a viable option.

A green roof is made up of a number of layers, generally comprising a waterproof layer, a root barrier, a drainage/reservoir layer, a water reservoir board, a filter blanket, a growing medium or substrate layer and the vegetation.

Where can they be used?

Provided the structure is capable of supporting the additional weight associated with a green roof (a structural engineer must confirm this), any roof, including a sloped roof, has the potential to be greened.

3.14.2   Living (green) walls

Benefits of living walls

Whereas roofs are often not a visible feature from the ground level, we are more aware of walls in our towns and cities. Living walls utilise plants in order to derive benefits, not only in visual terms, but also in regard to biodiversity, thermal efficiency and the reduction of pollutants. By providing shading from the sun, living walls can significantly reduce the external temperature of a building. Living walls can also provide a certain amount of insulation. Living walls also help reduce the urban heat island effect by intercepting heat which would otherwise be largely absorbed and radiated by the building surfaces back into the surroundings. They help to shield the surface from ultra-violet light, which could be an important consideration for some modern cladding materials.

Plants on buildings can potentially provide a food source for invertebrates on which, in turn, other invertebrates, bats and birds may feed. They also provide a breeding and nesting habitat for invertebrates and birds, and are ideal for including ready-made nest boxes.

Green roofs are particularly beneficial to the black redstart

Living walls can include provision for birds and bats. It is important that the box entrances are kept clear of vegetation

This living wall on Edgware Road, London, is being studied for the air purification benefits of the plants incorporated in the design

Living wall on residential property in London

Types of living wall

As with living roofs, there is nothing new in the concept of using plants to green buildings, but in recent years a variety of modern designs and techniques have been developed. Living walls can be separated into a number of categories that include:

- supported by a wall – self-supporting climbers
- supported by a structure on a wall – climbers on a trellis or wires
- purpose-made modules or blankets which are irrigated and which support a wide range of plants

Considerations in the use of living walls

The use of planted climbers, either self-supporting or in some way trained against a wall or similar structure, is not a new idea and, as long as the choice of plant is wise for the position and soil type, then it is a tried and tested and relatively inexpensive way of greening a wall. Irrigated modular or blanket walls can be spectacular but they are much more expensive and require frequent maintenance if they are to continue to look their best. Include native species planted in natural associations and plants that attract pollinators in order to benefit biodiversity.

Beneficial microclimates can be created against façades via living walls. Living walls reduce the maximum temperatures of a building by shading walls from the sun. They also provide protection from rain and reduce frost vulnerability, and evergreen climbers provide winter insulation, not only by maintaining a pillow of air between the plant and the wall, but by reducing wind chill on the wall surface.

Numerous wall-mounted growing trough systems of green walls are available on the market. They often need pumped irrigation which adds to running costs. Indigenous, nectar rich, berry bearing and drought tolerant species supporting indigenous species and pollinators should be encouraged. For true sustainability irrigation should be via rain or grey water systems.

A great deal more information can be found on the following websites:

- www.livingroofs.org
- www.london.gov.uk (search for 'living roofs' and 'walls pdf')
- http://naturalengland.etraderstores.com (search for living roofs)
- www.greenroofconsultancy.com
- http://www.greenroofcode.co.uk/
- Design Guidance for Biodiverse Green Roofs http://www.thegreenroofcentre. co.uk/Library/Default/Documents/GRC%20Biodiverse%20Design%20 small_634147160617860000.pdf
- Landscape and Urban Design for Bats and Biodiversity – Bat Conservation Trust

3.15 How much provision is enough?

There is never going to be a 'one-size-fits-all' answer to this question. Every building should be reviewed for its potential for built-in roosting/nesting opportunities. However, some locations in the development might be more suitable than others and provision could be more concentrated on appropriate structures. It is a case of taking the advice of an experienced ecologist who has carried out a survey of the site in question and its surroundings, and who can advise on the species for which it is appropriate to make provision and on how, where and how many potential roosts/nesting sites should be incorporated.

The latest guidance from the Town and Country Planning Association and The Wildlife Trusts, *Planning for a Healthy Environment: Good Practice for Green Infrastructure and Biodiversity* (2012), uses guidelines from Exeter City Council's Supplementary Planning Document Residential Design (available at: www.exeter. gov.uk/index.aspx?articleid=127302010). It recommends that nesting and roosting boxes be included as part of the fabric of the building for building-reliant birds (e.g. swift, swallow and house martin) and bats and birds associated with urban areas (e.g. house sparrow and starling). As a guideline, the number of built-in provisions of nest or roost sites per development should be approximately the same as the number of residential units. However, this provision would be located in the parts of the site suitable for the species in question and can be in residential or non-residential buildings.

Opportunities for species that need larger spaces (particularly in lofts), such as barn owls or bats requiring flight space, should be included where appropriate for the species and for the building location and type. Advice from a qualified ecologist will be required. For an example of guidelines that recommend specific numbers for roosting and nesting provision based on the type of development, consult Hackney Council's Advice Note for Biodiversity and the Built Environment, particularly the table in section 11 (available at: www.hackney.gov.uk/Assets/ Documents/1-3208993-Hackney_Advice_Note_-_Biodiversity_and_the_Built_ Environment.pdf).

CHAPTER FOUR

Designing for biodiversity in existing buildings

This chapter introduces the need and urgency for the existing building stock to be upgraded with extensive energy efficiency refurbishments, the programmes that government is using to drive this change and how this could reduce the potential roost and nest spaces for some species. It introduces some of the complications of working with both 'historic fabric' and more recent building methods and describes some of the potential solutions.

Birds and bats are protected under various pieces of UK and European legislation (see Chapter 2). If protected species are known (or suspected) to use a building (even occasionally) where refurbishment is to take place then a competent ecologist should be employed for advice and, in some cases, a European Protected Species (EPS) Mitigation Licence may be required. If protected species are discovered during building works, then work must stop immediately until the relevant Statutory Nature Conservation Organisation (SNCO) or the National Bat Helpline has been contacted and advice given. Local authorities are obligated to protect and enhance wildlife during the normal course of their duties.

> ENHANCEMENT OR MITIGATION?
> Although this chapter deals with existing buildings it is still focused on enhancement – it is not intended for situations where mitigation is required because a protected species is already making use of the space or enhancement.

4.1 Refurbishment – what are the issues?

Existing buildings contain many nooks, crannies and access points for birds, bats and other biodiversity.

A joint 'citizen science' survey by RSPB and BBC Radio 4's *Today* programme investigated the use of houses for nesting by swifts, house martins and house sparrows, and information was received across a range of house types and gradients from rural to urban (Wotton *et al.*, 2002). Pre-1919 houses were found most important for nesting birds, with house sparrows and common swifts recorded more frequently than in modern houses. Swifts and starlings were least likely to nest following recent roof repairs. The roof space or beneath the eaves were the most commonly reported nest-site locations. Modern houses, particularly in urban areas, are used infrequently by nesting birds.

> Visit the Roost website (http://roost. bats.org.uk) to view or upload case studies of bat roost mitigation.

Refurbishing buildings, especially under the new Building Regulations, means filling in or removing access points used by birds and bats, to make the building more airtight and thus energy efficient. Deliberate provision of roosting and nesting spaces that do not compromise airtightness of built structures is therefore essential for these building-reliant species.

The UK has the oldest housing stock in the developed world (see the housing stock statistics box). This poses a significant challenge for the reduction of carbon emissions.

In order to meet carbon dioxide/carbon (production and release to atmosphere) reduction targets driven by EU Directives, the UK has put some milestones into place through legislation (see Table 4.1).

Table 4.1: Carbon reduction targets based on 1990 baseline

Legislation	Reduction	Start point or deadline
	0%	1990
Climate Change Act 2008	34%	2020
Energy Act 2011	50%	2025
Energy Act 2011	60%	2030
Climate Change Act 2008	80%	2050

Based on these targets, seven million 'retrofits' or extreme energy refurbishments are needed by 2020, each with an 80% improvement in energy efficiency. How does this compare with current refurbishment statistics? Currently the UK spends £23 billion per annum on maintenance, but very little of this is on energy efficiency. In 2011, 20,000 houses were upgraded, compared with 700,000 properties that need to be upgraded each year to meet these carbon reduction targets. This is equivalent to 3,000 properties per day. The potential spend is in the order of tens of billions of pounds.

Table 4.2 lists government programmes aimed at improving the housing stock and reducing carbon emissions.

UK HOUSING STOCK STATISTICS
- One in five UK homes were built before 1918
- 20% of properties are over 100 years old and have solid walls
- 50% of homes are over 50 years old
- Six million homes are classified as 'non-decent'
- More than 800,000 properties are vacant and could be refurbished
- Existing housing stock generates 150 million tonnes of CO_2 per annum
- 27% of the UK's carbon emissions is generated by housing
- The average Standard Assessment Procedure (SAP) rating for UK housing (2010) is 52: the target is 80 (scale 0 to 100)
- 14 million UK homes could benefit from insulation
- 6.6 million properties are solid walled and 'hard to treat'
- 9.2 million properties have other elements that are 'hard to treat'

Table 4.2: Programmes relating to refurbishment and renewable energy

Government schemes	When	Who
Decent Homes Programme	Previous decade until 2010 and still running	Responsible Social Landlords' tenants 1 million 'non-decent homes' made decent, but not made sustainable
Carbon Emissions Reductions Target (CERT)	Until end of 2012	Householders
Community Energy Saving Programme (CESP)	Until end of 2012	Communities working together
Renewable Obligation Certificates (ROCs)	April 2002 (NI 2005)	Energy producers
Carbon Reduction Commitment (CRC), renamed Energy Efficiency Scheme	2008 onwards	Top 10% of UK consumers: government departments, government-funded buildings, biggest energy consumers
Feed-in Tariff (FIT) (renewable electricity)	April 2010 onwards	Richer individuals or companies investing now for return on investment and/or Renewable Obligation Certificates
Renewable Heat Incentive (RHI) (renewable heat)	2013 (to be announced)	Richer individuals or companies investing for return on investment and/or Renewable Obligation Certificates
Green Deal (GD)	April 2013 onwards	Everybody that pays bills can reduce their carbon emissions by insulating and adding renewable energy installations via a Green Deal Provider
Energy Company Obligation (ECO)	Oct 2012 onwards	Households who need financial support (more than 5 million households were in fuel poverty). August 2013: Government changed the definition of fuel poverty, reducing the number of households affected by 2 million Energy companies invest to reduce demand

4.1.1 Fabric first

Over the past decade, grants have been available for renewable energy (electricity and/or heat), electricity and heat installations that did not require the owner of the building to insulate the building, the hot water or heating pipes. More recently this has changed, so that insulation of the building is required by the grant in addition to the renewable energy installation. Building fabric needs to be insulated to the optimum level, thermal bridges need to be broken and air leakages needs to be brought under control before other energy installations are added. This has the potential to reduce the size and cost of the required heating, cooling or ventilation equipment, or their replacement renewable energy installations, and the long-term running costs. This is known as the 'fabric first' principle.

4.1.2 Build tight, ventilate right

As traditional buildings are adapted for the modern world we try to improve their fuel and energy efficiency, starting with airtightness at doors and windows. Making new or existing buildings airtight is often seen as a problem that is likely to result in high humidity, condensation, interstitial (occurring inside the wall) or surface condensation and growth of mould, including potentially toxic mould. Associated unhealthy conditions are thought likely to cause asthma, which can become life-threatening if not managed. This must be balanced with the need to minimise leakage of warm air from buildings; this is to maintain comfortable interior conditions, reduce heating fuel bills and reduce the carbon footprint of our existing housing stock.

Making buildings airtight needs to go hand in hand with deliberate managed mechanical ventilation with heat recovery (MVHR) on exhaust outlets. Passive ventilation can control humidity levels, but may not deal adequately with indoor air quality.

An alternative to passive ventilation or MVHR is the use of moisture permeable 'vapour-open' construction, also known in the UK, slightly confusingly, as 'breathing construction'. Vapour-open construction is commonplace in the EU, where in place of a vapour barrier, insulation and breather membrane and natural cross-ventilation, the practice is to use vapour-open airtight membranes inside, vapour-open insulation and vapour-open wind-tight membranes outside and no natural cross-ventilation. These approaches to construction can completely avoid the need for preservatives in timber framing.

Any membranes in the construction must be made airtight at all overlaps, at abutments with other elements at internal and external corners, at wall, floor and ceiling junctions (exactly where bats, birds and insects would have found a way in), and at all services penetrations; the latter issue can be simplified by the use of an insulated services zone close to the surface in wall construction.

One of the negative aspects of airtightness and vapour-open construction for biodiversity is the reduction in gaps allowing access to buildings for roosting or nesting – unless entrances, routes, boxes and roosts, enclosed by airtightness and thermal insulation, are deliberately created (see Drawings Nos 19 and 20, pages 112 and 114).

Historic buildings are protected by legislation and advisory organisations (see Table 4.3). These all look after the buildings, but their priorities are often in conflict with the need to reduce the carbon demand of buildings.

Table 4.3: Development control and historic buildings

Body or action	Influence over
Historic monuments	
Listed buildings	Buildings are listed for a variety of reasons: architectural merit, social or historic importance, contribution to townscape, etc.
	New extensions to listed buildings are automatically listed
	Listing puts in place barriers to prevent owners modifying buildings without reference to conservation specialists
Conservation areas	Streets, clusters or blocks of buildings, making up small or large parts of villages or cities, can be assigned 'conservation area' status, which protects everything within it, old and new
	External appearance and, sometimes, consistency of appearance are important here
English Heritage (and Irish, Scottish and Welsh equivalents)	Can set requirements for refurbishments that make energy improvements difficult
	Undertake research and publish reports that help to improve the fabric in appropriate ways
Society for the Protection of Ancient Buildings (SPAB)	Tries to ensure historic buildings are brought back into use, but that their essential character, details and craftwork are preserved, which is likely to go against extreme energy refurbishments
	Produces excellent technical guidance on methods of repair
Individuals	
Conservation officers	Can be particularly conscientious and on occasion can inadvertently delay or prevent thermal and energy upgrades of historic buildings
Conservation architects	Probably have SPAB qualifications and/or are on the RIBA register of conservation architects

4.1.4 Changing historic fabric

Traditional buildings, their methods of construction and the materials used have survived centuries of experimentation, resulting in methods that work best for the building and the users. Historic buildings and their walls, roofs and floors, or 'historic fabric', are those that are made with solid walls (pre-1919); many are made with hardwood frames, with stone or brick walls, using lime based mortar, and some with lime based render or plaster, and occasionally with animal dung as plaster or unfired clay or soil for wall construction.

The common characteristic of these materials is that they all 'breathe' or are 'vapour-open'. This means they have moisture vapour permeability through the whole wall, allowing both moisture to pass inwards and vapour to pass outwards, or vice versa, depending on internal and external conditions. 'Breathe' in this context does not mean the passage of air, in either direction, through leaky construction.

When thermal insulation is added to historic fabric we start to interfere with the natural flows of moisture through the construction and materials. It is critical that the walls can continue to breathe inwards and outwards according to the prevailing conditions. The materials chosen for thermal insulation must be selected for having moisture vapour permeability and moisture transport characteristics.

BAT ACCESS AND BARN OWL PROVISION AS ENHANCEMENT IN EXISTING BUILDINGS

In 2007, Warwickshire-based consultants ECOLOCATION were appointed by developers Walrus Projects to advise on ecology at a site central to a village in rural Leicestershire. Surveys showed no habitats or protected species issues requiring mitigation at the former farmyard site. However, ECOLOCATION were able to persuade the client to include opportunities for biodiversity enhancements in the design proposals despite this lack of evidence.

Consequently bat roosting opportunities were provided in two locations in external cavity walls of the dwellings, which were designed from new to resemble barn conversions, together with potential barn owl access to one gable close to open countryside, incorporating a barn owl nest box within a roof void.

Interestingly, a maternity roost of probable pipistrelles moved into one of the cavities left for bat use in the very first breeding season post-completion, with droppings being observed below the entrance to the roost on paving slabs. This confirms that even where there is no requirement for mitigation, voluntary provision by benevolent developers can provide significant advantages for creating more biodiverse development sites than would occur without such an open-minded outlook

ECOLOCATION's approach to the design of ecological enhancements, being part of a multi-disciplinary architecturally based consultancy, is to create less obtrusive features – which might perhaps have existed as architectural features of the building, or perhaps through what might appear to be a naturally occurring degree of disrepair – such that they do not stand out as incongruous. Using their ecologists' extensive collective experience, ECOLOCATION base their ecological enhancements closely on features known to be successful in the natural state, and evidence suggests a high take-up rate as a consequence.

Bat access was created by leaving 15 mm gaps into the cavity each side of the ridge

Gable end showing the owl entrance and bat ridge access

4.2 Methods to reduce heat loss and the impacts on biodiversity

4.2.1 Loft insulation

Roof lofts and attics are a major source of heat loss in buildings. Insulating at roof or ceiling level is a simple, and often inexpensive, way to improve thermal efficiency in an existing building. Insulating at ceiling level keeps the loft as a cold space and keeps it available as a potential roost or nesting space. Materials used include (UK normal practice) glass, stone or slag derived fibre insulation quilts and batts, or foamed plastics, but these do little to protect attics, attic rooms or upper floors from solar heat gain. EU common practice is to use cellulose fibre or dense wood fibre insulation boards to protect from winter heat loss, summer heat gain and noise; with tongued and grooved edges these dense materials can increase airtightness. European materials are increasingly available in the UK. When laying insulation at the ceiling level it is important to keep gaps at the eaves for passive ventilation of the roof and to allow bats and birds entry. Access into the roof void can be accommodated through access bricks in the gable ends (see page 43) or via special bat access roof tiles (see pages 30–32), which allow bats through the tiles and roofing felt. It is common building practice to limit access to roof voids by insects through the use of fine meshes, which permit passive ventilation but limit the opportunities for wasps, bees and birds to nest and bats to roost.

Insulating at roof level makes the loft a warm space, suitable for human habitation. This can remove opportunities for bats and birds that roost in roof voids, but the triangles at eaves and ridge can be set aside for nature. However, there may still be opportunities for crevice-dwelling bats to roost between the roof tiles and the roofing felt. Gaps can be made by lifting tiles with a wedge or by using special bat access roof tiles (see pages 30–32).

4.2.2 External thermal insulation

External thermal insulation wraps up the building with new finishes. These could include rainscreen, weatherboarding, render on foamed plastic, stone mineral fibre, cellular glass or wood fibre thermal and acoustic insulation. This minimises the effects of thermal bridges that may be difficult to change by other means. Internal heat warms the thermal mass and keeps the building fabric warm, which helps stabilise internal temperatures and minimises the thermal discomfort caused by cold walls. Solar gains through glazing will warm the interior space which in turn warms up the exposed thermal mass, which will then slowly release its heat back to the room and occupants after the sun has disappeared. If bats or birds are found in cavity walls, access to the cavity needs to be maintained, thus creating thermal bridges through the external thermal insulation. Internal insulation is another option to improve the thermal performance of the building while minimising the potential impact on biodiversity.

Impacts on opportunities for biodiversity
External insulation can block up or cover over crevices and spaces in the wall that have the potential to be used by bats and birds, either as nesting or roost spaces or for access into an internal roosting or nest space.

It is fairly easy to embed suitable habitat boxes into the construction (see the Mayville Community Centre case study, page 109). Consideration should be given to inserting enough efficient insulation around or behind the inserted box to ensure that it does not act as a thermal bridge through the surrounding thermal insulation. Of course, should the presence of protected species be found, all work should be stopped immediately until the relevant Statutory Nature Conservation Organisation or the National Bat Helpline has been contacted and advice has been received and acted upon. (See Drawing No. 18, page 110.)

4.2.3 Cavity wall insulation (CWI)

Post-1919 buildings (cavity walls)
One fundamental difference between post-1919 buildings and historic fabric buildings is the use of cavity walls in place of solid walls. Cavity walls were introduced to separate the rainscreen outer leaf of facing brickwork from the inner, loadbearing leaf of common brickwork, using a ventilated cavity between them. As the decades have passed the inner leaf has changed from common brick, via common concrete block, to insulating common concrete block, occasionally with a facing concrete block. During the past few decades, a timber framed panel inner leaf has been offered as part of a total timber panel construction. In the past five years a plethora of different block materials has been introduced and a large variety of loadbearing timber panel systems have arrived on the market.

MAYVILLE COMMUNITY CENTRE, PASSIVHAUS RETROFIT – INTEGRATED BAT AND BIRD BRICKS

The building was constructed in the 1890s as a generating station for London's tram network. In 1973 it was rescued from dereliction by the Mildmay Community Partnership, which turned it into a community centre for the local Mayville Estate. In 2006, bere:architects was commissioned to refurbish and extend the run-down building to Passivhaus standard.

The project took a holistic approach to the environment, incorporating rainwater harvesting, two native wildflower meadow roofs and ecologically sensitive gardens for community food growing projects. In addition, a number of bird and bat boxes were integrated into the external insulation.

Justin Bere says:

> It is easy to accommodate a bird or bat box into the typical Passive House thickness of external solid wall insulation that is required in the UK. Typically we need about 30 cm of insulation for the walls of a Passive House in the UK. So where the insulation is applied externally to a solid-wall building with a fine acrylic render coating, we find that using a keyhole saw it is easy to cut a recess in the insulation for nesting boxes. Squirting a little foam to fill any cavities around the nesting box also glues it permanently in place. The render can then be finished around the box for perfect protection and durability.

Walls were treated with 300 mm of expanded polystyrene block fixed to the external face of the brickwork and finished with Permarock render.

Schwegler bat tube placed on the south elevation. A second tube was installed around the corner on the west elevation

House sparrow brick box and terrace installed on the north elevation

Existing solid wall with internal insulation combined and external insulation

Top

1   Remove any existing internal moisture permeability resistant gypsum plaster or cement render

2.1 Option a1: New compressible moisture permeable, thermal insulation applied in close contact over whole area to inside face of external wall with no gaps, 200 mm

2.2 Option a2: New rigid moisture permeable, thermal insulation applied with a thick moisture permeable adhesive to whole surface area of external wall with no gaps 200 mm

3   Option b1: Moisture permeable magnesium oxide drylining board 12 mm

4   Option b2: Moisture permeable clay and reed drylining board 40 mm

5   Existing 9" 1 brick thick, brick wall with lime mortar bedding and perpends all joints fully filled

6   Reclaimed, locally grown, UKWAS or FSC temperate hardwood or durable softwood horizontal weatherboarding T&G jointed tongue uppermost 125 x 25 mm profiled to drip over entrance

7   Pressed metal drip below bat box above weatherboarding at entrance, 2 mm; use stainless steel if acidic timber species weather boarding

8   Building paper breather membrane applied to brickwork outerface

9   Schwegler Bat Box 1FE, wood-concrete, 300 x 300 x 80 mm. Supported by noggins (10)

10 38 x 38 mm battens zone with noggins to support bat box between battens

11 38 x 30 mm counter battens to hold breather membrane and support battens.

Middle

1   Existing 9" 1 brick thick, brick wall with lime mortar bedding and perpends all joints fully filled

2   Existing internal plaster made of moisture permeable lime, earth, animal dung, gypsum or clay left on or moisture impermeable cement render, left on

3   Option a2: New compressible moisture permeable, thermal insulation applied in close contact over whole area to inside face of external wall with no gaps, 50 mm

4   Option a3: Moisture permeable magnesium oxide drylining board 12 mm

5   Option a1 or b1: Thick moisture permeable adhesive to whole surface area of insulation

6   Option b2: New rigid moisture permeable thermal insulation to whole surface area of external wall with no gaps 50 mm

7   Option b3: Thick moisture permeable clay adhesive to whole surface area of insulation

8   Option b4: Moisture permeable clay and reed drylining board 40 mm

9.1 Moisture permeable dense wood fibre board thermal and acoustic insulation boards with T&G joints for airtightness, 3 layers x 50 mm staggered joints.

9.2 Aptus Wkret-met series fasteners to suit fixing pattern to manufacturer's requirements

10.1 Reclaimed, locally grown, UKWAS or FSC temperate hardwood or durable softwood wall mounting and spacer battens to receive Kent bat box

10.2 Fastener: in battens are acidic species use stainless steel, otherwise use galvanized steel

11.1 Option a1: 2 coat lime based render with reinforcment mesh if required

11.2 Option b1: Mineral based thick paint/thin render 5 mm

12 Option a2: Lime wash or lime based paint finish

13 'Kent Bat Box' reclaimed durable hardwood offcuts, stainless steel screws/nails, 200 (w) x 480 (l) mm x varying depth 250 x 160 mm lid, 15–25 mm tapered slots, stainless steel hanger and fastener

Bottom

1 Existing 9" 1 brick thick, brick wall with lime mortar bedding and perpends all joints fully filled

2 Existing internal plaster made of moisture permeable lime, earth, gypsum or clay left on or moisture impermeable cement render, left on.

3 Render options

3.1 Option a1: 2 coat lime based render with reinforcment mesh if required

3.2 Option b1: Mineral based thick paint/thin render 5 mm

4 Pressed stainless steel drip below bat box and climb surface

5 Cement-wood particle board, profiled, roughened/ grooved surface for climbing, fix with lost head fasteners through drip

6 Reclaimed, locally grown, UKWAS or FSC temperate hardwood or durable softwood profile over entrance

7 Matt brushed stainless steel or plastic render weather drip beading

8 Not used

10a Spacetherm aerogel high performance thermal insulation quilt 10 x 5 mm cut to size replacing one board of insulation behind bat box, no gaps

9 'Schwegler Bat Box 1FE 00748/3', wood-concrete, 300 x 300 x 100 mm. Supported by noggins,

10 Moisture vapour permeable dense wood fibre board thermal and acoustic insulation boards with T&G joints for airtightness, 4 layers x 50 mm staggered joints. (1 layer replaced behind bat box; see 8 above)

11 Not used, see (3) above

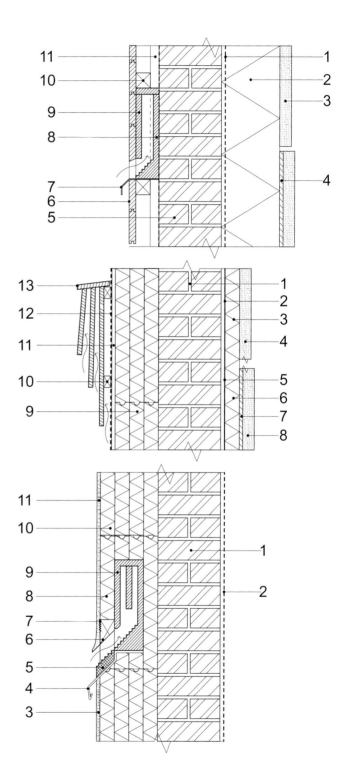

Drawing No.

19

Brick/block cavity wall construction; solid brick wall eaves detail and verge detail (room in roof, breathing roof, non-ventilated eaves)

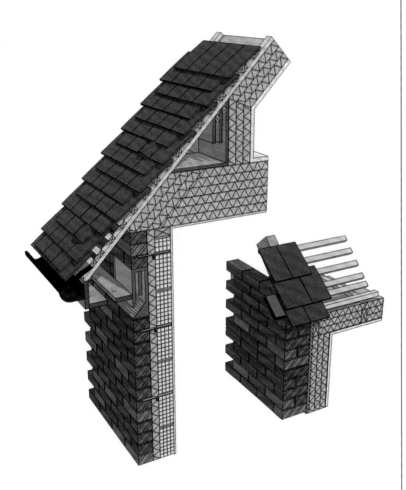

Eaves detail (left image)

1 Reclaimed, locally grown, UKWAS or FSC temperate softwood T&G jointed floor boarding, 125 x 25 mm

2.1 Reclaimed, locally grown, UKWAS or FSC temperate softwood existing ceiling joist, 100 x 50 mm

2.2 Reclaimed, locally grown, UKWAS or FSC temperate softwood floor joist, 200 x 50 mm

3 Drylining ceiling, clayboard 40 mm or gypsum plasterboard 12 mm

4 Reclaimed, locally grown, UKWAS or FSC temperate softwood existing wall plate, 75 x 100 mm with holding down straps

5 Blockwork inner leaf, 100 mm

6 Airtight clay, lime or gypsum plaster, 12 mm

7 'Schwegler Bat Box 1FE 00748/3', wood-concrete, 300 x 300 x 100 mm

8 Wall ties options:

8.1 'MagmaTech TeploTie Type 4', extruded basalt and fibre long wall tie, 200 x 6.5 dia. mm for 50 mm cavity

8.2 Wall tie, austenitic stainless steel (304 equivalent), 200 mm

9 Fired clay facing brick outer leaf, 102 x 215 x 65 mm

10 Reclaimed, locally grown, UKWAS or FSC temperate durable species softwood soffit

11 Reclaimed, locally grown, UKWAS or FSC temperate durable species softwood fascia

12 Gutter and brackets, galvanized steel, half round, Lindab Rainline

13 Rigid folded HDPE flashing into gutter

14 Reclaimed, locally grown, UKWAS or FSC temperate softwood tilting fillet, 50 mm x varies

15 'Bat access tile set', 18 mm gap x 165 mm long, gap in underlay below bat access tile set

16 Reclaimed, locally grown, UKWAS or FSC temperate softwood rafters (avoid trussed rafters), 150 x 50 mm (size to suit spans)

17 'Pro clima Solitex Plus' roofing underlay gap in underlay below bat access tile set

18 Reclaimed, locally grown, UKWAS or FSC temperate softwood roof tile counter battens, 25 x 50 mm

19 Reclaimed, locally grown, UKWAS or FSC temperate softwood roof tile battens, 25 x 50 mm

20 Medium density wood fibre thermal and acoustic insulation, compressed and released to close fit between rafters, 150 mm consisting of 3 No. x 50 mm (to suit rafter depth)

21.1 Option: UKWAS or FSC WBP weather and boil proof equivalent plywood 12 mm bottom, sides and back formation of bat/bird roosts

21.2   Option: Cement-wood particle board, roughened/ grooved surface for climbing and hanging

22   Clay handmade plain roof tiles 265 x 160 x 10 mm

25   Stone mineral fibre, full fill cavity thermal insulation, 50 mm.

Verge detail (right image)

1.1   Clay handmade plain roof tiles 265 x 160 x 10 mm

1.2   Clay handmade plain tile undercloak, 2 layers bedded in mortar, cantilevering over gable wall face 1/3 overhang 2/3 bearing

2   Reclaimed, locally grown, UKWAS or FSC temperate softwood roof tile counter battens, 25 x 50 mm

3   'Pro clima Solitex Plus' wind-tight, moisture vapour permeable roofing underlay

4   Reclaimed, locally grown, UKWAS or FSC temperate softwood roof tile battens, 25 x 50 mm

5.1   Medium density wood fibre thermal and acoustic insulation, compressed and released to close fit between rafters, 150 mm consisting of 3 No. x 50 mm (to suit rafter depth)

5.2   Moisture vapour permeable dense wood fibre board thermal and acoustic insulation boards with T&G joints for airtightness, 1 layers x 50 mm staggered joints fixed over rafters

6   Reclaimed, locally grown, UKWAS or FSC temperate softwood rafters, 100 x 50 mm (size to suit spans)

7   Drylining ceiling, clayboard 40 mm or gypsum plasterboard 12 mm

8   Pro clima Intello Plus ATL airtightness layer lapped + bonded to wall and roof

9   High-density wood fibre thermal and acoustic insulation, 150 mm consisting of 3 No. x 50 mm

10   Low density compressible wood fibre thermal insulation, thickness to suit to fit between rafter and external wall to close all gaps

11   Existing 9" 1 brick thick, brick wall with lime mortar bedding and perpends all joints fully filled

12   Not used, see (6) above

13   Reclaimed, locally grown, UKWAS or FSC temperate durable species softwood wall plate 100 x 75 mm with wall metal straps to secure to wall

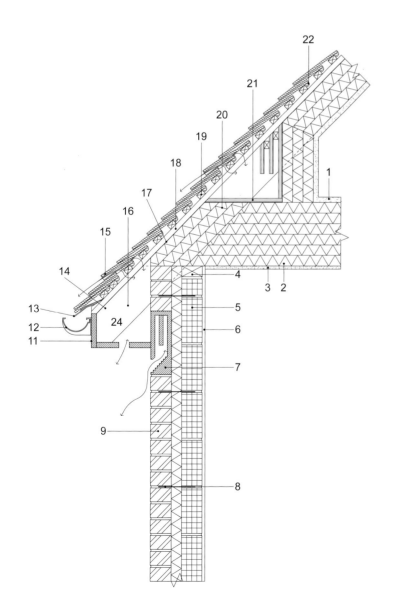

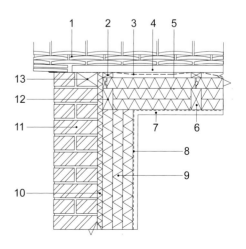

Drawing No.
20

Masonry 50 mm cavity wall
with retrofit cavity DIY bat box, outer leaf bat box and face fixed bat box

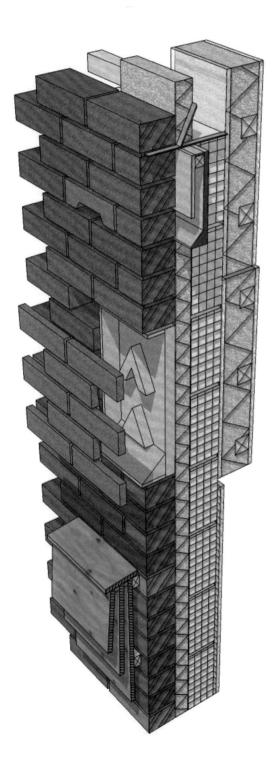

Retrofit cavity DIY bat box

1   Remove any existing internal moisture permeability resistant gypsum plaster or cement render

2   Reclaimed, locally grown, UKWAS or FSC temperate softwood cross battens, 2 No. layers 50 x 50 mm at 600 centres, 2nd layer at right angles to first

3   Compressible mid-density wood fibre thermal insulation, 2 No. layers 560 (w) x 50 (t) mm fitted between cross battens; fill all voids, no gaps

4   Not used, see (3) above

5   Magnesium oxide board lining 12 mm

13 Dense aggregate concrete block 100 mm (w) x 215 mm (h) x 440 mm (l)

20 Stone mineral fibre, full fill cavity thermal insulation, 50 mm

21 Ibstock bat brick entrance brick built into outerleaf at base of DIY cavity bat box to coincide with entrance of bat box

22 DIY bat box 50 mm overall to fit existing cavity: 20 x 20 softwood framing, ex 20 x 20 stepped triangle at base, 9 mm roughened plywood/cement particle board front and back, 10 mm. Aerogel insulation to back

23 Preformed proprietary retrofit cavity tray damp proof course, using plastic-memory to pull sloped surface down towards outer face of inner leaf

24 External leaf fired clay facing brick, 102 mm if laid in lime mortar, existing bricks removed to allow box and cavity tray insertion, reinstalled with lime mortar

18 'MagmaTech TeploTie Type 4', extruded basalt and fibre long wall tie, 200 x 6.5 dia. mm for 50 mm cavity

Outer leaf bat box

6   Existing internal plaster made of moisture permeable lime, earth, gypsum or clay left on or moisture impermeable cement render, left on

7   Reclaimed, locally grown, UKWAS or FSC temperate softwood cross battens, 2 No. layers 50 x 50 mm at 600 centres 2nd layer at right angles to first

8   Compressible mid-density wood fibre thermal insulation, 2 No. layers 560 (w) x 50 (t) mm fitted between cross battens, fill all voids, no gaps

9   Not used, see (7) above

10 Magnesium oxide board lining 12 mm

13 Dense aggregate concrete block 100 mm (w) x 215 mm (h) x 440 mm (l)

15 Stone mineral fibre, full fill cavity thermal insulation, 50 mm

18 'MagmaTech TeploTie Type 4', extruded basalt and fibre long wall tie, 200 x 6.5 dia. mm for 50 mm cavity

19 Habibat bat box, clay brick slip faced, built into outer leaf brickwork

24 External leaf fired clay facing brick, 102 mm with cut brick behind brick slips either side of box

Face fixed bat box

11.1 Option 1: Moisture permeable magnesium oxide drylining board 12 mm

11.2 Option 2: Moisture permeable clay and reed drylining board 40 mm

12 Thick moisture permeable adhesive and parge coat to whole surface area of drylining for airtightness

13 Dense aggregate concrete block 100 mm (w) x 215 mm (h) x 440 mm (l)

14 'MagmaTech TeploTie Type 4', extruded basalt and fibre long wall tie, 200 x 6.5 dia. mm for 50 mm cavity

15 Stone mineral fibre, full fill cavity thermal insulation, 50 mm

16.1 'Kent Bat Box' reclaimed durable hardwood offcuts, stainless steel screws/nails, 200 (w) x 480 (h) mm x varying depth 250 x 160 mm lid, 15–25 mm tapered slots, stainless steel hanger and fastener

16.2 Fastener: if hardwood are acidic species use stainless steel, otherwise use galvanized steel

17 Reclaimed, locally grown, UKWAS or FSC temperate hardwood or durable softwood wall mounting and spacer battens to receive Kent bat box

24 External leaf fired clay facing brick, 102 mm

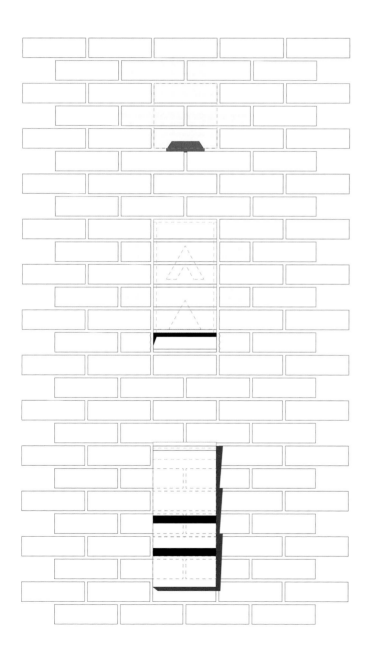

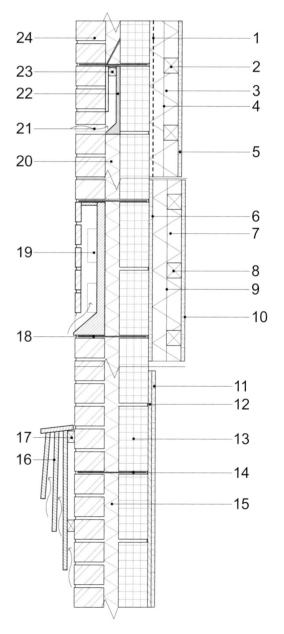

Cavities have also received different treatments; initially ventilated, then partially or fully filled with thermal insulation. Insulation has often been made inefficient by the ventilated cavity drawing heat out of the open-cell, closed-cell or even foil-faced thermal insulation, with the stack effect pushing the heat out of the top of the cavity. Moisture vapour permeable and resistant materials have both been used. The most extreme cavity wall so far in the UK is the 300 mm wide cavity, fully filled with hydrophobic, moisture vapour permeable thermal insulation and two-part wall ties, separate lintels in leaves and plywood window boxes lining the opening to allow cavity insulation close to the windows without cavity closer construction. New types of wall ties and lintels are even being experimented with to reduce the reliance on metal ties, which thermally bridge the cavity insulation at frequent intervals. Pultruded (from Pull = Pull through die and Extrude = Push through die) fibre-reinforced stone ties and lintels are now available.

Thermal insulation of cavity walls

Solid walls are described as 'hard to treat', which implies that existing cavity walls are easy to treat. In reality, to achieve an 80% carbon reduction in existing cavity walls is just as hard, if not harder, than in solid walls. This is because the width of the cavity – usually 50 mm – is insufficient to achieve the regulated or desired thermal insulation values (see Section 4.1.1) and additional insulation is therefore required internally, externally or both. Having two or three layers of insulation in different positions in a wall will complicate the interstitial condensation potential of the wall.

Impacts of CWI on biodiversity

Cavity walls are often used by birds and bats as nesting and roosting sites. If bats or other protected species are found or suspected, work must be stopped immediately until the relevant statutory nature conservation organisation or the National Bat Helpline has been contacted and advice has been received and acted upon.

Cavity walls can be retrofit-insulated using blown or injected materials. Holes are drilled at intervals through either the inner or the outer leaf brick or blocks through the mortar joint intersections, and using a 15–20 mm diameter nozzle attached to a hose and pump; insulation materials are blown or injected into the cavity, filling it from the bottom upwards.

Few materials are suitable for this purpose; they need to be hydrophobic (resistant to water entry) because rainwater can run down the inside face of the outside leaf of the wall.

Injected foams (low or zero urea formaldehyde) and blown-in stone, slag or glass mineral fibre are suitable, as are blown-in polystyrene balls. Cellulose fibre batts are available, but are an unlikely candidate in all but partially filled cavities (built in at the time of construction). All blown or injected insulation has the potential to entomb any wildlife living in the cavities, and superficial inspection of cavities is unlikely to detect them.

It should be noted that mineral fibre type and cellulose type insulation products are indicated as irritants and carcinogens. In some cases, contact has been thought to result in lesions, tumours and fatalities in swifts.

To reduce impacts of CWI on biodiversity, consider using internal insulation, instead of CWI. Partially insulated or uninsulated and ventilated cavity walls combined with external insulation will make the external insulation redundant and so should be avoided.

CAMDEN HOUSING ESTATES
(RETROFIT OF SWIFT BRICKS AS PART OF CAVITY WALL INSULATION)

The London Borough of Camden trialled an innovative process of retrofitting swift nest bricks by embedding them into the walls of high-rise flats in the Borough.

The Housing Sustainability team and the Nature Conservation Section identified the opportunity to combine the thermal insulation programme of housing estates with installation of the swift bricks. The work programme used records of swifts in the area to determine which buildings bricks should be added.

Twenty Schwegler Swift Box No. 17 single-cavity bricks were installed in pairs or threes on the stairwell walls of residential buildings across four estates in the Borough. Two approaches were trialled for the installation; the first method used abseilers from Avalon Abseiling, who had been contracted to inject thermal insulation into cavity walls. At the same time as injecting the thermal insulation, Avalon Abseiling installed ten swift boxes. A further ten boxes were installed by Bayer Group plc using a mobile work platform.

Swift bricks were cemented into the wall, flush with the outer surface of the brickwork, using a standard brick pointing mix to provide long-lasting nest sites. A layer one brick thick was left between boxes to provide additional support.

The work contributed toward targets in Camden's Biodiversity Action Plan to provide a variety of nesting habitats throughout the Borough.

More details can be found at:
www.camden.gov.uk/ccm/cms-service/download/asset?asset_id=2599851

Abseilers installing swift bricks

Swift bricks installed in cavity wall of lift shaft

Retrofitting nests/roosts into cavity walls

Retrofitting that includes provision for bat or bird roosts could be considered. This will be practical in walls made with lime mortar, which is easily removed and so allows bricks to be taken out whole; but since the bricks removed can be sacrificial (replaced by box), cement mortared walls can be modified using hammer and chisel carefully to minimise damage to surrounding wall. Purpose-made boxes can be installed, with very high performance insulation on the back, and with purpose-made retrofit cavity tray damp proof courses (DPC) installed over the boxes and bricks then reinstalled with matching mortar mix, colour and profile (Drawing No. 20, page 114).

4.3   Roofs and lofts

4.3.1   Timber barn roofs

Timber barn roofs are usually made of timber post and beam construction, with various framing techniques in the roof timbers spanning from post to post. They are clad with timber weatherboarding or surrounded by brick or stone solid walls. Roofs are tiled with slate or clay tiles or shingles on battens or are thatched with reeds. Modern thatch replacement will introduce a fire resistant lining below the thatch.

These roofs offer many ledges on which to perch, nest or roost, timbers from which to hang and, importantly, room to fly. Bespoke barn owl and bat lofts can easily be installed in the roof space (see Drawings Nos 5 and 19, pages 66 and 112).

(see Drawings Nos 5 and 19, pages 66 and 112)

4.3.2 Traditional cut roofs

These are roofs made in situ, with timbers cut on site, usually having rafters from eaves to ridge with intermediate purlins to reduce the span, with ceiling joists and binders creating an attic space that can be suitable for bats and birds and, if large enough, allow space for flying. Sometimes the roof is made to incorporate a room(s) and some will be converted to add one. In England, the underside of battens and tiles can be seen in older roofs, but roofing underlay is used in newer properties. In Scotland, where the temperatures are lower and with potentially stronger winds, roofs normally have softwood sarking boarded over the rafters, then counter battens, underlay and tile battens. Sarking could make the roof inaccessible to bats and birds, but workmanship quality usually means there are gaps large enough to allow access, while the space above underlay or sarking will also provide a place to roost.

The impacts of underlay felts on bats is the subject of an in-depth investigation at the University of Reading (see *Roofing membranes*, below).

Traditional roofs have timber lath and plaster ceiling, but newer ceilings will be plasterboard. Since thermal insulation thicknesses have been increasing, a vapour barrier may have been added below the ceiling joists and insulation. Increased thicknesses of roof insulation require a ventilation zone of 50 mm to be maintained between the eaves and the attic. Insect proof (and therefore bat and bird proof) ventilation strips are often added to eaves, and insect proof ventilation tiles have been added to pitched roofs to maintain drying conditions. In the past decade, breathable roofing membranes (BRMs) have been introduced to avoid the need for ventilation slots and tiles in the roof; however, tests have shown that BRMs are not performing and the new code of practice for control of condensation in buildings (BS 5250:2011) states that ventilation should be incorporated into roofs where breathable membranes are used.

Trussed rafters

Trussed rafters were introduced to reduce the time taken to construct roofs. Rafters and ceilings are factory prefabricated as triangular structural elements, which can either be craned into place one or more at a time or can be preassembled on the ground, allowing the whole roof to be craned into place as one.

The triangulation of the trussed rafter means these roofs less suitable for bat flight, although they still offer the opportunity for roosts at eaves, ridge and verges, among tiles, battens and underlay. This space can also be boxed off to create a bat loft (see Drawing No. 19, page 112).

(see Drawing No. 19, page 112)

External roof thermal insulation

The European approach to insulating roofs is appealing to UK designers and becoming more popular. The reason for this popularity is that wrapping the roof with insulation outside the roof timber framing means the insulation is not bridged by the timbers themselves, avoiding thermal bridges. The choice of insulation materials is also important. In this position there is an opportunity to effectively insulate the roof against solar gain as well as heat loss – avoiding rooms being cold in winter and hot in summer – and also providing acoustic insulation. Hygroscopic high-density, moisture vapour permeable (breathing, vapour-open) sheathing

PEREGRINE PLATFORM FOR EXISTING BUILDING

After noting the presence of peregrine falcons around County Hall in Aylesbury in 2006, Aylesbury Vale District Council's biodiversity team sought permission from Bucks County Council (the owners of the tower) to erect a nesting platform. The building lacked features on which the birds could nest so the installation of the platform was considered vital if birds were to breed on the tower. The project was considered to be beneficial both in terms of the conservation of the species and to provide a glamorous focal point demonstrating the importance of the urban environment for biodiversity.

There were a lot of problems to overcome relating mainly to County Council safety, maintenance and technical issues, which took over a year to resolve. The platform went up in 2008 and consisted of a marine ply structure filled with a nesting substrate (pea shingle), fitted into a specially constructed aluminium frame, which fitted onto the building. The design of the platform was influenced by the Hawk and Owl Trust, with input from the Bucks Bird Club and the British Trust for Ornithology (BTO). The birds investigated the platform almost immediately, but no breeding occurred for three years. During this wait adaptations were made to the platform to encourage occupation: a roof was installed, and netting was placed behind the box to minimise accidental visual disturbance.

The birds first attempted to nest in 2011. It may have been the condition of the platform prior to the alterations being made that led to the occupation, but was probably more to do with the fact that the resident birds were too young to breed. This was confirmed by the failure of the first nesting attempt, with only one egg being laid, which proved to be infertile. The failed attempt inspired the team to install two web cameras in preparation for the expected second breeding attempt the following year. The cameras were installed in early spring 2012 and were linked to the District Council's website to enable members of the public to see the footage in real time. Any particularly interesting events were captured and put on the Council's YouTube site.

The project has proved to be a spectacular success, in terms of both public engagement and peregrine conservation. Summer 2012 saw two chicks successfully hatched, reared, ringed and fledged, and there were thousands of hits on the website and YouTube site. In addition, several events, television appearances and radio interviews were conducted, which helped to advertise the project to a wide audience.

Peregrine on specially designed platform attached to council building

Peregrine looking at the webcam

insulating boards are appropriate, and dense wood fibre boards and batts are a suitable material; some grades are suitable for weather exclusion, avoiding the need for BRMs, while others need a wind-tight vapour permeable underlay to the tiles.

The simplicity of this method of insulating means it lends itself to refurbishment of existing roofs. It avoids the complications of working insulation around existing cut timber roofs and provides an effective insulation solution, but it does add the complication of weather-proofing party wall details in semi-detached or terraced buildings when removing and relaying tiles over the new external insulation.

This method will effectively close the roof void to bats and birds unless deliberate provision is made to incorporate roost spaces. If possible, roost spaces should be inside the external insulation line, but wrapped up with insulation to ensure a continuous U value envelope to the building.

Re-roofing

Depending on the result required, a number of options exist:

- retiling/re-slating, either reusing existing tiles/slates or replacing with new, with or without renewable energy systems being installed. If such systems are installed, roofing underlay is replaced with BRMs, wind-tightness layers or breathing sheathing boards;
- adding external thermal insulation over existing timbers and retiling/ re-slating;
- replacing the roof structure completely with a new timber roof or choice of panel systems.

Prefabricated panel systems

Part of the move away from traditional roof construction methods includes adoption of 'modern methods of construction' (MMC) and 'innovative methods of construction' (IMC), some of which include traditional methods with a modern twist. These focus on factory prefabrication to avoid construction in external site conditions, standardise quality of workmanship and help minimise waste.

Several different panel systems are available (see Table 4.4). These systems can be used to create whole new roofs in place of existing traditional or trussed rafter roof construction. These roof construction methods will exclude bats and birds from all areas other than the batten and tile zones. Gable walls above the highest ceiling-level thermal insulation may offer an opportunity to introduce bat or bird roost boxes: mounted to the external surface, within the cladding or inside the roof space.

Table 4.4: Applications for factory prefabricated panel systems

Panel system	Application	Thermal and/or acoustic insulation
Insulated structural panel systems (ISPS)	Floors, gables and pitched roofs for attics	Pre-insulated, either in the factory or on site Thermal and acoustic insulation options possible
Structural insulated panel systems (SIPS)	Gables and pitched roofs for attics Traditional or hybrid panels for floors	Thermal Insulation is bonded to the skins of the panel to add to the structural performance of the panel May also need solar heat gain thermal and acoustic insulation
Cross-laminated timber panel (CLTP) systems (glued solid softwood battens/ply)	Floors, gables and pitched roofs for attics	Thermal and acoustic insulation is added, usually outside of the panels, on site

Brown long-eared bats roosting against a breathable roofing membrane
(BRM) has resulted in 'fluffing' of the membrane

Roofing membranes

Over the past decade there have been several changes in the materials and methods used on roofing projects within the UK. Historically, underlays were not used in roofing. More recently, underlays – which sit beneath the tiles/slates – would have consisted of bitumen felt or wooden sarking boards (standard practice in Scotland). However, breathable roofing membranes (BRMs) are increasingly being used.

BRMs are manufactured using non-woven technology, in which extremely long fibres are compressed to form protective layers that can be applied to vulnerable core sheet materials. However, evidence shows that BRMs can pose a risk to bats. The fibres in a BRM are easily teased apart and create a 'fluff' on the membrane surface, which can lead to a bat's claws becoming entangled, resulting in death. There are also concerns over the differences in thermal conductivity, thickness and moisture permeability properties between traditional and new membranes; these could have an effect on the microclimate regime within a roof and therefore might affect roost suitability, either negatively or positively.

From an industry viewpoint, fitting of BRMs into locations where bats may eventually roost could lead to the premature deterioration of the product. It is possible that bats could tear or puncture the membrane (which will reduce the water-tightness properties), or that their fur oils and excreta could end up blocking the micro-channels that allow the membrane to breathe, thus reducing its effectiveness and increasing the risk of condensation.

Whilst, industry professionals believe that minor differences in performance due to the presence of bats should not alter overall roof conditions, the potential for localised problems such as water entry and increased risk of condensation (through reduced breathability), could prevent a membrane from functioning at its intended level.

Ongoing research will continue to investigate this matter. Until a suitable methodology or materials and techniques are found to make the use of BRMs suitable in bat roosts, it is recommended that these materials are avoided in potential roost areas. Traditional materials, such as bitumen roof felt and sarking boards, should therefore continue to be used.

It is sometimes wrongly stated that the use of bitumen felt in roofs does not comply with Building Regulations. Building Regulations state that contractors must "assess the condensation risk within the roof space and make appropriate provisions in line with part C relating to the control of condensation". Part C recommends meeting the recommendations made in BS 5250:2011. In that document it is made clear that both High resistance (bitumen) and Low resistance (BRM) underlays are acceptable as long as appropriate ventilation is provided.

4.4   Renewable energy

With the need to reduce carbon emissions and the introduction of the Green Deal in 2012/13, we can expect to see an increase in the adoption of renewable energy systems in buildings, both following and at the same time as the installation of thermal insulation. The planning system has put in place 'permitted development' rules to enable the adoption of such systems in the simplest of situations without the need for a planning application (except in important and historic buildings). See Table 4.3 and Renewable energy and historic buildings & Permitted development, above.

Solar panels

Solar thermal (ST) and photovoltaic (PV) panels generally fit the permitted development rules, whether installed above the roof tiling or integrated into the roof, replacing the tiling. Attics will always heat up in the summer unless they are shaded or protected from solar radiation. The placement of solar PV panels on roofs may have a substantial impact on the summer temperatures within a roof void and therefore affect its suitability for use by birds or bats.

In order for solar thermal (ST) (hot water/heating) panels to operate efficiently they must be adequately insulated internally and so should not lead to additional heating of the roof void, but they might lead to a lowering of the temperature in the roof space. However, inadequately insulated solar thermal panels and all solar PVs are likely to re-radiate heat downwards through roof coverings, membranes, low thermal mass short decrement delay thermal insulation, sarking boarding, etc. to overheat the roof void.

Integrating solar PV panels means their underside will not be as well ventilated as if they were installed above the roof finish; the performance of the panels will be reduced if they are not permitted to cool on the underside. Integrated panels will re-radiate their heat inwards, towards the roof void and, potentially, the top-floor rooms. Installing high-density thermal insulation below the panels can absorb some of this heat and protect the attic or rooms, but it might prevent the panel cooling; introducing phase change materials will probably not provide a solution either.

Photovoltaic panels with biodiverse green roof vegetation below

There is a third type of solar panel which is a hybrid of the first two: photovoltaic-thermal panels (PVTs). By introducing solar thermal (ST) panels below a PV panel – the heat in the PV can be removed by the ST lowering the PV temperature, allowing it to operate more efficiently; a well-insulated ST should reduce the heat reaching the roof void below. Further investigation is required to establish whether the net heat gains or losses will make potential bat roosts unsuitable. The heat that is removed needs to be used beneficially, such that the excess heat is stored inter-seasonally and not disposed of, which could lead to thermal pollution of the surrounding ground, air or water.

The placement of the meters and power inverters needs to be carefully considered if bats and birds are going to be attracted into a site with solar PV panels. Some models of inverter produce a high-frequency noise, which, if placed inside a roof void, may be disturbing to bats.

The combination of PVs and green roofs can also enhance the performance of PVs, on a number of counts:

- the PVs will be set at a slope on a frame to optimise the energy gain in relationship to the angle of the sun's path in the sky
- being raised above a flat roof leaves enough room for ventilation of the underside of the panels, allowing them to cool and perform nearer to their optimum
- evapo-transpiration from living roof planting will help to cool the roof, minimising stored and reflected heat (part of urban heat island effect)
- moist air rising from the living roof will help cool the PV panels and any condensation forming on the panels overnight will take heat out of the panels as it evaporates as the days warms up
- one provisio: ensure the planting choices will not grow high enough to shade the PV panels
- some of the multi-functional rural PV panel farms are being set at a height to allow sheep and cattle to roam freely below panel support frames.

Micro wind turbines

At the time of writing, permitted development rules prevent wind turbines being attached to terraced, semi-detached properties and blocks of flats for fear of vibration noise disturbing neighbours (which for the purposes of this guide could include bats and birds) until further research had been carried out. The planning portal website provides detailed guidance and will be the best source on the rules as they develop:

www.planningportal.gov.uk/permission/commonprojects/windturbines

Exceptionally bespoke aerofoil shaped buildings which concentrate undisturbed airflow through gaps or small apertures and through wind turbines can generate useful energy. More often than not wind turbines attached to roofs of buildings, especially in urban areas, receive disturbed air from surrounding buildings and trees and even due to disturbance of airflow over the building itself. Exceptionally off-the-shelf turbines mounted on normal rural roofs can be lucky enough to receive steady flows or air over a reasonable proportion of the available wind duration. As a result, the turbine will provide a smaller than expected return on investment, either in financial terms or as embodied energy/carbon versus renewable energy gained.

From a wind perspective, turbines should be mounted on a pole at least the same height as the building and at a distance equal to ten times the height of the building away from it, on the leeward side or on the prevailing side, and not in the shadow of any other buildings or obstructions, such as trees.

The siting of turbines is equally important from a biodiversity perspective. In addition to an unquantified risk of mortality, recent research (Minderman *et al.*, 2012) suggests that micro-turbines may act as a deterrent to both bats and birds. These findings support recommendations to site micro-turbines at least 20 m from potentially valuable bat habitat (including potential building roosts), especially in landscapes with limited available habitat. It is the obligation of the owner/occupier to seek the advice of the Statutory Nature Conservation Organisation when installing a microgeneration scheme where protected species are or are likely to be affected.

Further reading

British Standard (2011) BS 5250: 2011 Code of practice for control of condensation in buildings. British Standards Institution.

CHAPTER FIVE

Designing biodiversity into built developments

"Biodiversity is a key indicator of success in achieving sustainable development."

Brundtland Commission, 1987

The conservation of biodiversity in built developments is often characterised as the provision of nest and roosting boxes on buildings. However, such features are likely to be of little or no value if the surrounding landscape does not provide appropriate vegetation for foraging, cover and movement. Many new developments tend to be dominated by hard paving, with isolated patches of non-native planting that have little value to wildlife. These developments are of limited value for biodiversity. Fortunately, the changes needed to create places that work for both people and wildlife are often simple and inexpensive.

This chapter provides information about:

- large-scale planning and connectivity, including suggestions for the design, construction and post-construction phases;
- biodiversity principles and measures that can be incorporated into new developments and regeneration projects; and
- negative features for wildlife, including inappropriate artificial lighting and roads.

An example of where bat bricks were installed into the new houses and yet the surrounding landscaping lacks the necessary vegetation to link these enhancements within the site to the wider landscape

5.1   Large-scale design, planning and connectivity

5.1.1   What can be considered during the outline design stage

Beyond the buildings, the built environment can provide many opportunities for habitat retention and creation. As part of the outline design, it is important to incorporate incidental green spaces where possible, and for larger developments, parks should be planned. Natural England has developed Urban Greenspace Standards (Handley et al., 2003), which recommend that people living in towns and cities should have:

- an accessible natural green space less than 300 m (five-minute walk) from home;
- a local nature reserve at a minimum level of 1 ha per thousand population; and

- at least one accessible 20 ha site within 2 km of home, one accessible 100 ha site within 5 km of home and one accessible 500 ha site within 10 km of home.

Retaining habitats

It is strongly recommended that natural features should be retained wherever possible as these may be difficult to recreate and may contain established valuable wildlife, including invertebrate communities. Examples include hedges, ponds and ditches from former agricultural landscapes, mature trees, any remnants of semi-natural grassland and any streams. All of this should be viewed at a wider scale – consider how the development, large or small, sits within the existing landscape. Is there the possibility of enhancement? Can retained habitats be interconnected or connected to the wider surrounds?

Creating habitats

Besides parks and green spaces, other opportunities for habitat creation may be associated with footpaths and cycle paths, around car parks and amenity green space, alongside roads and within drainage features. Habitats to be created in this way can include woodland, grassland, hedges, tall herb, wetland, scrub/shrubberies and open mosaic habitat.

Take account of underlying geology and hydrology and the scope for modifying topography to create slopes, banks, humps and hollows. If you are in a limestone or chalk area, consider exposing the local subsoil to produce new limestone grassland or calcareous open mosaic habitat. If in a heathland district, consider exposing sandy soils to encourage acid grassland and heath.

The following guidance should be followed when creating habitats:

- The use of topsoil should be strictly avoided in order to promote plant diversity.
- Natural colonisation should be considered if high-quality habitat is nearby. If this approach needs to be augmented, seed or plant with native species of local provenance.
- Vegetation management should promote the structural diversity of invertebrate habitats, ensuring that some pupation and overwintering sites are provided every winter by leaving some areas uncut.

As well as considering the types of vegetation that might be most beneficial for invertebrates and other wildlife, it is worth keeping some sparsely vegetated or bare south-facing slopes which can support ground-nesting bees, wasps and associated parasites. Include water bodies and wetlands. These might be ponds, lakes, ditches and reed beds, which may be incorporated into the sustainable drainage system of the site. The boundary between open water and terrestrial habitats can be extremely valuable, so create gently sloping banks wherever possible with broad strips of native marginal and emergent aquatic vegetation.

In some parts of southern Britain, Stag Beetles exploit the decaying rootstocks of suburban trees.

5.1.2 Gardens

Private gardens collectively cover about 270,000 ha in Britain and make up the largest urban green space. The UK's 15 million gardens already provide important homes for wildlife, but the value of these areas for wildlife could be improved. Many creatures that are declining in the countryside, such as the common frog, song thrush and hedgehog, can thrive in domestic gardens and other urban areas if the right conditions occur. It is possible, with a little consideration, to make parts of gardens into areas that play a vital role in supporting biodiversity, either as a permanent home, a seasonal abode or a place to feed or breed.

- Arrange gardens so that habitat patch sizes are maximised and isolation minimised.
- Gardens should not be treated as individual units but rather as an interconnected habitat.
- The presence of adjacent gardens can increase the species richness of urban parks.
- Vegetation complexity needs to be maximised. The three-dimensional structure of garden vegetation is an important predictor of species abundance and diversity.

A pond is one of the most wildlife rich features to have in a garden

5.1.3 Accounting for wildlife during and after the construction phase

Development is often phased, which may allow for the formation of temporary habitats or ephemeral vegetation that can support wildlife. Careful planning and management can positively enhance temporary habitats and provide pioneer communities of invertebrates and other wildlife that will persist within the completed development. Measures to encourage this can include seeding with native wildflowers, the use of topographic features (banks, slopes, pits, pools, etc.) and the establishment of permanent wildlife corridors to encourage species movement.

It is important to ensure that the biodiversity element of sustainable place-making is continued beyond the direct involvement of the design and development team. Advice on increasing biodiversity in gardens and green spaces is provided by several conservation organisations. The RSPB and others offer a range of advice for planning and creating a wildlife-friendly garden, including on creating habitats, planting to attract wildlife and putting up bird boxes. Also, search for 'wildlife gardening' on the following websites, all of which have a host of information:

- www.rspb.org.uk
- www.wildaboutgardens.org.uk
- www.wildlifetrusts.org
- www.bats.org.uk
- www.buglife.org.uk
- www.naturalengland.org.uk (search for 'wildlife gardening' or 'wildlife on allotments')
- www.bigwildlifegarden.org.uk/
- www.rhs.org.uk/Gardening/Sustainable-gardening/Wildlife-and-the-gardener

Chapter 6 discusses ways to monitor biodiversity and engage with residents and employees.

Basic principles for biodiversity enhancing landscape design in developments

1. Retain existing vegetation and habitats where appropriate

- Find out what exists on the site already. It is uncommon to find sites that have no biodiversity value at all. For all sites, a survey for habitats and protected species should be undertaken by a suitably qualified and experienced person and a search by the local biological records centre should be commissioned.
- Retain mature trees (they provide potential nest sites for birds and can support roosting bats), hedges and vegetation of value to wildlife. In some situations it may be advisable to protect soils in situ or store and reuse soil.

2. Create new habitats

- Mimic natural habitats by using native species in natural associations. Non-native species should be avoided unless they have documented value for wildlife and are not invasive. Match planting to soils and avoid the use of rich topsoils, which depress species diversity.
- Types of habitat include woodland, wetland, grassland and sparsely vegetated stony communities.
- Some habitats, such as woodlands, need to be large in order to support the full range of species. Depending on the site it may be better to create a few large habitats than many small ones.
- Utilise otherwise wasted space, such as roofs, walls, balconies, road verges, cycle and footpaths, and parking areas.
- Increase roosting and nesting opportunities by providing artificial wildlife homes, such as bird/bat boxes/bricks, insect hotels and hives.

3. Connectivity

- Connectivity refers to the size and distribution of patches of habitat and the relative ease with which particular species can move through the landscape between the patches.
- Often, built structures or the artificial lighting associated with built areas can create unnecessary barriers to the movement of animals, so be aware of this and try to create routes for wildlife to move or disperse through the site. Aim to create 'dark green corridors' and unlit areas, especially in and around parks and tree-lined lanes, roads, and bridges that cross streams and rivers (see Section 5.2 for further information on lighting).
- Green corridors should be included to link habitats. Linking features include tree networks, stepping stone habitats (like green roofs) and effective road crossings, such as wildlife overpasses and underpasses (eco-passages).
- A small, isolated site is likely to have lower value than a larger site that forms part of a mosaic of green space.
- Linear features such as treelines, hedges, waterways, vegetated railway corridors, gardens and woodland edges are particularly important for bats and other mammals, birds and many of the more mobile invertebrates, e.g. butterflies, which use them as commuting routes.

4. Target species

- Check whether there are any particular species or habitats of which you should be aware in the local area (refer to the ecological survey, local experts and the local Biodiversity Action Plans). It may be that you can provide new habitats for endangered or priority species or protect or expand important habitats. As well as helping the local authority to meet its biodiversity duty and targets, this could become an attractive feature of the new development.
- Bat and bird populations are considered to be a good indicator of the broad state of wildlife and landscape quality because they utilise a range of habitats across the landscape and are sensitive to pressures in urban, suburban and rural environments. Targeting bats and birds as beneficiaries of landscape design will benefit a host of other wildlife and will ensure there is a biodiverse, multi-functional green infrastructure.

5. Incorporate tree planting

- Species should be predominantly native and, where possible, of local provenance or climate-adapted provenance. It is also recommended that disease-resistant strains are considered.
- 30% of trees to be planted should be large tree species as they provide greater wildlife benefits and ecosystem services.
- Create lines and groups of trees to create 'woodland patches' and woodland edge habitat.

6. Wildlife-friendly planting

- Planting should benefit a wide array of wildlife by providing larval food plants, food (nectar, pollen, fruit/berries, leaves) and/or shelter in the form of cover or nesting habitats, with flowering occurring from spring to autumn.
- Native species are often more beneficial for wildlife, but there are non-natives with documented value to wildlife, some of which may provide benefits for a longer time period. Avoid the use of non-native invasive species (www.defra.gov.uk/wildlife-pets/non-native).
- Wherever possible, ensure that new areas of planting are next to existing vegetation. The connectivity and quality of habitat are more important than the total area.
- If there are opportunities for new planting on the scheme, consider making some of the plants edible for both humans and wildlife. This includes fruit trees (which require soft landscape below), nut trees, berry bushes and salad and vegetable plants.
- Diversify grassland areas by reducing the fertility of the soil and re-seeding with suitable native mixes or plug-planting with wildflowers.
- Gardens not only play an incredibly important role in biodiversity protection, but also reduce the likelihood of flooding by retaining rainfall.

7. Multi-functional green infrastructure (GI)

- GI is the network of natural and man-made green (land) and blue (water) spaces that sustain natural processes. GI includes playing fields, parks, gardens, squares, verges, rivers, canals and street trees as well as vegetation on buildings, such as green roofs and living walls.
- GI should be designed and managed as a multi-functional resource that provides a full range of ecosystem services, as well as quality of life benefits for society. GI will not be biodiverse unless designers and managers *design it in* by considering the setting for and situation of each scheme as well as the planting and management.

8. Sustainable drainage systems (SuDS)

- SuDS is an approach to surface water drainage that takes account of water quantity, water quality and amenity issues by mimicking nature.
- All new development should use SuDS.
- SuDS can improve a development by creating habitats that encourage biodiversity and simultaneously provide open space while delivering features to filter and store water.
- The biodiversity value of SuDS will be greatest in schemes that utilise green roofs, swales, ponds and wetlands as these provide wildlife habitats.
- Remove or reduce the amount of impermeable surfaces by using permeable paving, gravel, sections of lawn or flower beds. This mediates flood risk and restores natural processes, such as nutrient cycling.

9. Artificial lighting

- Outdoor lighting is disturbing to a wide range of wildlife, including bats, birds, invertebrates and amphibians.
- Designing wildlife-sensitive lighting schemes has knock-on benefits, including decreased light pollution, increased energy efficiency, lower carbon emissions and reduced maintenance.
- See Section 5.2 for more detail.

10. Community involvement

- Involve local communities in the monitoring and management of their wildlife. Experience shows that not only does this help with community cohesion, but it is also a healthy outdoor activity which improves mental and physical well-being. Increasing awareness of wildlife could also result in valuable information being collected on species found in an urban environment. See Chapter 6 for more information on monitoring.

WILDLIFE TOWER – BARN OWL TRUST

The wildlife tower was designed by the Barn Owl Trust to incorporate provision for barn owls, little owls, kestrels/stock doves, sparrows, reptiles and amphibians. In addition, it incorporates three separate chambers which allow a variety of bats to use the site for breeding and winter hibernation. Within only seven weeks of completion the building was naturally colonised by a little owl, hibernating butterflies, lacewings and other insects. After 14 months a barn owl started roosting and in the fourth year barn owls and kestrels nested simultaneously and were both successful.

The building described was constructed from limestone with a breezeblock and wood inner structure and a pitched slate roof. It is 5 m tall at the apex.

EAST-FACING WALL: The barn owl entrance hole is 3.5 m above ground level and leads into a generous deep nest box. To maximise chances of occupation the hole overlooks open ground and is therefore highly visible to any passing owl. In addition, areas of rough tussocky grassland are provided for owls to hunt over.

WEST-FACING WALL: Kestrels prefer a shallow open-fronted nest cavity (just under the apex in the picture opposite). Directly below the kestrel nest is a small hole leading to a small, deep nest box for little owls to use. A perch is provided just below and in front of each owl-hole. This, plus the generous roof overhang, makes the site safer for emerging fledgling owls.

SOUTH-FACING WALL: On the warmer south-facing wall are numerous cavities in the mortar to suit a range of invertebrates (spiders, wasps, etc.).

ALL FOUR WALLS: On all four sides, the building has a variety of sparrow-sized openings for hole-nesting bird species. Piles of stones were left at the foot of the refuge to provide a habitat for amphibians and reptiles.

BATS: The lower half of the building is a hibernation area for bats, designed to be permanently dark, cool and damp, with a simple earth floor. A variety of bat species can access this through a wide horizontal slot situated just below the level of an internal floor, which separates the top half of the building from the hibernation area. A second bat hibernation space is accessed through a smaller horizontal slot at the top of the north-facing wall. Breeding bats need a much warmer cavity so the third area for bats (the bat nursery) is situated behind the top of the south-facing wall. This extends right up to the roof tiles. Its entrance hole is at the bottom, thus trapping warm air.

Wildlife tower

For more information:
http://www.barnowltrust.org.uk/infopage.html?Id=202

Table 5.1: Biodiversity features and interventions for landscape design

Feature	Action/How to do it	Benefit
Trees and woodlands	• Mature and veteran trees are important throughout the landscape. Retain and manage sympathetically and encourage continuity through appropriate management of younger trees. • Retain standing and fallen dead and decaying wood, where safe to do so. • Encourage or retain dense understory within woodland. • In some places, deer browsing can impact on woodland understory and regeneration. Where this occurs, control browsing or protect shrubs and saplings. • Maintain woodlands and seek opportunities to create new woodlands where appropriate. • Create or retain lines of trees. These help link up fragmented habitats and can be used by wildlife as corridors. • When planting new trees, select native species of UK provenance and appropriate to the location. • Use a variety of species to provide different height and structure through their growth characteristics and a protracted supply of pollen, nectar and fruit. • For informal tree planting, avoid straight lines and use irregular spacing of 3–4 m centres. • Trees planted in hard surfacing should make use of tree pits or tree trenches. • Do not artificially light trees or treelines.	• Trees and shrubs provide shelter and foraging opportunities for a range of wildlife. • Their flowers provide nectar for bees and other insects and their fruits, food for birds and mammals. • Native and veteran trees support more insects than non-native and immature trees. • Mature trees with holes, dead and decaying wood are particularly valuable for wildlife such as bats, birds, insects and fungi. • Trees provide a number of ecosystem services including carbon capture, surface run-off capture, regulation of temperature, filtering pollutants and acting as noise barriers.
Scrub and shrub	• Plant native species of UK provenance and appropriate to the location. • To create natural spacing between plants and to increase structural diversity, avoid planting in rows and space shrubs irregularly. Avoid replacing all shrubs that die in the first years after planting. • A variety of age and physical structure in scrub and shrub beds will maximise the potential wildlife values. Rotational management of scrub and informal areas of shrubs is important. • Manage over an eight to twelve year cycle. For example, cut a third of a stand every four years or a quarter every three. In formal shrub beds, some species such as dogwood may require a shorter rotation. • Where appropriate and there is a good seed source, encourage natural generation of scrub, for example adjacent to existing wildlife rich habitat. • To maximise the wildlife potential, vary the shape (sinuous edges), size (small groups of bushes to large continuous blocks) and density of stands (scattered, open and closed canopy), avoiding straight rides which can cause wind tunnelling.	• Provides somewhere for wildlife to feed, shelter and breed. • Invertebrates will feed on the foliage and nectar from flowers, while birds and mammals will feed on the foliage, fruits and seeds and also on the insects and invertebrates living on the foliage and among the leaf litter beneath the bushes. • Meanwhile, using the sheltered sinuous edges of stands, bats will forage at night on insects.
Climbing plants	• Locate climbers to cover otherwise bare walls and fences on all aspects. • Where appropriate, incorporate climbers into hedge and shrub planting. • Native climbers include ivy, clematis, honeysuckle and wild rose.	• Climbers can provide nesting sites for birds as well as fruit and insect food. • They are a haven to insects for year-round shelter and as a source of nectar.
Hedges	• Include hedges even in built-up areas as they are important linking features. Locate new hedges so that they will contribute towards forming a local wildlife habitat network with neighbouring hedges, trees, shrubs, scrub, wildflower rich grassland and watercourses. • Provide a variety of hedge structure throughout a site. Height and width are important and utilised in different ways by different wildlife. • Fill gaps with native deciduous species. • Use a range of hedgerow species, preferably native, to provide food throughout the year. • Hedges should be cut every three or four years – annual flailing severely impacts some species of butterfly and moth. It also reduces the amount of flowers and fruits and creates gaps. • Cut only a proportion of hedges in any one year, preferably in late winter (February) after fruits have been eaten and before birds begin nesting in March. • Place standard trees within hedgerows. • Encourage flowers and grasses at the base and margins of hedgerows.	• Many bat and bird species use hedges as commuting flight paths. • Frogs, toads, newts and lizards like dense growth at the base of hedgerows for food, cover and places to hibernate. • Many invertebrate species overwinter in hedges and in associated grass margins. • Thick, dense hedges provide safe roosting and nesting places for birds like thrushes and finches.

continued overleaf

TABLE 5.1 CONTINUED

Feature	Action/How to do it	Benefit
Grassland	• Varying sward height is important. Maintain a mosaic of grasslands over a site. In local parks and green spaces this could mean a mix of short, intermediate and long grass. Where possible, maintain areas of grass cut on a three or four year rotation. • Retain areas of long grass over winter, particularly where adjacent to hedges, shrub and scrub, and beneath trees. • Amenity grassland may be enhanced with spring flowering bulbs, planted in the preceding autumn, re-seeding with wildflowers, plug-planting, green-hay strewing or other appropriate techniques applicable to the site. • Create new flower-rich grasslands by seeding low-fertility substrates. • Avoid cutting flower-rich grassland until after the plants have dropped their seed. Remove cuttings and do not apply any fertilisers. • Compartmentalise grassland areas and stagger rotations to ensure a permanent mosaic of sward structures. Ensure that these mosaics include areas of permanent rough grassland with a litter-layer of 'thatch' at least 7 cm deep.	• Long grass provides habitat for invertebrates in which to shelter and breed as well as a refuge for the eggs, larvae or pupae of some insects such as butterflies and moths to overwinter. • Wildflowers provide nectar and aesthetic value. • It provides a source of insect and seeds for birds and small mammals as well as insects for amphibians and reptiles. • Patches of sparse, open vegetation are important for many insect species as somewhere to bask and for other insects, birds and mammals to forage. • It can protect shrubs and scrub from drying winds, maintaining humidity within and beneath the bushes as well as provide insects that have been feeding on the foliage of bushes somewhere to pupate and complete their life-cycles. • Beneath trees, grass protects the roots from drying, maintains humidity and provides somewhere for insects to pupate after feeding on the foliage of the trees above.
Ponds, lakes, rivers and wetlands	• Avoid development and hard landscaping adjacent to watercourses. • Where required and appropriate, enhance and restore the naturalness of an existing water course. Re-profile steep sides (but see below), buffer with flower-rich grassland, marginal vegetation, trees and shrubs planting and remove culverts. • Manage adjacent trees and shrubs appropriately to provide shelter and prevent them from excessive shading of extensive stretches of the main water body. Consider introducing a suitable management programme for existing tree and shrub cover if required. • Manage marginal and submerged vegetation on a rotational basis, removing about a third each year. • Ditch sides should be cut alternately in a two-year rotation. • On larger areas, encourage development of wet grassland, wet woodland and reed beds where appropriate. • Provide dead wood piles as a habitat for invertebrates, reptiles and small mammals. Replenish as required but do not remove existing material. • Some wildlife, such as water vole and kingfisher, require steeper banks in which to breed. This should be taken into consideration when designing or enhancing wetlands. Where these species occur in an area appropriate work can be targeted. • Restrict or remove artificial lighting from river footpaths as many bat species associated with water avoid light.	• Water features provide important feeding areas for birds, bats and other wildlife. • They have an important role to play as corridors linking the built environment with the surrounding landscape and allowing wildlife to move freely. Buffer strips and marginal vegetation reduce leaching and run-off of pollutants. In conjunction with submerged vegetation, they help maintain water quality.
Gardens	• Managing gardens 'extensively' retains their aesthetic value while being relaxed enough to provide more niches for wildlife. • Reduce reliance on, or avoid the use of, insecticides, herbicides and fertilisers (except see below). • Select flowers, shrubs and trees that are the most useful pollen and nectar sources and provide a long foraging season with something in flower for much of the year. • Preferentially use native species, and a selective variety of non-native plants with documented value to wildlife, taking care to avoid invasive species such as cotoneaster and buddleia which are likely to cause damage by spreading to sensitive habitats in the wider countryside. • Avoid hybrid cultivars where the effort has been put into producing colourful, long-lasting showy flowers at the expense of pollen and nectar. • On a limited budget, scattering a cheap packet of mixed flower seeds onto bare ground can provide a makeshift nectar source and insect-rich addition to the garden with minimal effort and skill required. • Create ponds and small wetlands for the many invertebrates that like water, wet mud or wetland plants. • If and where possible, create different lengths of grass to encourage more insects. • Retain dead and decaying wood where possible. Consider creating ornate horizontal or vertical landscape features from logs around which may be planted nectar-rich flowers and shrubs. Other features that can provide breeding, overwintering sites and year-round shelter include rubble piles and compost heaps. • Where possible plant native hedges as boundaries and avoid the use of fences. • Make use of containers and planters on paved areas such as patios, balconies or terraces. Cluster in groups of different height and shapes and preferably adjacent or near to a water butt. Plant with a mix of nectar-rich flowers and shrubs into peat-free compost. Tubs will need to be fertilised regularly.	• Helps wildlife move safely through the landscape and better links public green space • Can provide a prolonged source of nectar for insects • If managed well can provide somewhere safe to nest for some species of bird

| TABLE 5.1 CONTINUED |

Feature	Action/How to do it	Benefit
Sustainable Drainage Systems (SuDS) – management train includes biodiverse green roofs, living walls, rain gardens, filter strips, bioretention planters, detention, retention basins and wetlands, swales	**SuDS manage rainfall by replicating natural processes of slowing and cleaning water flows and allowing natural percolation into the ground, preventing flooding and pollution.** • The underlying principle to SuDS is its management train which is a series of stages (see left-hand column) mimicking natural processes to incrementally reduce pollution and slow flow rates. • SuDS should be created above ground where they are cheaper to create and manage. Each stage of the train is linked by a conveyance feature such as a swale or in hard landscape, an ornamental rill.	• SuDS can benefit the local environment by reducing the risk of flooding and pollution, and can provide healthy living space of high wildlife value
	Biodiverse green roofs: Discussed in more detail in Chapter 3 • Developments should, where feasible, incorporate green roofs. Retrofitting existing green roofs is also sometimes possible (subject to approval by a structural engineer). The design and planting of green roofs should be informed by local conditions and species of interest. • It should be noted that green roofs provide a different type of habitat to trees and some other habitats and therefore do not directly compensate for their loss. • Roof gardens can also attract wildlife in the way gardens do. Think carefully about the plant species used.	• Biodiverse green roofs provide 'Open Mosaic' pioneer and dry grassland habitats as well as a feeding and foraging area for birds and invertebrates. They provide habitat for breeding invertebrates and a stepping stone habitat in urban areas. There is also potential for small water features to be included
	Living walls: Discussed in more detail in Chapter 3 • Living walls are usually irrigated or are designed to receive run-off from roofs. Living walls should be irrigated by rainwater or grey water and not potable water. • Climbers and creepers on a trellis or cable system often make a more cost efficient and flexible form of living wall which may not require irrigation. • Careful consideration of aspect (orientation) is important as walls planted in sunny locations are prone to drying out rapidly.	• Living walls provide cover for nesting birds. Their flowers can attract nectar feeding insects which in turn provide foraging for bats and birds. Bird, bat and invertebrate boxes and chambers can be located among the vegetation
	Rain gardens • Are shallow depressions with free-draining soil, or planter box. They receive rainfall from downpipes or paved areas (but not car parks; see bioretention planters). • Slows rainfall run-off and improves water quality. • Planted with species able to tolerate short periods of inundation. • Variety of scales and locations from domestic to public realm. • Plants selected for rain gardens must be able to tolerate extremes. Most perennial native plants will do well in rain gardens, including wildflowers, sedges, rushes, ferns and shrubs.	• Flowers can attract nectar feeding insects. Invertebrate 'hotels' can be added along with other habitat features. Acts as a 'stepping stone' habitat in urban areas
	Filter strips • Vegetated areas of broad, flat and gently sloping land that intercept rainfall run-off from a site as overland sheet flow. Can be used anywhere except over vulnerable groundwater aquifers. • Can be sown with native plants to create wildflower meadows, with tussocky grassland.	• Provide habitat for invertebrates, reptiles and amphibians
	Bioretention street planters • Landscaped shallow depression to capture and bio-remediate polluted run-off from paths roads and car parks. • Can be formally landscaped with colourful shrubs and herbaceous plants.	• Provide invertebrate cover and nectar for insects when landscaped with suitable plants as well as foraging areas for birds and other wildlife
	Detention basins • Vegetated depressions which temporarily hold water. • Some designs may hold water longer than others. • Can be sown with native wildflowers and wetland plants.	• Provide habitat for wetland plants and nectar source for insects if seeded with suitable wildflower mix. Will benefit those plants and animals that require ephemeral water bodies as part of their life cycle
	Swales • Swales are linear, shallow channels that transport water from one part of the SuDS management train to the next. • Shallow pools within swales can be created by using small check dams. • Can be under drained. • Can be incorporated into hard landscape as a rill or other concrete channel. • Can be sown with native plants to create wildflower meadows, with tussocky grassland. • Can be planted with native wetland plants, taking care not to impede storm water passage and visibility.	• Provide shelter and somewhere to forage and breed for invertebrates, birds and mammals. Shallow pools upstream of check dams provide opportunities for wetland plants

continued overleaf

| TABLE 5.1 CONTINUED |

Feature	Action/How to do it	Benefit
Artificial nesting and roosting sites	• Incorporate a range of artificial nesting and roosting sites, with the number reflecting the size and scale of the development. • Integrated or built-in features such as roosting or nesting bricks are preferable in new developments; as well as blending in with the structure they provide longer-lasting benefits and require minimal maintenance (see Chapters 3 and 4). • Target species should be selected based on the ecological survey and in liaison with the local authority and wildlife trust. Ensure the size and type of box/brick is appropriate for the target species. • Ensure the location is right for the species (see Table 3.1); birds have different requirements to bats. Think about the height from the ground, direction of sunlight and wind, and ensuring the box/brick is away from disturbance. • Buildings over 7 m high should include a band of swift and/or bat bricks around the top of the building. • Invertebrate features can be incorporated through the use of 'bug hotels' or habitat walls. These are discreet features that are easy and inexpensive to install. • Where appropriate, developments near to watercourses should install kingfisher and/or sand martin features in the watercourse. • Provide habitat for the target species. It is particularly important to provide foraging areas for bats and bees in the landscape design.	• Artificial nesting/roosting boxes provide opportunities for shelter and breeding for wildlife in areas which may have few/reduced options due to habitat disturbance, lack of mature trees/vegetation or changes in building use/practices.

5.1.4 Stepping stones and linkages

One of the greatest negative impacts of development is division of the landscape, resulting in habitat fragmentation. Fragmentation not only blocks the movement of wildlife, but also reduces ecological function as some habitats need to be above a threshold size in order to function properly. This effect can be mediated through the use of linking features, such as tree networks, hedgerows, wildlife corridors, linear parks and eco-passages. If patches cannot be physically linked then 'stepping stone' habitats can be used. These stepping stones are smaller, unconnected areas of preserved or restored habitat, which ease movement through the landscape without necessarily creating direct links. They can take many forms, including any green space, such as gardens, parks, green roofs and living walls. The closer they are to other stepping stones, the more likely they are to act as a continuous corridor.

Buildings, gardens and urban green spaces have considerable potential to contribute to larger and more complex habitat mosaics operating at a landscape scale. Indeed, it is more valuable to consider them in this way than simply as self-contained packages of land.

Green infrastructure, such as gardens, urban green space, living walls and green roofs, has the potential to provide specific nectar and pollen sources for species of invertebrate breeding in nearby woods, meadows or wetlands and therefore create foraging opportunities for bats and birds. Indeed, they have potential to be key foraging areas in landscapes that are otherwise relatively hostile, such as intensive arable settings. For invertebrates, the built environment may provide what is not available in the wider countryside, such as walls and gardens, and encourages colonisation by new species, which can then forage more widely in the surrounding countryside.

With careful planning, it ought to be possible to create an integrated approach to landscape design and management that allows a strong ecological interplay between the built environment and any nearby farmland, woodland, semi-natural grassland, wetland or riverine habitat for a wide range of wildlife. Advice from an experienced ecological advisor should be sought.

Wildflower meadow

5.2 Artificial lighting and wildlife

5.2.1 The bigger picture

Wherever human habitation spreads, so does artificial lighting. However, this increase in lighting has been shown to have an adverse effect on our native wildlife, particularly on those species that have evolved to be active during the hours of darkness. So any development needs to consider carefully what lighting is necessary and minimise any unnecessary lighting, both temporally and spatially. The good news is that, when the impacts on a range of species groups are reviewed, the solutions proposed have commonalities that form the basis of good practice. The following sections review the impacts of artificial lighting on British species groups then offer advice on how to minimise its effects.

5.2.2 Artificial lighting and invertebrates

Artificial light significantly disrupts natural patterns of light and dark, disturbing invertebrate feeding, breeding and movement, which may reduce and fragment populations. Some invertebrates, such as moths, are attracted to artificial lights at night. Moths are known to fly to light from distances varying from 3 m to 130 m, but greater distances up to 500 m have been observed. It is estimated that as many as a third of flying insects that are attracted to street lights will die as a result of their encounter. Insects can die or become injured when they collide with a hot lamp or they can become disoriented and exhausted, making them more susceptible to predation. In addition, the polarisation of light by shiny surfaces attracts insects, particularly egg-laying females, away from water. Reflected light has the potential to attract pollinators and impact on their populations, predators and pollination rates. Many invertebrates depend on the natural rhythms of day–night and seasonal and lunar changes to light levels.

Observations of 337 species of moth between 1968 and 2002 show that 67% of common and widespread species have declined and 21% are endangered or vulnerable (Fox *et al.*, 2006). Changes in extent and quality of habitats are likely to be the cause of this decline, along with pesticide use, eutrophication (the depletion of oxygen in water due to excessive nutrients in water, usually from fertilisers or sewage) affecting plant composition, climate change and light pollution. When looking at population levels, it is not always easy to disentangle the effects of lighting on moths from other impacts of urbanisation. However, we do know that ultra-violet (UV), green and blue light, which have short wavelengths and high frequencies, are seen by most insects and are highly attractive to them. Where a light source has a UV component, male moths in particular will be drawn to it. Most light-induced changes in physiology and behaviour are likely to be detrimental. Even without a UV element, the mere presence of even near monochromatic light will affect the behaviour of certain moth species. They discern it to be 'light', so they do not fly to feed or mate.

5.2.3 Artificial lighting and birds

When considering the impacts of lighting on birds, there are several aspects of bird behaviour to take into account. The phenomenon of robins and other birds singing by the light of a street light is well known, and research has shown that singing does not have a significant effect on the bird's body mass regulation (Pollard, 2009). However, it was felt that the continual lack of sleep is likely to be detrimental to the bird's survival and could disrupt the long-term circadian rhythm that dictates the onset of the breeding season. It also has the potential to cause hormone disruption.

Other UK bird species that are particularly sensitive to artificial lighting are long-eared owls, black-tailed godwit and stone curlew. In a study in Spain over an eight-year period (Rodríguez *et al.*, 2006), it was found that long-eared owls selected nest sites that were not in lit areas.

Some birds have changed their behaviour to adapt to artificial lighting. Edward Drewitt, a researcher based in Bristol, has found that the peregrine falcons that have moved into our cities and use our tall buildings as a substitute for cliffs have made a further adjustment in their behaviour. In looking at the prey remains taken from a number of feeding sites, Drewitt and Dixon (2008) found clear evidence of prey species being caught at night.

Another opportunist bird, the gull, has also found street lighting can be to its advantage. In our towns and cities, gulls are known to leave at dusk to roost elsewhere, only to return hours later to feed on the discarded takeaways before the refuse collectors have a chance to clear them.

Many species of bird migrate at night and there are well-documented cases of the mass mortality of nocturnal migrating birds as they strike tall lit buildings.

5.2.4 Artificial lighting and mammals

A number of our British mammals are nocturnal and have adapted their lifestyle so that they are active in the dark in order to avoid predators. Artificial illumination of the areas in which these mammals are active and foraging is likely to be disturbing to their normal activities and so their foraging areas could be lost in this way. It is thought that the most pronounced effect is likely to be on small mammals due to their need to avoid predators. However, this in itself has a knock-on effect on those predators.

The detrimental effect of artificial lighting is most clearly seen in bat populations. Our resident bat species have all suffered dramatic reductions in their numbers over the past century. Light falling on a bat roost exit point, regardless of species, will at least delay bats from emerging, which shortens the amount of time available to them for foraging. As the main peak of nocturnal insect abundance occurs at and soon after dusk, a delay in emergence means this vital time for feeding is missed. At worst, the bats may feel compelled to abandon the roost. Bats use the same roosts over many years and disturbance of this sort can have a significant effect on the future of a colony. It is likely to be deemed a breach of the national and European legislation that protects British bats and their roosts.

In addition to causing disturbance to bats at the roost, artificial lighting can affect the feeding behaviour of bats and their use of commuting routes. There are two aspects to this: one is the attraction that UV light has to a range of insects; the other is the presence of lit conditions.

As mentioned above, many night-flying species of insect are attracted to lamps that emit a UV component. Studies have shown that noctules, serotines, pipistrelle and Leisler's bats take advantage of the concentration of insects around white street lights as a source of prey, but that this behaviour is not true for all bat species. The slower flying, broad-winged species, such as long-eared bats, barbastelle, greater and lesser horseshoe bats and the *Myotis* species (which include Brandt's,

LIGHTING – WARREN FOOTPATH, RICHMOND, LONDON

The Warren Footpath runs along the Thames River between Richmond and Twickenham in south London. Richmond upon Thames Council needed to replace the existing low sodium lighting but wanted a solution that would reduce the impact on the bat species that use the river for foraging. The council worked with the Thames Landscape Strategy, the Bat Conservation Trust and Philips Lighting to deliver an intelligent lighting innovation that could deliver bright white LED light, which would ensure that residents feel safe and secure when using the footpath but would not flood the area with too much light and disturb the nocturnal wildlife living in the area.

THE SOLUTION

The centrepiece of the lighting scheme introduced by Philips was LumiMotion, an LED outdoor lighting technology detector, control device and communicator all in one. By intelligently sensing activity around it, LumiMotion adjusts the lighting to a maximum level when there is activity and to extremely low levels when there is no activity – when someone approaches, light levels will rise from 20% to 100%, or to any level in between those percentages as required. The system is also programmed to recognise and communicate to neighbouring street lighting fittings via radio, so that presence and absence is relayed. Thus, a 'carpet of light' is created as a person walks along the stretch of path where the system has been installed, guiding them along.

The system incorporates a sensor and camera within the fitting which is able to detect activity within a 20–30 m diameter circle – minus the area that is in shadow of the mast. The video detection is based on pixel changes instead of images. The system can be tailored to take into account differing street widths, light levels and even obstacles such as trees or construction in streets.

Richmond upon Thames Council, like all local authorities, is under pressure to improve energy efficiency in order to comply with legislation and carbon reduction targets. The lighting system introduced by Philips will save the Council up to 80% in energy costs and reduce light spill by more than 50%. This LED lighting solution focuses light on the footpath rather than into the trees or onto the river, where nocturnal wildlife shelter and forage, ensuring there is no light wastage. Ken MacKenzie, Project Implementation Manager for the Thames Landscape Strategy comments:

> *Philips' innovative lighting solution introduced along Warren Footpath has transformed the area to the benefit of both local people and wildlife, and helped us take a step forward in meeting our sustainability targets. The initial results look extremely promising – not only are we saving energy and cutting costs, but those bat species that shy away from light are being seen again in greater numbers since LumiMotion was installed.*

Before showing glare of sodium lighting on the Warren Footpath

After showing cutoff providing by LED lighting on the Warren Footpath

New intelligent lighting on the Warren Footpath

The intelligent LED lighting system on the Warren Footpath has a directional cutoff ensuring minimal light spillage as well as motion sensors that detect when to increase and decrease brightness.
Credit: Philips Lighting

whiskered, Daubenton's, Natterer's and Bechstein's bats) generally avoid street lights. It is also known that insects are attracted to lit areas from further afield. This could result in adjacent habitats supporting reduced numbers of insects, causing a further impact on the ability of light-avoiding bats to feed. It is noticeable that most of Britain's rarest bats are among those species listed as avoiding light.

Lighting can be particularly harmful if it illuminates important foraging habitats, such as river corridors, woodland edges and hedgerows used by bats. Studies have shown that continuous lighting along roads creates barriers that some bat species cannot cross. Stone *et al.* (2009) used an experimental approach to provide the first evidence of a negative effect of artificial light pollution on the commuting behaviour of a threatened bat species. High-pressure sodium lights were installed that mimic the intensity and light spectra of street lights along commuting routes of lesser horseshoe bats. Bat activity was reduced dramatically and the onset of commuting behaviour was delayed in the presence of lighting, with no evidence of them acclimatising to the light. These results demonstrate that light pollution may have significant negative impacts upon the selection of flight routes by bats. Current research is looking at whether light in the amber part of the spectrum (> 500 nm) could be less disturbing to bats.

These are just a few examples of the effects of artificial lighting on British wildlife, with migratory fish, amphibians, some flowering plants, a number of bird species, glow-worms and a range of other invertebrates all exhibiting changes in their behaviour as a result of this unnatural lighting.

5.2.5   Skyglow

The detrimental effect of artificial lighting on our wildlife is not the only reason for reviewing its provision in the built environment. The Campaign for Dark Skies (CfDS), an initiative of the British Astronomical Association launched in 1989, is campaigning against skyglow, which has steadily increased since the 1950s. Usually the result of poorly designed street lights shining above the horizontal into the sky, skyglow is exacerbated by carelessly mounted security lights and sports lighting. It is the shared aim of the CfDS, those concerned about our carbon footprint, conservationists and the Institution of Lighting Professionals to minimise the use of artificial lighting.

5.2.6   How to minimise the impact of artificial light

- Do not provide excessive lighting. Use only the minimum amount of light needed for safety.
- Minimise light spill. Eliminate any bare bulbs and any upward-pointing light. The spread of light should be kept near to or below the horizontal. Flat cutoff lanterns or accessories should be used to shield or direct light to where it is required.
- Use narrow-spectrum bulbs to lower the range of species affected by lighting. Use light sources that emit minimal UV light and avoid the white and blue wavelengths of the light spectrum so as not to attract lots of insects. Lights should peak higher than 550 nm or use glass lantern covers to filter UV light. White LED lights do not emit UV, but they have still been shown to disturb slow-flying bat species (Stone *et al.*, 2012).
- Reduce the height of lighting columns. Light at a low level reduces impact. However, higher mounting heights allow lower main beam angles, which can assist in reducing glare.

- For pedestrian lighting, use low-level lighting that is as directional as possible. It should be below 3 lux at ground level, but preferably below 1 lux.
- Increase the spacing of lanterns.
- Use embedded road lights to illuminate the roadway and light only high-risk stretches of roads, such as crossings and junctions, allowing headlights to provide any necessary illumination at other times.
- Limit the times that lights are switched on to provide some dark periods. Use timers to reduce the hours lit and tailor this specifically to wildlife that would be affected, as compatible to human health and safety requirements.
- Use lighting design software and professional lighting designers to predict where light spill will occur.
- Avoid using reflective surfaces under lights.
- Use temporary close-boarded fencing until vegetation matures, to shield sensitive areas from lighting.
- Some locations are particularly sensitive to light pollution and so lighting schemes in these areas should be carefully planned. In particular, lighting should not be installed near ponds, lakes, rivers and the sea, areas of high conservation value, sites supporting particularly light-sensitive species of conservation significance (e.g. glow-worms, rare moths, slow-flying bats) and habitat used by protected species.
- The potential impacts of light pollution on wildlife should be a routine consideration in the Ecological Impact Assessment process. Risks should be eliminated or minimised wherever possible.

Further information

More information on lighting and wildlife can be obtained from the following sources.

Organisations:
- Institution of Lighting Professionals (ILP): www.theilp.org.uk
- Bat Conservation Trust (BCT): www.bats.org.uk
- Campaign for Dark Skies (CfDS): www.britastro.org/dark-skies; and
- Bats and Lighting Research project: www.batsandlighting.co.uk/index.html.

Publications:
- Bruce-White, C. and Shardlow, M. (2011) *A Review of the Impact of Artificial Light on Invertebrates.* Buglife.
- Royal Commission on Environmental Pollution (2009). *Artificial light in the environment.* London: HMSO.
- Rich, C. and Longcore, T. (eds) (2006) *The Ecological Consequences of Artificial Night Lighting.* Washington, DC: Island Press.

5.3   Roads and wildlife

Roads can harm wildlife, not only through direct collisions with vehicles, but also through loss of roosts, nests and foraging habitats and by fragmentation of the landscape. Roads create open spaces that many species are reluctant to cross. The barrier effect of roads is further increased by the sudden movement and noise of traffic, road and vehicle lighting, and collisions with vehicles.

Roads also affect flying animals. Most species of bat fly relatively close to the ground or close to trees and hedges. Those that do cross roads typically do so at traffic height; therefore the risk of collision is high. Recent research has shown that roads also have a major negative impact on bat foraging activity and the number of species present (Berthinussen and Altringham, 2011). Roads can impact wildlife in the following ways:

- fragmenting habitat through barrier effects;
- severing wildlife commuting routes;
- collisions with vehicles;
- disturbance from lights;
- sudden movement and noise;
- decreasing foraging activity: feeding areas can be lost or reduced in quality along the route of the road and in the surrounding area.

Awareness and mitigation of the impacts of roads is an essential part in the planning and design of developments. If at all possible, design vegetated crossing points near existing wildlife paths and commuting routes. These eco-passages (also called 'animal bridges' or 'wildlife crossings') can be in the form of different types of underpass (tunnels and culverts) and overpass (hop-overs, elevated verges and green bridges). They should not be artificially lit and should be screened (using vegetation or boarding) from lights and noise.

Roads are not the only structures causing habitat fragmentation. Railways, canals, electricity power lines and pipelines also create divides. The use of eco-passages should also be considered in these cases. The effectiveness of such schemes in helping biodiversity should be monitored, pre and post construction, to inform the design of future crossings.

5.4 Bird collisions with windows and buildings

Birds collide with windows and other glass installations on a regular basis, because they cannot see the obstacle created by the glass. Many die as a result of the impact. Many people have, understandably, concerns about the effect that such collisions might have on UK bird populations.

There are a number of things people can do to reduce the negative impacts of a building they are in charge of:

- In domestic houses in particular, silhouettes of birds and other such figures on the outside of the window will help break the illusion and reduce the number of collisions.
- While silhouettes may also work on larger buildings, they might not be practical. American Bird Conservancy has produced a booklet containing a range of ideas on how to make a building more bird-friendly.
- Birds can see UV light. A new type of glass called Ornilux, marketed by a German company, incorporates into the glass a web of strands that reflect UV light. Birds can see these strands and, according to a number of tests, successfully avoid collision. Concerned individuals can check local planning applications for tall glass-fronted office blocks, express their concern to the consenting authority and request that the planning consent specifies the use of Ornilux glass in the new building.
- When planning new buildings along birds' existing daily flight and migration routes, the collision risk should be established, and either the design or arrangement of buildings along the flight path adjusted to minimise impact, or such areas avoided altogether.

Birds, dead through collision with buildings, recovered by FLAP volunteers at a handful of buildings in Toronto during the 2009 spring and fall migration seasons. For more information visit: http://flap.org

- Turning lights off when office buildings are not occupied not only saves energy, but also cuts down the number of birds that get attracted to and collide with the building.

5.4.1 Further reading

- Drewitt, A. L. and Langston, R. H. W. (2008) Collision effects of wind-powered generators and other obstacles on birds. *Annals of the New York Academy of Science*, 1134, pp. 233–266.
- Sheppard, C. (2011) *Bird-friendly Building Design*. The Plains, VA: American Bird Conservancy. Available at: www.abcbirds.org/abcprograms/policy/collisions/pdf/Bird-friendly_Building_Guide_WEB.pdf

5.5 The impact of wind turbines on biodiversity

Wind farms and wind turbines are important for the development of sustainable energy. However, it is imperative that their possible harmful effects on bats, birds and other wildlife (both direct and indirect) are taken into account before deciding on the siting of wind turbines, large and small.

It is widely accepted that wind farms and wind turbines generally present three main areas of potential risk to bats and birds:

- displacement through indirect loss of habitat: bats and birds avoiding the wind farm and its surrounding area due to turbine operation and maintenance or visitor disturbance. Displacement can include barrier effects, in which wildlife are deterred from using their normal routes to feeding or roosting grounds;
- death through collision or interaction with turbine blades: this includes barotrauma in bats (fatal lung damage resulting from the sudden drop in air pressure close to the turbine blades); and
- direct habitat loss: through construction of wind farm infrastructure.

Proper surveys should be done to determine the correct siting of wind turbines to mitigate adverse impacts to wildlife.

5.5.1 Further reading

- www.bats.org.uk/pages/wind_turbines.html
- www.snh.gov.uk/docs/B999258.pdf
- http://publications.naturalengland.org.uk/publication/35010
- www.rspb.org.uk/ourwork/policy/windfarms/index.aspx
- www.snh.gov.uk/planning-and-development/renewable-energy/onshore-wind/windfarm-impacts-on-birds-guidance

FURTHER INFORMATION
Additional sources of information regarding designing for biodiversity are provided in the References. The following internet resources may also be helpful:

- Bat Conservation Trust, Landscape and Urban Design for Bats and Biodiversity: www.bats.org.uk/pages/landscapedesign.html
- Buglife: www.buglife.org.uk/getinvolved/gardening/gardencreepycrawlies
- Bumblebee Conservation Trust: bumblebeeconservation.org/get-involved/gardening-for-bees/
- Butterfly Conservation: www.butterfly-conservation.org/downloads/48/gardening.html
- Exeter Residential Design Guide: www.exeter.gov.uk/CHttpHandler.ashx?id=14277&p=0
- RSPB Homes for Wildlife: www.rspb.org.uk/hfw
- www.floralocale.org
- www.puddleplants.co.uk
- www.raingardens.info
- www.susdrain.org
- www.wildseed.co.uk

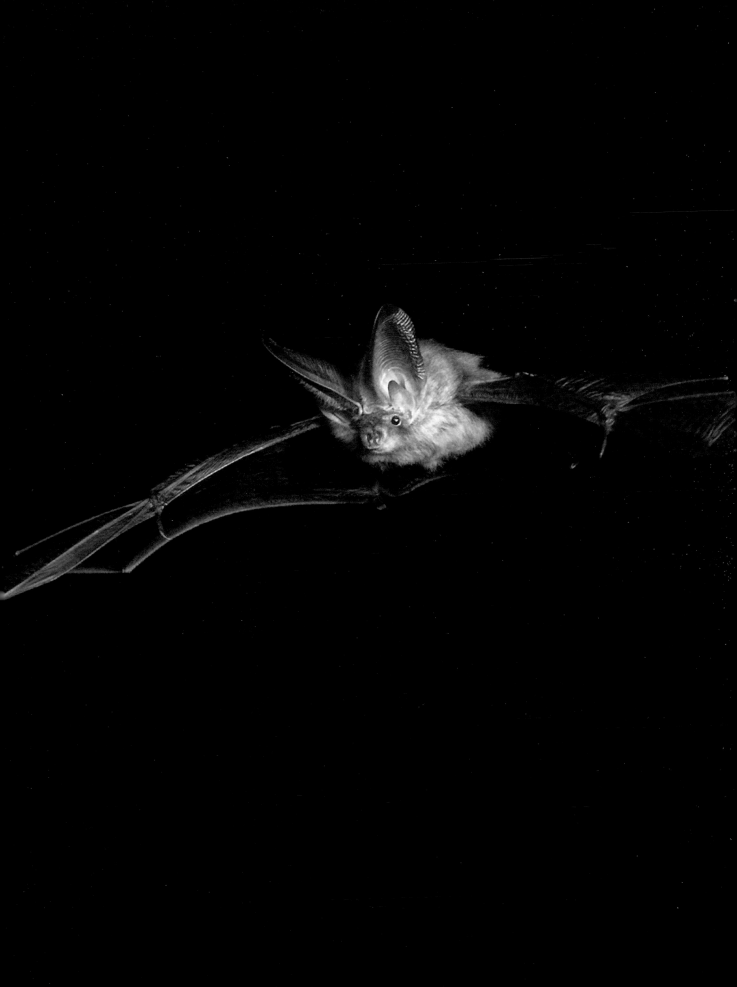

Engagement and monitoring

The completion of a building development is just the start of creating a living built environment. Steps should be taken to ensure that the principles of integrating biodiversity are continued beyond the direct involvement of the design and development team. Wildlife is a great way to connect people with their environment. Buildings with design features for encouraging wildlife can give occupants the chance to engage with their environment and provide opportunities to get involved with the ongoing maintenance, monitoring and improvement of the features built for biodiversity.

Not all biodiversity features can or should be easily accessible (some green roofs, for example) but by thinking about engagement and which features can or need to be accessed by the public, building users or occupants, opportunities for engagement and monitoring can be maximised.

In the nascent field of building for biodiversity it is important that sites are monitored so that lessons can be learnt, success gauged and sites improved and modified. Monitoring biodiversity can also inform the management and maintenance of the site; for example, by identifying bat roosts, nest sites and other flora and fauna they can be protected and conserved. The growth of 'citizen science', where the community can contribute biological records and participate in biodiversity surveys, brings together monitoring and engagement with the environment. There are now a range of initiatives that allow people to engage with their local environment, from guerrilla gardening to bird watches.

6.1   Community involvement

Getting involved with the environment is good for health, well-being and community cohesion. Biodiverse buildings and developments provide great opportunities for enjoying wildlife and getting active outdoors and in shared spaces in the local area. Approximately 80% of the population of the UK live in urban areas (according to the Office for National Statistics), and for most of these people local green spaces provide the best opportunities for contact with nature.

Environmental projects with community involvement have become increasingly popular and there is a wealth of resources and organisations working in this area. Projects can include gardening schemes, allotment projects and park planting, as well as biodiversity monitoring projects. These projects establish connections with nature, and they use the natural environment to engage with and benefit people and communities. Environmental projects, in particular, have proven to be successful in involving the public, encouraging volunteering, raising awareness and educating and engaging with new people – all of which bring substantial benefits to individuals and the wider community alike.

Transition Towns are an exciting initiative, started in the UK but now spreading globally. A Transition Town is a place where there is a community-led process that helps that city, town, village or neighbourhood to become stronger and happier by starting up projects relating to food, transport, energy, education, housing, waste, arts, etc. These are small-scale local responses to the global challenges of climate change, economic hardship and shrinking reserves of cheap energy.

More information on setting up a community involvement project is available by searching the following websites:

www.bats.org.uk/batsforall
www.wildlifetrusts.org
www.cabe.org.uk (see the publications *It's Our Space* (2007), *Making Contracts Work for Wildlife* (2006) and *Start with the Park* (2005).
www.transitionnetwork.org

Bat Box building with community groups

6.1.1 Gardens

There are a number of garden projects which encourage community involvement. The British Trust for Ornithology (BTO) runs a Garden BirdWatch programme which requires only basic knowledge and involves collecting simple records of birds seen in a garden. The BTO also runs a Nest Record Scheme, which uses simple techniques and so is accessible to everyone, helping to encourage and involve newcomers in a community group. Similarly, BTO runs a project called the Nest Box Challenge. Community groups (or individuals) can register nest boxes in their local area and record what is inside at regular intervals. The Royal Society for the Protection of Birds (RSPB) runs a number of garden-related projects, including The Big Garden Bird Watch. It also runs Homes for Wildlife, which is an online community providing advice and encouragement to individuals or groups who want to make their gardens and local green spaces richer in wildlife by getting involved in practical activities such as digging ponds and planting trees.

Register the location of your integrated bat box with the Bat Conservation Trust at www.bats.org.uk/boxplot.

The Wildlife Trusts and Royal Horticultural Society run The Big Wildlife Garden – a national competition to garden for wildlife. The Big Wildlife Garden is free for anyone of any age to join and is open to individuals, schools and community groups.

www.bats.org.uk/garden
www.bto.org/volunteer-surveys/nrs
www.bto.org/volunteer-surveys/gbw
www.rspb.org.uk/birdwatch/
www.rspb.org.uk/hfw/
www.bigwildlifegarden.org.uk

6.1.2 School involvement

Many of the major conservation charities run programmes for schools and have educational resources available on their websites to support engagement with the environment in the classroom and beyond. In addition, there are a number of initiatives dedicated to supporting schools which are getting involved with their environment, including 'ecoschools', which seeks to embed sustainability into every aspect of a school, and a National Framework for Sustainable Schools.

Many education resources may be found on the RSPB 'For schools' homepage. In addition, the RSPB runs the Big Schools' Birdwatch and the Wildlife Action Awards and provides advice to make school grounds better places for wildlife.

www.bats.org.uk/education
www.keepbritaintidy.org/ecoschools/aboutecoschools
http://se-ed.co.uk/edu/sustainable-schools
www.rspb.org.uk/schools
www.rspb.org.uk/schoolswatch
www.rspb.org.uk/youth/learn/waa
www.rspb.org.uk/ourwork/teaching/schoolgrounds

6.2   Monitoring and research

Understanding the effects of a development on the biodiversity found within and adjacent to its footprint is important for reporting on biodiversity change as a result of planning consents (see Section 2.2) – this type of investigation may well be carried out by the project ecologist. However, any information about changes in the abundance and diversity of species and habitats that is recorded in a methodical way will also prove valuable for learning about the impacts of particular aspects of development and how best to maximise positive outcomes. A selection of recording techniques available to all is included below, a number of which could additionally help to encourage community involvement and cohesion.

6.2.1   The National Bat Monitoring Programme (NBMP)

The NBMP, organised by the Bat Conservation Trust since 1996, runs a number of national annual surveys through its volunteer network, which comprises over 2,000 dedicated volunteers. The core surveys are: the Colony Roost Count Survey (volunteers count bats emerging from roosts at sunset); the Hibernation Survey (licensed bat workers identify and count bats found in hibernation sites, such as

Tate Modern Peregrine Watch with the RSPB

tunnels and caves in winter); and the Field and Waterway Surveys (volunteers count bat passes while walking transects). These are aimed at all skill levels, from beginner to expert, and repeat visits are carried out at each site in order to produce statistically robust long-term trends (www.bats.org.uk). Online recording pages are being developed for all of these surveys, starting with the roost count and hibernation surveys. This enables volunteers to download the survey forms and instructions, input their data online, and view summaries of the data from each site they monitor.

Another survey, the Sunset/Sunrise Survey, is designed to engage new volunteers in bat monitoring through collecting basic information on the presence of bats and where they are roosting. Participants do not need previous experience or special equipment, as the survey method involves using simple visual clues to record bats in flight and swarming at their roosts. Experienced bat surveyors have also taken part in this survey in order to track down where bats are roosting in their local area. The majority of participants record seeing bats in flight, and several new roosts are located each year through spotting bats swarming around structures before sunrise. Participants who have discovered roosts that they can visit on an annual basis are encouraged to then take part in the Colony Roost Count Survey. The more detailed information they collect on bat numbers at the roost can then be fed into UK species population trends.

Training workshops and online resources are provided so that volunteers are equipped with the bat detector and species identification and survey skills required to carry out NBMP surveys. The aims are to improve survey coverage across the UK, refresh volunteers' existing skills and knowledge, and help volunteers develop new skills, so that they can begin taking part or progress to more advanced surveys within the NBMP and other voluntary bat monitoring projects.

More information on NBMP surveys, results and training is available at www.bats.org.uk.

Detecting bats on a bat walk

Get involved with bat conservation in your area by joining a local bat group: www.bats.org.uk/pages/find_your_local_bat_group.html

6.2.2 The RSPB National Swift Inventory

The National Swift Inventory is a map-based conservation tool for local authorities, architects, developers and ecologists to use to find out about reported sightings of swifts and their nests. The Inventory helps the targeting of protection measures into those places where the birds occur and may be most threatened.

The Inventory seeks two sets of information from members of the public:

- sightings of 'screaming swifts' at roof level: this behaviour usually indicates that the birds are nesting somewhere close by;
- sightings of birds entering buildings: this indicates the presence of nesting birds, but is generally more difficult behaviour to observe.

Other details that are recorded for sightings include the age of building and if the site is considered under threat in any way; for example, if the building is derelict.

Submitting records to the National Swift Inventory

Members of the public are encouraged to enter details online, reporting where swifts may potentially be or are known to be nesting. The information can be entered on the RSPB website at: www.rspb.org.uk/helpswifts

Records from anywhere in the country can be entered by an individual. It is usually only necessary to enter one record per site each year. However, the recording of sites annually is encouraged where possible. In so doing, the inventory is kept up to date.

Using the Inventory to protect sites and target provision of new sites

The data gathered are uploaded annually to the National Biodiversity Network (NBN) website. The information is then available online, and can be used to help inform where to target nest protection and provision for swifts when planning building or renovation work.

What if I put up a new nest for swifts?

If you provide a new nest of any kind, or have put up one in recent years, you are invited to notify the RSPB. A form for this purpose can be downloaded from the RSPB's website: www.rspb.org.uk/thingstodo/surveys/swifts/newnestsites.aspx. The information obtained will ultimately be used to analyse patterns of occupancy from variables of box design and location in order to improve future advice about nest requirements.

6.2.3 Garden bird surveys

Both the RSPB and the BTO run monitoring programmes. These are appropriate for a variety of skill levels, and require varying amounts of time commitment. For example, the RSPB's Big Garden Birdwatch requires just one hour of your time on one day in January. Others, such as the BTO's Garden BirdWatch programme and Nest Record Scheme, require only basic knowledge but a longer commitment of time, including enough time during each week to observe birds in the householder's own garden. Other surveys include the Breeding Bird Survey (which is the main source of population trends information about the UK's widespread birds), BirdTrack and the Nest Box Challenge (www.bto.org and www.rspb.org.uk).

6.2.4 Butterfly transects and counting moths

Butterfly Conservation runs ongoing programmes to monitor butterflies in the UK, involving over 10,000 volunteer recorders. The data gathered are used by the Government to indicate the health of the environment. The surveys are aimed at both beginners and experienced recorders. Data are collected annually to monitor changes in the abundance of butterflies, using the well-established transect methodology – volunteers walk a transect and record butterflies along the route on a regular basis over a number of years. Other surveys simply require volunteers to submit records of sightings from their back garden. There are also regular counts of moths, organised to improve knowledge about the larger moths in the UK and hence their conservation. These are based on a simple survey methodology, and moth sightings are submitted online to Butterfly Conservation (www.butterfly-conservation.org).

6.2.5 Online recording and species identification

A number of websites enable registered users to upload photographs of wildlife sightings, together with details such as location and likely species identification, and have the species verified by other users, including designated experts. The websites also enable searches to be carried out by geographic area so that users can find out which species have been recorded in a specific locality. These sites are useful tools for verifying species records at a site and for finding out what else has been recorded in the vicinity, although species that are difficult to photograph or where a licence to disturb would be required, such as bats, are largely excluded.

- www.ispot.org.uk
- www.brc.ac.uk/irecord
- www.inaturalist.org

Species record searches can also be carried out on the National Biodiversity Network Gateway (data.nbn.org.uk), which contains publicly accessible records from a wide variety of recording schemes across the UK.

JARGON BUSTER

The authors wishes to acknowledge use of material from the Scottish Environmental Design Association (SEDA), the Ecos Renews, Environmental Building Solutions, EESC '11 and CIRIA RP656 Design for Deconstruction (Bill Addis)

AIR BARRIER
Comprises materials and/or components which are air impervious or virtually so, separating conditioned spaces (heated, cooled or humidity controlled, usually inside) from unconditioned spaces (unheated, uncooled, humidity uncontrolled, usually outside).

AIR EXFILTRATION
The uncontrolled outward leakage of indoor air through cracks, discontinuities and other unintentional openings in the building envelope. In winter the air is likely to be heated, and heated air exfiltration will result in uncontrolled heat loss and potential interstitial condensation risk.

AIR INFILTRATION
The uncontrolled inward leakage of outdoor air through cracks, discontinuities and other unintentional openings in the building envelope. In winter the air is likely to be cold, and cold air infiltration will result in uncontrolled draughts, leading to thermal discomfort and condensation risk.

AIR LEAKAGE PATH
A route by which air enters or leaves a building, or flows through a component, and can destroy the integrity of the fabric's acoustic, fire, thermal, wind, weather, water and airtightness performance. During the heating season, air passing through air leakage paths will carry heat, increase energy demand and increase the carbon footprint of the building and its occupants.

AIRTIGHTNESS
This relates to the 'leakiness' of a building. The smaller the leakage for a given pressure difference across a building, the tighter the building envelope.

AIRTIGHTNESS LAYER
A layer built into the external envelope to minimise air infiltration/exfiltration.

BAP – BIODIVERSITY ACTION PLAN
Describes the UK's biological resources, and commits a detailed plan for conserving and enhancing species and habitats, in addition to promoting public awareness and contributing to international conservation efforts.

BARS – BIODIVERSITY ACTION REPORTING SYSTEM
This is the UK's Biodiversity Action Plan reporting system. It includes national, local and company Biodiversity Action Plans (BAPs) and all UK Biodiversity Strategies and Action Plans. Reports on status and trends, as well as targets and outcomes for species on the UK BAP list are available to download on the Biodiversity Action Reporting System website (www.ukbap-reporting.org.uk/default.asp).

BIODIVERSITY
Biodiversity (biological diversity) is the number and variety of all living organisms, including genetic, species and ecosystem diversity. It includes all wildlife, plants, bacteria and viruses, and their habitats, and this variety is vital to a well-functioning ecosystem.

BOCC (BIRD OF CONSERVATION CONCERN)
The UK's leading bird conservation organisations have worked together on the third quantitative review of the status of the birds (BOCC3) that occur regularly here. A total of 246 species have been assessed and placed on one of three lists – green, amber and red – indicating an increasing level of conservation concern.

BREEAM
BREEAM (BRE Environmental Assessment Method) is a sustainability assessment tool. Sustainability assessment tools are used to measure the sustainability of a construction or building, including the contribution played by recycled and secondary aggregates, via an index or scoring system.

CARBON SEQUESTRATION
Carbon sequestration in construction usually refers to building products derived from plant materials such as wood and hemp, where CO_2 is absorbed as part of the growing process.

CELLULAR BLOCK
(see Extruded cellular fired-clay block construction)

CEMENT PARTICLEBOARD
Contains particles of wood fibre (like chipboard (wood particle board)) bound together by cement. It has strength, moisture resistance, durability and thermal mass.

CLTP – CROSS-LAMINATED TIMBER PANELS
A method of construction which makes use of forest thinnings of small diameter.

CODE FOR SUSTAINABLE HOMES
An environmental assessment method and national standard for rating and certifying the performance of new homes.

DECREMENT DELAY
Refers to the time it takes for heat generated by the sun to transfer from the outside to the inside of the building envelope and affect the internal conditions.

ECOLOGICAL ASSESSMENT
A comprehensive assessment of the likely ecological impacts of proposed developments on a site. This can take place on any type or size of site.

ECOLOGY SURVEY
A survey providing baseline information about the ecological characteristics of a site, including the presence or potential for protected species and their habitats.

ECOSYSTEM SERVICES
These refer to the benefits that humankind receives from natural ecosystems including many resources and processes.

EIA – ENVIRONMENTAL IMPACT ASSESSMENT
For larger projects or for those in more sensitive sites where projects are likely to have a significant environmental effect, an Environmental Impact Assessment (EIA) will be a legal requirement. An EIA covers a broad range of factors, such as the effects on soil, water, air, climate and landscape, and the effects on humans, as well as species and habitat considerations.

EMBODIED ENERGY
The components of embodied energy are the growing or mining, manufacturing, transportation, assembly or installation, demolition and disposal energy.

EPI – ENVIRONMENTAL PERFORMANCE INDICATORS
Environmental Performance Indicators (EPI) are needed when evaluating the environmental performance of, for example, activities, processes, hardware and services.

EUROPEAN PROTECTED SPECIES (EPS)
Certain types of animal and plant are recognised as species of European Community interest and in need of strict legal protection. The list of species protected under European law includes bats, otters and newts.

EUROPEAN PROTECTED SPECIES (EPS) LICENCE
Some activities or works can affect protected species or their habitats, and in these instances a licence is necessary. To make sure you do not break the law, you must apply for a licence if you propose to do anything that would affect protected species or their breeding, resting or shelter places in ways the legislation makes illegal.

EXTERNAL INSULATED RENDER SYSTEMS (EIRS)
External finish to external solid walls (historic (where permitted): stone or brick; modern: brick or blockwork).

EXTERNAL WEATHER ENVELOPE
Consists of roof (pitched shallow or flat roofs) or roof terraces and recessed balconies, external walls and doors, windows and roof lights. Occasionally there are also soffits to projecting or bridging rooms over drives and passageways, or a soffit of suspended ground floors.

GREEN INFRASTRUCTURE (GI)
A term used to refer to the living network of green spaces, water and other environmental features in both urban and rural areas.

HABITAT
The area or environment where an organism or ecological community normally lives or occurs.

HABITAT CREATION
The establishment of a new habitat, often required as compensation for development and loss of an ecosystem. Can include bat box installations and pond creations.

LUMINAIRE
Light fitting or unit designed to distribute light from a lamp.

MOISTURE MASS
Walls with absorbent surfaces are said to have moisture mass. Materials with moisture-absorbent properties, for example unfired clay, can be used as a plaster skim or finish on walls and ceilings. If there is a sufficient amount of the material and when the air is saturated, the clay can absorb moisture from the atmosphere and hold it in the body of the material until conditions improve, then release the moisture again.

MOISTURE TRANSPORT
The ability of a material to transport moisture from one place to another, for example a place where interstitial condensation or moisture ingress is occurring to a place where it can evaporate away when conditions permit.

PARGE COAT
A single base coat of plaster applied to the inside face of masonry walls to achieve a level of airtightness before applying plasterboard drylining.

PASSIVE SOLAR ORIENTATION
Orientating towards or facing the sun, and positioning rooms, roosts or boxes on the correct side of the building to gain the heat. Overshadowing by other building and trees can complicate this process.

PV – PHOTOVOLTAIC CELLS
A module incorporating a semiconductor that generates electricity when exposed to daylight or sunlight.

RAINSCREEN CLADDING
A design principle involving cladding made of screens with open joints that predominantly drains rainwater down the outside face but permits some wind-driven rainwater to pass through the open joints creating internal air pressure to resist most of the rain passing through the remainder of the joints.

SIPS STRUCTURAL INSULATION PANEL SYSTEM
A panelised MMC (modern method of construction) using foamed insulation as a part of the structural performance of the panel, thus enabling reduced thickness of panel while maintaining strength.

SOLAR BLINKERS
These are sunlight and daylight shading blades besides windows, usually placed to the south of east- or west-facing windows.

SOLAR GAIN
Direct solar radiation from the sun's rays passing through windows, roof lights and glazed areas to provide warmth to rooms and spaces. Optimal gains come from south to south-west-facing glazed areas. Solar rays falling on opaque external masonry will warm the masonry and after a long period will start to warm the interior. Solar rays falling on opaque external lightweight building fabric like timber frame and metal cladding will pass through to warm the interior relatively quickly.

SOLAR SHADING SHELVES (BRISE SOLEIL)
These are sunlight and daylight shading shelves above windows.

SUSTAINABLE DRAINAGE SYSTEMS (SUDS)
Surface water drainage methods that take account of water quantity, water quality and amenity issues are collectively referred to as sustainable drainage systems (SuDS). SuDS components can include soakaways, ponds or wetlands but also permeable paving, green roofs, bioretention trenches, swales, rain gardens, etc. For more info visit: http://www.susdrain.org/

THERMAL MASS
The ability of construction materials to absorb, store and release heat. Buildings constructed of dense materials, such as bricks or concrete, usually have a better thermal mass than lightweight buildings, such as timber, but choice of finishing materials can provide it.

THERMAL STORE
A thermal store is a structure typically made from a material with high thermal mass. These materials are capable of absorbing and retaining heat, for example usually, but not solely, from the sun, and slowly releasing the heat back into the building when space temperature falls.

TIMBER FRAME
Timber frame as we know it is not timber post and beam construction used in traditional building construction. Today the term is used to describe timber stud framework, usually panelised (sometimes known as cassette panels), which may or may not be pre-insulated. It is usually available as kits or to bespoke designs.

U VALUE
This is a measure of thermal transmittance through the fabric of a building. U values give a measure of air-to-heat transmission (loss or gain) due to the thermal conductance of the material, for example from inside to outside a building. The lower the U value, the lower the building fabric's thermal conductance (k value) and the better the material performs thermally. Approved Document L to the Building Regulations and the Code for Sustainable Homes dictate the maximum U value of elements of buildings; designers can improve on these.

U VALUE ENVELOPE
This refers to all the parts of the external envelope of the building that keep the heat in and the cold out. It is not always the same as the external envelope.

UNIMPROVED GRASSLAND
This is permanent grassland either that has never been subject to agricultural improvement or where that improvement was insignificant and the effects have now disappeared.

ZERO CARBON
Since the publication of the Government's plans to achieve zero carbon in all new homes from 2016, and in all new non-domestic buildings from 2019, there have been calls from the industry for a clear definition of 'zero carbon'. The basic definition is that a zero carbon home is one whose net carbon dioxide emissions, taking account of emissions associated with all energy use in the home, is equal to zero or negative across the year, as outlined by the then Minister of State, John Healey MP, in August 2009.

REFERENCES

*Barn Owl Conservation Handbook, in Barn Owls and Rural Planning Applications –
a Guide*, and also via the Barn Owl Trust website (www.barnowltrust.org.uk).

Barn Owl Trust (2012). *Barn Owl Conservation Handbook.* Exeter: Pelagic
Publishing.

Bat Conservation Trust (2012) *The State of the UK's Bats.* London: Bat Conservation
Trust. Available at: www.bats.org.uk/pages/results_and_reports.html

Berthinussen, A. and Altringham, J. (2011) The effect of a major road on bat activity
and diversity. *Journal of Applied Ecology,* 49(1), pp. 82–89.

British Standard (2011) BS 5250: 2011 Code of practice for control of condensation
in buildings. British Standards Institution.

Christie, T. H., Cooper, R., Fazey, I., Dennis, P., Warren, J., Colombo, S. and Hanley,
N. (2011) *Economic Valuation of the Benefits of Ecosystem Services delivered
by the UK Biodiversity Action Plan.* London: Defra. Available at: http://archive.
defra.gov.uk/temp/sffsd0702-economic-valuation-uk-bap.pdf

Commission for Architecture and the Built Environment (CABE) (2005a) *Does
Money Grow on Trees?* London: CABE.

Commission for Architecture and the Built Environment (CABE) (2005b) *Start
with the Park. Creating Sustainable Urban Green Spaces in Areas of Housing
Growth.* London: CABE.

Commission for Architecture and the Built Environment (CABE) (2006) *Making
Contracts Work for Wildlife. How to Encourage Biodiversity in Parks.* London:
CABE.

Commission for Architecture and the Built Environment (CABE) (2007) *It's Our
Space. A Guide for Community Groups Working to Improve Public Spaces.*
London: CABE.

Convention of Biological Diversity (CBD) (2010) *The Strategic Plan for Biodiversity
2011–2020 and the Aichi Biodiversity Targets.* COP10 Decision X/2.

Department for Business, Enterprise and Regulatory Reform (BERR) (2008) *Strategy
for Sustainable Construction.* HM Government in association with the Strategic
Forum for Construction. London: BERR.

Department for Communities and Local Government (2012) *National Planning
Policy Framework.* London: DCLG.

Department for Environment, Food and Rural Affairs (Defra) (2007a) *Guidance for
Local Authorities on Implementing the Biodiversity Duty.* London: Defra.

Department for Environment, Food and Rural Affairs (Defra) (2007b) *Conserving
Biodiversity – The UK Approach.* London: Defra.

Department for Environment, Food and Rural Affairs (Defra) (2008) *Populations of
Butterflies in England.* England Biodiversity Strategy Indicators (Part H1(b)).
London: Defra.

Department for Environment, Food and Rural Affairs (Defra) (2012a) *UK Biodiversity
Indicators in Your Pocket 2012.* London: Defra.

Department for Environment, Food and Rural Affairs (Defra) (2012b) *Defra National
Statistics Release: Wild bird populations in the UK, 1970 to 2011.* London:
Defra.

Drewitt, E. J. A and Dixon, N. (2008) Diet and Prey Selection of Urban Dwelling Peregrine Falcons in Southwest England. *British Birds*, 101, pp. 58–67.

European Commission (2011) *Our Life Insurance, Our Natural Capital: An EU Biodiversity Strategy to 2020*. Brussels: Publications Office of the European Union.

European Communities (EC) (2008) *The Economics of Ecosystems and Biodiversity*. Brussels: Commission of the European Communities. Available at http://ec.europa.eu/environment/nature/biodiversity/economics/.

Forest Research (2010) *Benefits of Green Infrastructure. Report by Forest Research*. Farnham: Forest Research.

Fox, R., Conrad, K. F., Parsons, M. S., Warren, M. S. and Woiwod, I. P. (2006) *The State of Britain's Larger Moths*. Wareham: Butterfly Conservation and Rothamsted Research.

Fuller, R. A., Irvine, K. N., Devine-Wright, P., Warren, P. H. and Gaston, K.W. (2007) Psychological benefits of greenspace increase with biodiversity. *Biology Letters*, 3, pp. 390–394.

Joint Nature Conservation Committee (JNCC) and Department for Environment, Food and Rural Affairs (DEFRA) (on behalf of the Four Countries' Biodiversity Group) (2012) *UK Post-2010 Biodiversity Framework*. Peterborough: JNCC.

Hackney Council's Advice Note for Biodiversity and the Built Environment (www.hackney.gov.uk/Assets/Documents/1-3208993-Hackney_Advice_Note_-_Biodiversity_and_the_Built_Environment.pdf).

Handley, J., Pauleit, S., Slinn, P., Barber, A., Baker, M., Jones, C. and Lindley, S. (2003) *Accessible Natural Green Space Standards in Towns and Cities: A Review and Toolkit for their Implementation*. English Nature Research Reports Number 526. Peterborough: English Nature.

Horwitz, P., Lindsay, M. and O'Connor, M. (2001) Biodiversity, Endemism, Sense of Place and Public Health: Inter-relationships for Australian Inland Aquatic Systems. *Ecosystem Health*, 7, pp. 253–265.

Margerison, C. (2008) *A Response from the British Ecological Society and the Institute of Biology to the Environmental Audit Committee Inquiry into 'Halting UK Biodiversity Loss'*. London: The British Ecological Society.

Millennium Ecosystem Assessment (2005) *Ecosystems and Human Well-being: Biodiversity Synthesis*. Washington, DC: World Resources Institute.

Minderman, J., Pendlebury, C. J., Pearce-Higgins, J. W. and Park, K. J. (2012) *Experimental Evidence for the Effect of Small Wind Turbine Proximity and Operation on Bird and Bat Activity*. PLoS ONE 7(7): e41177. doi:10.1371/journal.pone.0041177.

Mitchell-Jones, A. J. (2004) *Bat Mitigation Guidelines*. Peterborough: English Nature.

Morgan, C. (2006) *Design and Detailing for Airtightness. SEDA Design Guides for Scotland: No. 2* Edinburgh: Scottish Ecological Design Association (SEDA).

Natural Economy Northwest (NEN) (2008) *The Economic Value of Green Infrastructure*. Natural Economy Northwest. Available at www.naturaleconomynorthwest.co.uk/resources+reports.php.

Office of the Deputy Prime Minister (2005a) *Biodiversity and Geological Conservation – Statutory Obligations and their Impact within the Planning System*. Government Circular 06/2005. London: HMSO.

Office of the Deputy Prime Minister (2005b) *Planning Policy Statement 9: Biodiversity and Geological Conservation*. London: HMSO.

Office of the Deputy Prime Minister (2006) *Planning for Biodiversity and Geological Conservation: A Guide to Good Practice*. London: HMSO.

Planning Service (1997) *Planning Policy Statement 2: Planning and Nature Conservation*. Belfast: The Planning Service.

Pollard, A. (2009) *Visual Constraints on Bird Behaviour*. University of Cardiff.

Ramsden, D. and Twiggs, M. (2009) *Barn Owls and Rural Planning Applications. What needs to happen – A Guide for Planners*. Barn Owl Trust: Ashburton.

Rodríguez, A., García, A. M., Cervera, F. and Palacios, V. (2006) Landscape and anti-predation determinants of nest-site selection, nest distribution and productivity in a Mediterranean population of Long-eared Owls, *Asio otus*. *Ibis*, 148(1), pp. 133–145.

Schofield, H. W. (2008) *The Lesser Horseshoe Bat Conservation Handbook*. Ledbury: The Vincent Wildlife Trust.

Scottish Government (1999) *National Planning Policy Guide 14: Natural Heritage*. Edinburgh: Scottish Government.

Scottish Government (2000) *Planning Advice Note 60: Planning for Natural Heritage*. Edinburgh: Scottish Executive Development Department.

Shawyer, C. R. (1987) *The Barn Owl in the British Isles: Its Past, Present and Future*. London: The Hawk Trust.

Stone, E. L., Jones, G. and Harris, S. (2009) Street lighting disturbs commuting bats. *Current Biology*, 19, pp. 1–5.

Stone, E. L., Jones, G. and Harris, S. (2012) Conserving energy at a cost to biodiversity? Impacts of LED lighting on bats. *Global Change Biology*, 18: 2458–2465. doi: 10.1111/j.1365-2486.2012.02705.x

Town and Country Planning Association (2009) *Biodiversity positive: Eco-towns Biodiversity Worksheet*. London: TCPA. Available at www.tcpa.org.uk/data/files/etws_biodiversity.pdf.

Town and Country Planning Association (TCPA) and The Wildlife Trusts (2012) *Planning for a Healthy Environment: Good Practice for Green Infrastructure and Biodiversity*. London: TCPA.

UK National Ecosystem Assessment (2011) *The UK National Ecosystem Assessment: Synthesis of the Key Findings*. Cambridge: UNEP-WCMC.

Welsh Assembly Government (2009) *Technical Advice Note 5: Nature Conservation and Planning*. Cardiff: Welsh Assembly Government.

Wembridge, D. (2007) *Living with Mammals*. London: People's Trust for Endangered Species and Mammals Trust UK.

Wotton, S., Field, R., Langston, R. and Gibbons, D. (2002) Homes for birds: The use of houses for nesting by birds in the UK. *British Birds*, 95, pp. 596–592.

USEFUL RESOURCES

Arnott, S. (2007) *Wildlife on Allotments*. Peterborough: Natural England.

Balmer, D. E., Adams, S. Y. and Crick, H. Q. P. (2000) *Report on Barn Owl Release Scheme: Monitoring Project Phase II*. BTO Research Report No. 250. Available at www.defra.gov.uk.

Bat Conservation Trust (2006) *A Review of the Success of Bat Boxes in Houses*. Scottish Natural Heritage, Commissioned Report No. 160. Inverness: Scottish Natural Heritage.

Blakesley, D. and Buckley, G. P. (2010) *Woodland Creation for Wildlife and People in a Changing Climate: Principles and Practice*. Pisces Publications.

Bray, R., Gedge, D., Grant, G. and Leuthvilay, L. (2012) *Rain Garden Guide*. RESET Development. Available at: http://raingardens.info/wp-content/uploads/2012/07/UK-Rain-Garden-Guide.pdf

Buglife (2012) *Creating Green Roofs for Invertebrates: A Best Practice Guide*. Available at: www.buglife.org.uk/Resources/Buglife/Creating%20Green%20Roofs%20for%20Invertebrates_Best%20practice%20guidance.pdf

Dixon, N. and Shawyer, C. (2005) *Peregrine Falcons – Provision of Artificial Nest Sites on Built Structures. Advice Note for Conservation Organisations, Local Authorities and Developers*. London: London Biodiversity Partnership. Available at www.lbp.org.uk/downloads/ Publications/Management/peregrine_nest-box_advice.pdf.

Dunnett, N. and Clayden, A. (2007) *Rain Gardens: Managing Water Sustainably in the Garden and Designed Landscape*. Portland, OR: Timber Press.

Dunnett, N. and Kingsbury, N. (2008) *Planting Green Roofs and Living Walls*. Portland, OR: Timber Press.

Dunnett, N., Gedge, D., Little, J. and Snodgrass, E. C. (2011) *Small Green Roofs: Low-Tech Options for Greener Living*. Portland, OR: Timber Press

Early, P., Gedge, D., Newton, J. and Wilson, S. (2007) *Building Greener. Guidance on the Use of Green Roofs, Green Walls and Complementary Features on Buildings*. London: CIRIA.

Fox, R., Conrad, K. F., Parsons, M. S., Warren, M. S. and Woiwod, I. P. (2000) *The State of Britain's Larger Moths*. Wareham, Dorset: Butterfly Conservation and Rothamsted Research.

Gedge, D., Dunnett, N., Grant, G. and Jones, R. (2007) *Living Roofs*. Peterborough: Natural England.

Graham, A., Day, J. Bray, B. and Mackenzie, S. (2013) *Sustainable Drainage Systems: Maximising the Potential for Wildlife and People: A Guide for Local Authorities and Developers*. Wildfowl and Wetlands Trust/RSPB.

Grant, G. (2012) *Ecosystem Services Come to Town: greening cities by working with nature*. Wiley-Blackwell.

Gunnell, K., Grant, G. and Williams, C. (2012) *Landscape and Urban Design for Bats and Biodiversity*. London: Bat Conservation Trust.

HM Government (2009) *Strategy for Sustainable Construction Progress Report*. Crown copyright.

Ketchin, M. of Simpson and Brown Architects (1998) *The Design and Construction of Bat Boxes in Houses – A Guide to the Installation of Roost Boxes for Bats in Existing Scottish Houses*. Perth: Scottish Natural Heritage.

Mitchell-Jones, A. J. and McLeish, A. P. (2004) *Bat Workers' Manual*, 3rd edn. Peterborough: JNCC.

National Trust (2013) *When Nature Moves In: A guide to managing wildlife on buildings.*

Oxford, M. (2001) *Developing Naturally: A Handbook for Incorporating the Natural Environment into Planning and Development.* London: Association of Local Government Ecologists.

Pelsmakers, S. (2012) *Environmental Design Pocketbook.* RIBA Publishing.

Ponds Conservation Trust (2003) *Maximising the Ecological Benefits of SUDS Schemes.* Oxford: Ponds Conservation Trust.

Ramsden, D. and Twiggs, M. A. (2009) *Making Provision for Barn Owls. A Guide for Planners, Applicants and Developers.* Ashburton: Barn Owl Trust.

Rich, C. and Longcore, T. (eds) (2006) *Ecological Consequences of Artificial Night Lighting.* Washington: Island Press.

Royal Commission on Environmental Pollution (2009) *Artificial Light in the Environment.* London: HMSO.

Royal Society for the Protection of Birds (RSPB) (2002) *Unravelling the Web: The Global Value of Wild Nature.* Sandy, Bedfordshire: RSPB. Available at www. rspb.org.uk/Images/Global%20values_tcm9-133024.pdf.

Royal Society for the Protection of Birds (RSPB) (various dates) RSPB Advisory Sheets:
Managing Urban Green Space for Wildlife
Managing Urban Green Space for Wildlife: Formal and informal grass
Managing Urban Green Space for Wildlife: Creating and managing flower-rich grassland in parks and green spaces
Managing Urban Green Space for Wildlife: Wildlife seed mixes for parks and gardens
Managing Urban Green Space for Wildlife: Formal and informal shrub beds and flower borders. RSPB advisory sheet
Managing Urban Green Space for Wildlife: House sparrow
Pond Management
Scrub Management
Managing Scrub on Chalk and Limestone Grassland
Managing Wet Scrub

Symes, N. and Currie, F. (2005) *Woodland Management for Birds: A Guide to Managing for Declining Woodland Birds in England.* Sandy, Beds: RSPB.

Swift, S. M. (2004) *Bat Boxes: Survey of Types Available and Their Efficiency as Alternative Roosts, and Further Progress on the Development of Heated Bat Houses.* The Bat Conservation Trust and Mammals Trust UK.

Town and Country Planning Association (TCPA) and The Wildlife Trusts (2012) *Planning for a Healthy Environment: Good Practice for Green Infrastructure and Biodiversity.* London: TCPA. (Annex C: Model polices and approaches.)

UK Green Building Council (2009) *Biodiversity and the Built Environment. A Report by the UK-GBC Task Group.* London: UK Green Building Council. Available at www.ukgbc.org.

Wembridge, D. (2012) *Urban Mammals: a concise guide.* People's Trust for Endangered Species, Whittet Books Ltd, London.

Wilby, R. L. and Perry, G. L. W. (2006) Climate change, biodiversity and the urban environment: a critical review based on London. *Progress in Physical Geography*, 30(1), pp. 73–98.

Winspear, R (ed.) (2007) *The Farm Wildlife Handbook.* Sandy, Bedfordshire: RSPB.

Winspear, R. and Davies, G. (2005) *A Management Guide to Birds of Lowland Farmland.* Sandy, Bedfordshire: RSPB.

INDEX

IMAGE CREDITS

Cover images: (front) CG image of housing, courtesy of zedfactory.com
(back) Steve Parker © Bat Conservation Trust